WARTIME ENTERTAINMENT

WARTIME ENTERTAINMENT

HOW BRITAIN KEPT SMILING THROUGH THE SECOND WORLD WAR

ANTON RIPPON & NICOLA RIPPON

PEN & SWORD HISTORY

AN IMPRINT OF PEN & SWORD BOOKS LTD.
YORKSHIRE – PHILADELPHIA

First published in Great Britain in 2024 by
PEN AND SWORD HISTORY
An imprint of
Pen & Sword Books Ltd
Yorkshire – Philadelphia

ISBN 978 1 39903 484 5

A CIP catalogue record for this book is available from the British Library.

Typeset in Times New Roman 11.5/14 by
SJmagic DESIGN SERVICES, India.
Printed and bound in the UK by CPI Group (UK) Ltd.

Pen & Sword Books Limited incorporates the imprints of Atlas, Archaeology, Aviation, Discovery, Family History, Fiction, History, Maritime, Military, Military Classics, Politics, Select, Transport, True Crime, Air World, Frontline Publishing, Leo Cooper, Remember When, Seaforth Publishing, The Praetorian Press, Wharncliffe Local History, Wharncliffe Transport, Wharncliffe True Crime and White Owl.

For a complete list of Pen & Sword titles please contact
PEN & SWORD BOOKS LIMITED
George House, Units 12 & 13, Beevor Street, Off Pontefract Road,
Barnsley, South Yorkshire, S71 1HN, England
E-mail: enquiries@pen-and-sword.co.uk
Website: www.pen-and-sword.co.uk

or

PEN AND SWORD BOOKS
1950 Lawrence Rd, Havertown, PA 19083, USA
E-mail: uspen-and-sword@casematepublishers.com
Website: www.penandswordbooks.com

MIX
Paper | Supporting responsible forestry
FSC® C013604

Contents

Chapter 1	This Country is at War…	1
Chapter 2	Here is the News…	6
Chapter 3	This is the BBC Forces Programme	15
Chapter 4	It's That Man Again	24
Chapter 5	Mr Wu's an Air Raid Warden Now	30
Chapter 6	More Than One Forces' Sweetheart	40
Chapter 7	Sing As We Go and Let the World Go By	48
Chapter 8	Great Symphonies and Concertos	58
Chapter 9	Soft Lights and Sweet Music	68
Chapter 10	In the Mood	83
Chapter 11	Over the Rainbow	88
Chapter 12	Now Showing – Target for Tonight	108
Chapter 13	No Better National Service	124
Chapter 14	Tonight and Every Night	129
Chapter 15	I'll Be Home for Christmas	136
Chapter 16	Smiling Through Coupon Monday	151
Chapter 17	Holidaying at Home	157
Chapter 18	A Sporting Life	169
Chapter 19	A Land of Begin Again…	184
Sources		191
Index		192

Chapter 1

This Country is at War…

> We caught sight of hurrying cars, loaded with baggage as mothers and children were raced to an even safer place … and heard at frequent intervals the voices of the BBC announcers telling of the madness that had got out of hand.
>
> *Sunday Mercury*

It was the BBC that brought the news. For months everyone had expected it, dreaded it, and now, on the morning of Sunday, 3 September 1939, listeners across Britain fiddled with the dials on their wireless sets to hear Neville Chamberlain confirm it: for the second time in a generation, Britain was at war with Germany.

For many months it had seemed certain that Adolf Hitler's overriding desire for territorial expansion would see him attack somewhere, and Civil Defence exercises, the feverish building of air-raid shelters and the distribution of gas masks appeared to confirm people's worst fears: Britain would be pulled in again. Poland looked the most vulnerable to Hitler's ambitions, and on 31 March 1939 the prime minister, Neville Chamberlain, told the House of Commons: 'In the event of any action which clearly threatened Polish independence, and which the Polish government accordingly considered it vital to resist, His Majesty's government would feel themselves bound at once to lend the Polish government all support in their power.'

Five months later, on Friday, 1 September, Germany invaded Poland, and throughout the hot and humid weekend the feeling of anxiety in Britain was almost tangible. This was no time for the flag-waving patriotism of August 1914. Memories of the horrors of the First World War were still far too raw for that.

The BBC announced that between 7.00 am on the Sunday and 12.15 am the following day it planned to broadcast a single miscellaneous programme – its National Programme and various regional programmes now combined and called the Home Service – in which the times of news bulletins would be as on weekdays. Transmissions would be on two wavelengths only – 391 metres and 449 metres – and, subject to last-minute alterations, the day's programming would include a talk by Anne Beaton entitled *Making the Most of Tinned Food*, Sandy McPherson playing the BBC theatre organ, and J. B. Priestley reading part one of his new novel *Let The People Sing*. Priestley did not normally allow serialisation before publication, but the book had been specially commissioned by the BBC for broadcasting every Sunday evening for twelve weeks.

In the Author's Note, Priestley explained, 'I agreed to let the BBC have a novel partly because I felt we might go to war in the autumn – when they were going to serialise it – and that broadcasting then might be extremely valuable to the public.' He felt that the later chapters were better because they were written 'in the anxious and darkening days of August'.

Priestley told the newspaper columnist 'Tuner' that he was looking forward to it because of its experimental nature. 'The BBC asked me to do this, and I agreed. They are paying me what they think is a lot of money for it, but I think otherwise.' *Let The People Sing* is set in the small English town of Dunbury where one character, Daisy Barley, responds to an anti-semitic remark with '… I don't care what shape their noses are, n' if you an' Hitler don't like it, major, I'm sorry but you'll have to lump it. Good night.'

If there was any special news on that Sunday, then the BBC advised that it would be broadcast at 1.00 am, 11.00 am, 3.00 pm, and so on. Of course, there would be special news – the Luftwaffe was still bombing Warsaw and German tanks were still rolling over the Polish border – and throughout the morning announcers urged listeners to stay tuned ready for more announcements.

The BBC's fledgling television service had closed down rather abruptly shortly after noon on Friday, 1 September 1939, following a Mickey Mouse cartoon, *Mickey's Gala Premier*. It was thought that the strong signal from the Alexandra Palace transmitter would provide a navigational aid for the Luftwaffe. One of the programmes that would never air was an Air Raid Precautions (ARP) lecture planned for that evening when W. P. Matthew, a handyman who wrote a column in the *News Chronicle*, would broadcast from a specially constructed room at Alexandra Palace where he would show 'how the ordinary householder could protect his home, arrange windows and doors to secure proper blackout conditions, and devise scoops from shovels and other ways of getting ready for an emergency'.

The author of the 'Round and About' column in the *Belfast News-Letter* was not impressed by the radio scheduling:

> I wish that the BBC could be induced at times of grave crisis to broadcast its news at stated intervals and adhere rigidly to the timetable. The morale of the nation is a vital consideration, and it is not helped if households keep their radio sets going practically all the time, less something important should be missed. That, I am afraid, happens all too frequently and I can think of nothing more upsetting in its effects, particularly in the case of women. Not only do listeners hear the same news – bad as well as good – over and over again but they are kept on the qui vive [on the alert], the war atmosphere gets hold of them, and nerves begin to suffer. A year ago, I thought the BBC responsible in no small measure for what may be called the 'jitters' period, and although things are better now, it would be well if the authorities were to give this matter their serious consideration. And while on the subject I may remark perhaps that the method of broadcasting Mr Chamberlain's speech in Parliament on Friday was by no means inspiring. It would have been far better to wait until a comprehensive summary was available than to give a series of short snippets punctuated by the playing of gramophone records.

At 10.00 am that Sunday, the Home Service reported that Sir Neville Henderson, the British ambassador in Berlin, had handed the German government a final note stating that unless Germany agreed by 11.00 am to withdraw their troops from Poland, a state of war would exist between Britain and Germany. When listeners were further told that the prime minister would broadcast to the nation at 11.15 am, it was clear that Britain would soon be at war.

All across the country, people gathered around their nearest wireless set. In London, at the Russell Hotel – half a mile from King's Cross and 'made of reinforced concrete', the establishment boasted, not all that reassuringly – the Sunderland football team that had lost 5-2 at Arsenal's Highbury the previous afternoon crowded into the foyer along with other guests awaiting the prime minister's address to the nation. The England player Raich Carter's first thoughts were of how they would get back home. Would the trains still be running if there was a war on?

The BBC had not always been in the business of presenting hard news. Although its first bulletin had been delivered in November 1922, a national morning newspaper circulation war had seen influential owners persuade the government to ban the Corporation from broadcasting news bulletins before early evening. The BBC also had to use the newspapers' wire services until, in 1934, it was allowed to create its own news department. Even then there was still a ban on broadcasting news before 6.00 pm.

In May 1938, for instance, a typical day's listening included a daily religious service, a programme for schools, and then Arthur Salisbury and his Orchestra, a selection of gramophone records, the Bernard Crook Quintet, and a recital on two pianofortes by 'Alleyne and Leonhardt' (pseudonyms adopted by two English pianists who created their own arrangements of the lighter classics and British folk songs and ballads) before, at 6.00 pm, the 'First News', a twenty-minute bulletin that included a weather forecast. There followed more music, a magazine programme which included excerpts from books, yet more music, the week's sports news, a documentary programme on the cinema, a serialised play *The Count of Monte Cristo*, and still more music before another twenty-minute news bulletin at 9.00 pm. A programme about world affairs, some poetry readings, Bram Martin and his Dance Orchestra, and Jack Hylton and his Orchestra brought down the radio curtain at midnight.

Those wanting to tune in to foreign commercial stations such as Radio Luxembourg, Radio Athlone and Radio Normandy managed to do so despite government pressure on newspapers not to print overseas stations' programme schedules and the BBC being discouraged from employing presenters and artistes who had appeared on Continental stations. In 1936, a broadcasting committee set up by the government had reported that 'foreign commercial broadcasting should be discouraged by every available means'. Nonetheless, in 1938, Radio Luxembourg, which was enjoying substantial revenue from advertising, had 45 per cent of the UK's Sunday listening audience against the BBC's 35 per cent. Of course, the Luxembourg transmitters and others would soon fall into Nazi hands and the BBC would have the airwaves to itself, unless listeners wanted to amuse themselves with German propaganda broadcasts.

Britain's radio audience had been relatively small. But it was growing. In 1930, there were some 5 million wireless sets among a population of 46 million. In 1939, 9 million wireless licences would be issued among a population of 47 million.

Cost was a major factor. In 1938, a typical set, with aerial and installation, might cost up to £10 when the average weekly wage for a working man was only £3 10s (£3.50), although they could also be hired through firms like Radio Rentals at just under 2 shillings (10p) per week.

Sales of sets increased dramatically after Hitler invaded Czechoslovakia in March 1938 and again in September that year when Neville Chamberlain visited Munich where he and France's prime minister, Édouard Daladier, both signed an agreement confirming their willingness to pay Hitler's price – the annexation of the Sudetenland in western Czechoslovakia – for a peace that turned out to be of short duration.

The year 1938 had been one of firsts for BBC radio. In January it broadcast its first foreign-language service, in Arabic. There followed, in March, a Latin American service broadcasting in English, Spanish and Portuguese, and during that fateful September, the start of a European service in French, German and Italian.

One year later, it was Anne Beaton's advice on the best use of tinned food that had to give way to Mr Chamberlain. At 11.15 am, the BBC faded out the sounds of Bow Bells being played from Studio 'BA' in Broadcasting House and switched to 10 Downing Street from where Chamberlain told a hushed nation that Henderson had delivered the ultimatum, but 'I have to tell you now that no such undertaking has been given and that, consequently, this country is at war with Germany.' Thousands of Germans also heard Chamberlain's words. They had defied a government decree threatening with death or hard labour to those who listened to foreign wireless stations.

After the prime minister had finished speaking, there was a brief reprise of Bow Bells before a BBC announcer advised that, as soon as they heard a warning siren, everyone should take shelter. Raich Carter and his Sunderland teammates would be able to get back to the North-East all right, but when they would be able to play football again was anyone's guess: sports events would be banned immediately. Venues such as cinemas, theatres and dance halls would also be closed. Like every other aspect of British life, entertainment was going on a war footing.

Chapter 2

Here is the News...

> The maintenance of public morale should be the principal aim of wartime programming and for this the continuance of a reliable news service is obviously of first importance.
>
> BBC sub-committee report, January 1939

Shortly after 2.00 am on Tuesday, 5 September 1939, night owls who had inadvertently tuned in to the 449 metres wavelength on which the BBC's Northern Home Service was broadcast were surprised to hear a voice, speaking in perfect English, announce a German news bulletin for listeners in Britain. The newsreader ended with the customary 'Goodnight, goodnight,' of BBC announcers. A BBC official said that their attention had been drawn to the matter, which he thought probably originated from a Cologne station broadcasting on its usual 455 metres wavelength compared to the BBC's 449 metres, and that they would 'have to take steps about it ... we could jam it out by simply switching to dance music'. However, there was nothing sinister about it, he said. 'We do not feel that there was any attempt to gate-crash the BBC wavelength.'

'During the early hours, when reception is particularly good when the BBC programme was not in operation, it would be very easy by the slightest turn of the dial to get Cologne under the mistaken impression that it was the BBC wavelength.'

Bizarrely, that same day British newspapers were still advertising German radio schedules. Under the heading 'Today's Continental Fare' in the *Nottingham Evening Post*, besides schedules for stations in Barcelona, Paris, Stockholm and Oslo were programme details for Berlin, Cologne, Hamburg and Munich. Anyone who didn't fancy the Leslie Bridgewater Quintet on the Home Service could put patriotism aside for an hour or so, and twiddle the dials to hear Emmi Goedel-Dreising and her children's chorus direct from the capital of Germany.

Meanwhile, the BBC now found itself charged with a new responsibility – lifting everyone's wartime spirits. And that did not mean simply providing light entertainment. Keeping the nation appraised of events was now paramount, for whatever the news, good or bad, there was nothing more likely to cause dismay and panic than wild rumour. The decision was made that, wartime censorship allowing, the BBC would simply tell the unvarnished truth. There would be no propaganda.

This was not always well received. In September 1940, columnist 'Odd Man Out', writing in 'A Shieldsman's Diary' in *The Shields Gazette*, blamed the BBC for painting too grim a picture of life in Britain as the Blitz began. Commenting on the negative impression formed by a former newspaper colleague, 'Bobstay', who was visiting South Shields while on leave from the Merchant Navy, 'Odd Man Out' said:

> Regrettably, this fault I lay at the door of the BBC. He and his shipboard colleagues came back to this country firmly believing that we here were starving and our towns in ruins. That seems to be a false conclusion gained by most deep-sea men away from these shores for any length of time.
>
> The BBC Overseas News Service, they say, is all very well in its way, but presents a poor side of the picture from Britain's point of view. Such sailors are astonished to find that our menus have suffered little and our homes scarcely at all. If the overseas news has them believing the opposite, what must be the thoughts of those who have no opportunity to see for themselves? Everywhere, 'Bobstay' assures me, there is a real desire that Britain shall win. It is a desire especially strong among natives in the Middle East. We should do nothing to dampen that spirit.

When it came to providing the nation with information, thanks to the agreement with those overbearing newspaper owners, the BBC had hitherto never broadcast news until early evening. But with war clouds gathering, on 25 August 1939 daily morning and lunchtime news bulletins were added. For the first time, listeners became acquainted with the names of newsreaders who they now needed to trust as never before. Alvar Liddell, born in Surrey of Swedish parents, had introduced Neville Chamberlain when he told the nation that it was now at war with Germany. 'Here is the news, and this is Alvar Liddell reading it,' became another catchphrase. John Snagge, a voice already well known as the commentator for the Oxford–Cambridge Boat Race, became the BBC's presentation director, making announcements of national importance as the war unfolded. Former singer Frank Phillips was another voice to become familiar to millions as his unmistakable baritone announced the ever-changing tide of war. On 26 January 1936, Stuart Hibberd had delivered the words: 'The King's life is moving peacefully towards its close.' He, too, now became a vital link.

The BBC was not just speaking to the Home Front. In between the normal programmes of music, comedy and drama, radio listings now carried items such 'The News in German' and 'The News in Norwegian'. Behind that was a major development for the BBC, whose pre-war Empire Service had, since November 1939, been known as the Overseas Service. Staffing for non-domestic output had risen from 103 in 1939 to almost 1,500 by the end of 1940.

Top ensure the continuity of all BBC services, staff were often required to sleep in makeshift dormitories in basements and wherever else there was room at Broadcasting House. This was especially so during the Blitz of 1940–41. It was no surprise that the BBC would be a prime target for German bombers. On 15 October 1940, the *Daily Mirror* reported that the BBC's director of variety, John Watt, was that night taking his turn on fire-watch duty on the roof of Broadcasting House in Portland Place. Watt told the newspaper, 'It is cold and uncomfortable, and there is not much more to say about it, but I am doing it because it is the only way to keep broadcasting alive when Jerry is about, and I think that's worthwhile.'

That evening, Broadcasting House received a direct hit. At 8.05 pm, a 225 kg (496 lbs) delayed-action bomb penetrated the seventh floor, destroying the BBC switchboard before coming to rest in the fifth-floor music library. At just after 9.00 pm, the bomb exploded. Six people were killed instantly and a seventh died in hospital. In a basement studio, Bruce Belfrage, a former BBC casting director, was reading the news when listeners heard a muted explosion.

Ironically, a few hours before the bombing, an order had been placed with Decorative Painting Contractors Ltd of Hounslow to camouflage Broadcasting House. A number of local residents had complained that, on moonlit nights, the white Portland stone building presented an easy target for the Luftwaffe.

A few weeks later, at just after 10.00 pm on Sunday, 8 December 1940, a parachute mine exploded near the entrance to Broadcasting House. One police officer was killed, and several people were injured. Damage to BBC equipment was more severe that sustained during the October bombing. There was a small fire on the third floor, windows were blown out, and studios flooded from fire hoses. As a result, the Overseas Service was moved a few miles away, to a disused skating rink in Maida Vale. But it had a glass roof, and so some sections were moved again, this time to Wood Norton Hall in Worcestershire, which the BBC had purchased in 1939, as a relocation centre. The European Service – which regularly transmitted coded messages to resistance groups in German-occupied countries – was transferred back to London, to Bush House between Aldwych and the Strand, and near to Fleet Street, then the heart of the British newspaper industry. Although Broadcasting House was spared further direct hits, during subsequent raids several BBC employees were killed in surrounding streets, and in June 1944, during the 'flying bomb war', Bush House suffered external damage from a V-1 rocket.

As the Blitz continued across Britain, other BBC centres were attacked. In November 1940, three staff at a transmitter in Birmingham were killed. In February 1941, the Swansea studios were burned down. Variety staff at the BBC's Bristol studio were relocated to Bangor and Weston-super-Mare, while music staff were moved to Bedford.

During the Blitz, the BBC announced that it was considering plans to reduce the interruption of its programmes when air-raid sirens sounded, and for more live shows to be broadcast during the actual warning period. At the moment, gramophone record programmes were substituted for the show in progress at the time of the alert, but, popular as they usually were, the BBC said that it was aiming for something better.

At least one man, however, thought that, far from ignore them, the BBC should be used to advertise air-raid warnings, and for sirens to be banned altogether. Speaking at the National Trade Union Club in London, dockers' veteran leader Bob Tillett said, 'The sirens are a curse, and as a result of them many hours of useful work are being lost.' Tillett did not believe that the sirens had saved lives. It was a clumsy and barbarous machinery, he said. There were good alternatives – the BBC wireless, the telephone, the ARP and other agencies which could give warning so that factories could still carry on. Every day, he said, the Germans came over and won bloodless victories. 'I want to make this protest: the government must be alive to the criminal waste of energy and labour. Nerves have been destroyed by the sirens without any results.'

The sirens, of course, continued, and the BBC carried on with its programmes. By the end of 1940, it was broadcasting in thirty-four languages. Each day, seventy-eight news bulletins were broadcast, and new services included Icelandic, Albanian, Hindi, Burmese and the dialect of Luxembourg. Danish and Norwegian language news bulletins had begun in April 1940, on the day the two countries were invaded; the service in Dutch began in June, a month after Holland was occupied. Because Belgium's population was divided into two language areas – French and Flemish – each language was featured on alternate nights. The German service posed a particular dilemma because it made use of refugees, and it was felt that German listeners would assume that they were therefore Jewish. The BBC did also not want to give the impression that it was broadcasting propaganda promoted by refugees but that it was 'the sincere expression of an English point of view'. The overseas broadcasts were also available to listeners sitting by their own British firesides, in the unlikely event that they would tune in in preference to comedians Ben Lyon and Bebe Daniels taking aim at 'Lord Haw-Haw', the American-born Anglo-Irishman William Joyce who, in 1946, would be hanged at Wandsworth prison for treason after a war spent broadcasting Nazi propaganda from Germany.

As the war progressed, the BBC entered more and more into the business of true journalism, presenting eyewitness accounts rather than simply reporting events that had already happened. BBC reporters were getting right to the heart of the conflict, and were present at many of the most critical moments. On a still summer's evening in July 1940, Charles Gardner and his crew set up their recording equipment in a house overlooking the port at Dover. Their brief was to see whether the Luftwaffe would appear. Suddenly the skies above them began to fill with the sound of aircraft. Gardener began to record:

> Well, now the Germans are dive-bombing a convoy out at sea … there are one, two, three, four, five, six, seven German dive-bombers, Junkers 87s. There's one going down on its target now … Bomb! No! He missed the ships. It hasn't hit a single ship … there, you can hear our anti-aircraft going at them then now … I can't see anything … No! We thought we had got a German one at the top then, but now the British fighters are coming in … you can hear our guns going like anything now…

Listeners to the BBC's Home Service suddenly realised that the Phoney War really was over. Gardner was reporting on the start of the Battle of Britain.

In September 1943, Wynford Vaughan-Thomas broadcast from a Lancaster bomber on a raid over Berlin. He described it as 'the most beautifully horrible sight I've ever seen'. Vaughan-Thomas also described a night raid on Anzio in January 1944 – this time he was on the ground – and from Lord Haw-Haw's broadcasting studio in Berlin. In April 1945, he reported on the liberation of Belsen concentration camp, as did Richard Dimbleby, who told listeners:

> One woman, distraught to the point of madness, flung herself at a British soldier who was on guard in the camp on the night that it was reached by the 11th Armoured Division. She begged him to give her some milk for the tiny baby she held in her arms. She laid the mite on the ground, threw herself at the sentry's feet and kissed his boots. And when in his distress he asked her to get up, she put the baby in his arms and ran off crying that she would find milk for it because there was no milk in her breast. And when the soldier opened the bundle of rags to look at the child, he found it had been dead for days. I have never seen British soldiers so moved to cold fury as the men who opened the Belsen camp this week.

His ten-minute radio piece was so shocking that, at first, the BBC would not play it. 'It was,' said Dimbleby, 'the most horrible day of my life.'

For D-Day, the BBC created its War Reporting Unit, and on 6 June 1944 its reporters boarded ships and landing craft heading across the Channel to be embedded with the invasion force. Australian war correspondent Chester Wilmot was delivered to Normandy by glider. Howard Marshall had to wade ashore after his landing craft hit a mine.

Guy Byam, who as a member of the Royal Naval Volunteer Reserve was one of the few survivors when HMS *Jervis Bay* was sunk in the North Atlantic in November 1940, joined airborne troops and parachuted in. Byam was one of two BBC journalists who paid the ultimate price for their courage in reporting the war under battle conditions. In February 1945, he was killed when the US 8th Air Force Flying Fortress, from which he was reporting on a daylight raid over Berlin, was shot down.

After the war, his widow, a BBC studio manager, married Robert Dougall, who would become a familiar face reading the news on BBC television.

Kent Stevenson perished in June 1944 when the RAF bomber from which he was covering an attack on an oil refinery near Cologne was one of a number that did not return. Stevenson, who was 36, was buried, along with the crew of the aircraft, at Rheinberg War Cemetery in Germany.

BBC journalists were now using the revolutionary Midget Recorder, recording their reports on to twelve 10 in (25 cm) discs. The machines were relatively sophisticated: a flickering light told the reporter that they were speaking at the correct level; different recording modes limited background noise or allowed all sounds of battle to be heard. Despite the name, each one weighed 18 kg (almost 40 lbs) and each disc had only three minutes' recording time, a light warning the user when their time was nearly up. The reports could not be edited, and so reporters had to learn to censor any sensitive information. And the discs broke easily in cold weather; in the winter, reporters kept them warm inside their coats.

That was not a problem during the summer days of the Battle of Normandy, and by the evening of D-Day reports were already flowing in from various parts of the battlefield. That night the BBC's pioneering *War Report* programme was heard for the first time. It continued nightly for 235 editions until the German surrender in May 1945, broadcasting more than 1,500 despatches from journalists who went on assault course training and learned new skills such as map-reading, aircraft recognition, and even gunnery.

In September 1943, John Snagge, one of the definitive voices of the BBC, spoke to Haywards Heath Rotary Club, giving them an insight into wartime broadcasting. Snagge had been involved in Minister of Information Brendan Bracken's plan to introduce British regional accents rather than Received Pronunciation – 'BBC English' – in a bid to avoid enemy infiltration into the broadcasting service. Never mind the Germans, it appeared that the initiative also confused some home listeners.

Snagge said that Wilfred Pickles, the Halifax-born son of a builder who had come to the BBC's attention when he was appearing in amateur dramatics, was chosen because of his North Country accent, but, curiously enough, he did not produce in his reading a fully-fledged North Country accent. Pickles told Snagge that this was because the bulletins were not written in the 'idiom of the north'. The BBC then tried a Scotsman, said Snagge, 'but listeners could not understand whether he was saying "Burma" or "bomber"'. Everyone laughed.

A problem which would never be solved, said Snagge, was the pronunciation of foreign names and places. Newsreaders had been faced with some 6,000 fresh pronunciations since the war began. Whether they gave a place its native pronunciation or its anglicised pronunciation, somebody said it was wrong. The trouble was that if they gave foreign places their native pronunciations, these would not be recognised by most listeners.

Snagge told how the BBC's job in wartime had grown out of all proportion, until Broadcasting House accommodated only a small percentage of the entire staff. There were 168 hours in week, he said, but by some elastic means the BBC managed to get in over 800 hours of transmission. In addition to the Home and Forces Programmes, there were the Overseas Service, the European transmission – which daily broadcast 150 news bulletins in different languages – and the division responsible for listening to enemy-controlled stations and supplying digests of the propaganda to government departments. He thought that the effectiveness of the European Service was due to the fact that, throughout the war, the BBC had told Europe nothing but the truth.

Recalling the days of the Blitz, when Broadcasting House was hit, Snagge told his audience that during all the bombing not a single announcer has failed to arrive at a studio and carry through a programme, and not one left the studio to go to a shelter.

On the morning of 3 September 1939, a *Sunday Mercury* columnist, commenting on the BBC announcement 'This is the Air Ministry weather forecast for the next twenty-four hours,' had wondered what the future held:

> My mind travels forward a quarter of a century – fifty years – a hundred; it is impossible, with the world in chaos, to say whether the BBC will still be functioning or to guess what will have replaced it. But probably – as we have been listening by radio back to 4 August 1914 – our successors will be hearing reconstructions of the hours through which we are now passing. One imagines the news bulletins which have grown more and more ominous during the past week, flying again across now peaceful countrysides, filling the

> listeners of that new day with wonder at the former follies of mankind. What will amaze them most, however, will be the words which head this column. I wonder if they will think that really, with the heavens themselves falling, we cared first of all about the weather.

In fact, it would be 9 May 1945 – the day after VE Day – before the next weather forecast would be published – 'warm and thundery with bright intervals in most districts' – as the European war ended.

Chapter 3

This is the BBC Forces Programme

> It's being so cheerful as keeps me going.
>
> Mona Lott, *ITMA*

Two days after Neville Chamberlain had delivered the news that no one wanted to hear, the *Radio Times* assured listeners that all-day live BBC programmes 'of probably a higher standard than in peacetime' would now begin.

The BBC was carrying on, and there was every prospect that the new, decentralised, system would be successful by using a number of smaller 'radio cities' in distant parts of the country. In these centres, which had been reserved for nearly a year, would be leading members of the BBC Symphony Orchestra, a team of variety favourites, a team of actors and producers and other staff performers. Many had been signed on for the war period.

Over that last weekend of peace there had been much recorded music. The following day's programme would now include the BBC Northern Orchestra, the Boulevard Players, Sandy McPherson at the BBC theatre organ, a play, a schools broadcast, *Children's Hour*, the BBC Orchestra, conducted by Sir Adrian Boult, a concert party item, and songs from the shows. The BBC was ready.

For the first few months of the Second World War, however, not a lot happened. Between the German invasion of Poland in September 1939 and Hitler's attack on the Low Countries in May 1940, the only military land operation was the brief excursion into Germany's Saarland by French forces soon after war had been declared. Poland quickly subjugated, Germany was then able to launch a counteroffensive and the French soon withdrew. In Britain, although air-raid sirens wailed and hospitals prepared for hundreds of thousands of casualties, there was no bombing offensive by the Luftwaffe. And so for those eight months the British people endured an uneasy calm during what became known as the 'Phoney War'.

Everything was about to change. In April 1940, Germany invaded Norway before, on 10 May, the Nazis began to overrun Belgium, the Netherlands, Luxembourg and France. Between 26 May and 4 June 1940, 338,000 Allied troops were evacuated from the beaches at Dunkirk after being surrounded during the six-week Battle of France. In late June, the French signed an armistice, leaving Nazi Germany a firm base from which to invade Britain which now stood alone, its newly formed armed civilian militia, the Local Defence Volunteers – soon to be known as the Home Guard – its last line of defence. On 7 September, the Blitz began, a sustained campaign of aerial bombardment on Britain's towns and cities that lasted until late May 1941, after which Hitler turned his attention to Russia and to targets in the Mediterranean. During those nine months, more than 43,500 civilians were killed during bombing raids. Although the Blitz was over, less intense bombing continued for the remainder of the war, notably the so-called Baedeker Blitz where cultural centres such as Bath, York, Exeter and Canterbury were targeted, and the V-1 and V-2 'flying bomb war' between June 1944 and March 1945 when more than 9,000 people were killed by the 'doodlebugs' that terrified the population.

As life on the Home Front became less tedious and instead much more difficult and dangerous, so entertainment became increasingly important in providing some form of escape, however fleeting. Information, too, was vital. The BBC's radio broadcasts provided both. The pre-war National Programme and various regional programmes now merged into the BBC Home Service and provided news, public information, and music, and as the months of the Phoney War went by and troops found themselves in barracks, both in France and at home, with nothing much to do, in February 1940 the BBC launched its Forces Programme to provide popular music, comedy, drama and general variety shows. The civilian population could also hear this rich mixture of entertainment and it was soon proving more popular than the Home Service. After France fell and the war came much closer to Britain, the BBC decided to continue broadcasting the Forces Programme to the entire United Kingdom. It was now the light entertainment station of choice for the nation.

Initially the Forces Programme aired from 11.00 am to 11.00 pm daily, but from 16 June 1940 it began at 6.30 am every day. Programmes that had been designed for specific services – such as *Garrison Theatre*, which starred Jack Warner, for the army, and *Ack Ack, Beer Beer*, which featured RAF officer Kenneth Horne and began as a series of special programmes for anti-aircraft, balloon barrage and searchlight units – soon became essential listening for civilians too.

BBC producer Harry S. Pepper, and orchestral conductor Charles Shadwell, who had been an entertainments officer in the West Yorkshire Regiment during the First World War, devised *Garrison Theatre*, which first aired on 10 November 1939, a forty-five-minute show running between *Private Smith Entertains* and the nine o'clock news followed by a documentary, *The Shadow of the Swastika*, 'the story of the Nazi Party'.

With *Garrison Theatre*, Pepper and Shadwell created a radio version of the homespun revues that had entertained troops on the Western Front between 1914 and 1918. Invited audiences of servicemen and servicewomen soon recreated the raucous atmosphere of those earlier times. Jack Warner's regular 'Letter from Syd', in which he read out letters purporting to be from his brother who was serving in France, proved immensely popular. Sometimes an obvious expletive was replaced with the words 'blue pencil', which delighted Warner's audience, who were all too familiar with the censor. *Garrison Theatre* made a star of Warner – who was the brother of Elsie and Doris Waters, whose comedy double-act playing 'Gert and Daisy' had already ensured their fame – and the show's catchphrases such as 'Mind my bike!' (each week Warner would arrive on a bicycle which would always be in the way) and 'little gel' (referring to the character of an usherette, played by Shadwell's daughter, 21-year-old Joan Winters) were soon in common use.

Garrison Theatre ran on the radio for a year before transferring to a stage tour of the country. On Christmas Eve 1940, the *Nottingham Journal* reviewed the show that had begun a two-week run at the city's Empire Theatre:

> That Jack Warner's microphone reputation is fully deserved is the first and immediate impression made by 'Garrison Theatre' … played before two equally appreciative audiences last night. One novel feature of the presentation was the fact that real members of HM Forces occupy special box seats on the stage, and the Navy, the Army, and the Air Force were represented last night.
>
> Jack Warner, assisted and supported by Joan Winters and a chorus of 'Little Gels', gave us many examples of the new style of verbal humour which he has perfected, including

> the story of the fishmonger and the seals, an imitation of Maurice Chevalier, and a letter from Brother Syd, who has apparently migrated to Ireland!

The *Nottingham Evening Post* reviewer thought that 'if "Garrison Theatre" is good on the radio – and who will deny it? – it is even better on the stage and at the Empire audiences will find that their radio favourites grow in their affection through the contact that can be made over the footlights'. The reviewer continued:

> Jack Warner, that pleasant, average, 'rough diamond' private, is even more likeable, his 'Little Gel', Joan Winters, has a personal appeal of which her radio prattle is but a pale reflection, the twelve little WAAF girls might easily explain the male enthusiasm for the RAF, while the Garrison Theatre Band conducted by Fred Bretherton, plays popular melodies with a verve that is infectious.

Ack Ack, Beer Beer began broadcasting on 1 July 1940, twice weekly on Mondays and Thursdays. The BBC announced that the programmes would consist 'generally of sketches, parlour games, talks, recordings of singsongs and concerts, and record recitals based on requests' but also asked for ideas from the service personnel at whom it was targeted. Kenneth Horne, hitherto a member of the Royal Air Force Volunteer Reserve, was called up to the RAF full-time upon the outbreak of war. In charge of a barrage balloon unit, during the Phoney War he formed a concert party.

Early in 1942, BBC producer Bill McLurg asked whether the balloon station at which Horne was stationed could put on an edition of *Ack Ack, Beer Beer*. Thus, Horne, now a squadron leader, made his broadcasting debut on 16 April 1942. The talent was not particularly high, but Horne impressed McLurg with his presentation, especially when hosting the show's quiz. Horne was invited to be its regular quizmaster and by early 1943 was presenting the entire show. In March that year, he was posted to the Air Ministry with the rank of wing commander but continued to work on *Ack Ack, Beer Beer*, writing sketches for the programme and working on other BBC shows and stations including the Overseas Recorded Broadcasting Service (ORBS), which was part of the Entertainment National Service Association (ENSA), to provide troops with mostly fifteen- and thirty-minute programmes taken from or based upon previously transmitted works. That brought Horne into contact with Squadron Leader Richard 'Stinker' Murdoch, who he once jokingly introduced as 'the station commander of Much-Binding-in-the-Marsh', a name that, towards the end of the war, was going to be so familiar to radio audiences.

Ack Ack, Beer Beer came to an end in February 1944, when the BBC abandoned the specific entertainment need of barrage balloon crews to concentrate on the general armed forces. On 27 February, the *Sunday Sun*'s radio critic Ronald Strode told readers:

> The radio will take on a fresh interest for listeners from today when the new General Forces Programme makes its aerial bow. Many new features, strange newsreaders and announcers, and new times for the broadcasting of familiar broadcasts will puzzle and intrigue listeners for a time. However, when the novelty has worn off, I'm afraid many home listeners will wish they could have backed the old Forces programme again…

Horne and Murdoch now presented the idea of a programme about a fictitious RAF station called Much-Binding-in-the-Marsh. Horne would play the part of a dim-witted station commander with Murdoch as his long-suffering second-in-command. *Much-Binding-in-the-Marsh* first aired as a segment in *Merry-go-Round* in March 1944 before enjoying a life of its own in various formats between then and 1954, the RAF station becoming a country club. Horne would continue to be a household favourite well after the war with programmes such as *Beyond Our Ken* and *Round the Horne*, the latter running until 1968.

The pre-war *Band Waggon* – the first comedy shows to be designed specifically for radio – starring Arthur Askey and Richard Murdoch continued in popularity until the middle of 1940 – the year that a film version of the show was released – when it ended because Murdoch joined the RAF, while Askey went off to pursue a film career.

On Sunday, 26 May 1940, as the evacuation from Dunkirk got under way, a new radio show aired on the Forces Programme. *Hi Gang!* was the idea of American film actor Ben Lyon who, with his actress wife, Bebe Daniels, had been travelling around Britain entertaining troops and workers alike in theatres, army camps and factories. Lyon suggested to the BBC's head of light entertainment, Pat Hillyard, that a light comedy programme on radio would reach so many more people all at the same time and would help to boost morale as the war took a disturbing new turn. Austrian-born British actor and comedian Vic Oliver agreed to join them. Daniels wrote most of the script, there was a new song every week, and the show delighted its audience by poking fun at Hitler and at 'Lord Haw-Haw', the Anglo-Irish anti-British propagandist whose voice was now as familiar on the wireless as that of any comedian.

After the show made its radio debut, the *Daily Mirror*'s Bernard Buckham praised it:

> If you ask me for an example of something 'light and bright' I would cite Bebe Daniels, Ben Lyon and Vic Oliver fooling around in the new Forces feature 'Hi Gang'. Some of the dialogue was not so hot, but all three have that vitality and distinctive personal appeal which makes a poor joke sound good, and a good joke sound a million dollars. It must be a gag-writer's paradise to find a bunch of such clients. Here is a typical Vic Oliver crack. 'She was at home yesterday busy with her spring cleaning. Yes, she discovered four new rooms.' And the way Vic says it makes it sound like a real bit of information, confidentially imparted. I liked Bebe's new song. All the crooners will be after it, but if any of them sing it as well as she does, I should be glad – and surprised.

Hi Gang! would see out the war and continue being broadcast until 1949.

Radio was increasingly seen as a way to improve morale throughout the country and in June 1940 the *Radio Times* announced: 'This coming week there will be, twice every day, half an hour's music meant specially for factory workers to listen to as they work. You will find it in the programme pages for each day under the title "Music While You Work".' And so, at 10.30 am on Sunday, 23 June 1940, a new half-hour radio programme began on the BBC. It first aired on the Home Service that day and featured the theatre organist Dudley Beaven. The second edition went out at 3.00 pm that afternoon, on the Forces Programme when it was sandwiched between *All Sorts of Music*, in which gramophone records were played, and a variety show starring, among others, Cyril Fletcher and Morton Fraser 'from the stage of a cinema'.

On that first day, newspaper listings applied the name *Music While You Work* to only the afternoon slot, which featured a trio, the Organolians, with Harry Farmer playing the Hammond organ, Jack Moss the drums, and Jimmy Leach the piano. Leach would later take over the organ and the band, and in September 1967 Jimmy Leach and his Organolians would play the final tune of the final edition of *Music While You Work.*

Back in June 1940, however, at the same time as the Organolians were getting into the swing of things, the Home Service offered a concert featuring the BBC Orchestra (Section B) followed by a talk from the Very Reverend F. A. Iremonger entitled 'From a Deanery Window'. As *Music While You Work* was the result of a suggestion by the government, that if cheerful music was piped into the nation's factories then it would improve morale and thus lead to better production, it is unlikely that, on this Sunday afternoon, many munitions factories were opting for the bass tones of Norman Walker and a talk about religious books and events.

Music While You Work was to be broadcast in two half-hour programmes daily, one at 10.30 am and the other in the middle of the afternoon, halfway through shifts when production might be flagging. A different band, orchestra or ensemble would play each day and the best choice of music would be that which encouraged workers to whistle or sing along. A great deal of thought went into each playlist. At the best of times, factories can be noisy environments, and the music played over a public-address system had to be loud as well as of a constant pitch. The tempo also had to be just right. Nothing too slow, obviously, but nothing too fast either. It was felt that this might unsettle workers. So the BBC issued a set of rules to which producers had to strictly adhere.

Banned completely were numbers with predominant rhythm, insufficient melody, or other unsuitable characteristics; numbers that were lethargic or unsuited to any speeding up of tempo; all modern slow waltzes, due to their soporific tendencies. There was also a list of numbers that were deemed unsuitable for other reasons, such as 'Deep in the Heart of Texas' whose clapping motif, it was felt, would encourage workers to bang their spanners on the machinery, causing damage to the same. Initially *Music While You Work* had different signature and signing-off tunes but in October 1940 it adopted permanently for both 'Calling All Workers', composed by Eric Coates, whose name would one day become synonymous with the 'Dam Busters March'. Eventually, as twenty-four-hour shifts were introduced in armaments factories, *Music While You Work* was broadcast three times daily.

The programme was a huge success, and by the end of the war more than 9,000 factories broadcast it through loudspeakers to workers. The *BBC Year Book* for 1941 commented:

> Programmes of music for factory workers have been broadcast since the end of June as a help to lessen strain, relieve monotony, and thereby increase efficiency. The initiative came from the factories, and in collaboration with recognised authorities the BBC carried out research among workers to discover their preferences, and among factories to establish their special needs. The result was the mid-morning and mid-afternoon programmes *Music While You Work.*

In March 1941, *Workers' Playtime* – 'a lunch-hour entertainment for factory workers relayed from a factory somewhere in Britain' – made its debut, building on a similar show, *Works Wonders*, that had been broadcast in November 1940. *Workers' Playtime* would be heard three times a week, the Ministry of Labour choosing the factories from which it would be broadcast, and the Minister of Labour and National Service, Ernest Bevin, appeared on it several times, congratulating workers for their efforts. *Workers' Playtime* went on to become one of the BBC's longest-running radio shows, airing until 1964, the venues, of course, by then disclosed. Throughout its twenty-three years, *Workers' Playtime* was produced by Bill Gates, who always ended the show by wishing, 'Good luck, all workers!'

Throughout the war, Henry Hall, the pre-war leader of the BBC Dance Orchestra who had formed his own orchestra, played for troops, both through live performances with ENSA and through his radio programmes, and gave concerts in factories, cinemas and theatres all over Britain. In February 1939, when they fulfilled a four-week contract at the Scala Variety Theatre in Berlin, he apparently agreed to drop tunes composed by Jews. Nevertheless, Henry Hall continued to be a regular, and welcome, sound on the BBC during and long after the war.

After the United States entered the war, and American troops were stationed in Britain, from March 1942 listeners to the BBC benefited from the addition of programmes like *The Bob Hope Show* and *The Jack*

Benny Programme to the domestic schedule, although when reports on American sports were later included there were accusations that Britain's national broadcaster was in danger of becoming 'Americanised'. Acknowledging the wider range of entertainment, in February 1944, as more and more US troops arrived to prepare for the invasion of Europe, the BBC created the General Forces Programme, which replaced the Forces Programme and ran until the end of 1946, after which the Light Programme came into being.

It was not only the introduction of American sports items that made some people feel that, when it came to Britain's cultural heritage, this 'invasion' by GIs had gone too far. In May 1943, in his 'Listening Post' column in the *Daily Herald*, Spike Hughes complained:

> Now that we got so many genuine Americans on the air over here, I do think it's time we were given a rest from the pseudo-American accents affected by so many dance band singers and others. We surely have enough dialects of our own in the English language without having to borrow from the States … this ridiculous Americanisation of our language is something the BBC should not encourage. Not because American hasn't its points but because we have a rich language of our own which should be good enough for British programmes for British people, particularly overseas. But listen to any dance band programme and you hear even British tunes sung with a bogus accent by people who've never been any further west than Shepherds Bush Empire.

When asked on D-Day what the 'fighting forces' thought of the General Forces Programme, the Minister of Information, Brendan Bracken, told the House of Commons, 'The evidence in the hands of the BBC shows that the programme is very acceptable to the Fighting Forces.'

Chapter 4

It's That Man Again

> Such sunshine Tommy Handley radiated into millions of homes through years when little of any other sort could be snatched from the events and environments oppressing them.
>
> *Birmingham Gazette*

Throughout the Second World War, the radio show that it seemed no one wanted to miss was *It's That Man Again*. *ITMA*, as it was universally known, had begun broadcasting on 12 July 1939, initially as four shows to be aired fortnightly. It took its name from the ever-increasing use of the phrase during the early months of that year to describe Hitler, specifically in a *Daily Express* headline of 2 May, over an article written by Bert Gunn who had begun to use it when talking about the increasingly alarming behaviour of the Führer on the international stage. New Zealand-born Ted Kavanagh wrote the *ITMA* scripts which generally followed the adventures of Tommy Handley, a Liverpool-born variety artiste and himself a scriptwriter who during the First World War had served in a kite balloon section of the Royal Naval Air Service.

At the age of 14, Handley had been apprenticed to a merchant at Liverpool Corn Exchange, but he had no heart for such work. His spare time was given to amateur theatricals and playing the mouth organ at local concert parties before he earned an audition with a touring company. His radio career had started in 1925, in the 2LO Days – the first official broadcasts were transmitted by London station 2LO from Marconi House Studios on the Strand – of the BBC. Engaged as a singer, he soon revealed his gift for comedy.

In those early days of his career he met Jean Allistone, a young soprano. They kept their romance a secret before surprising everyone by their marriage in 1929. Before the Second World War, he was already known as the 'Winterbottom' of what the *Bradford Observer* described as 'the fast moving, sophisticated and deliriously inconsequential crosstalk act "Murgatroyd and Winterbottom", in which his outrageous puns and verbal capers were ably matched by Ronald Frankau [an English comedian who started in cabaret and made his way to radio and films]'.

Handley, then, was already a veteran of radio entertainment, having worked in the medium in its infancy. Now, thanks to *ITMA*, he was to become a national treasure.

However, after listening to the first airing of *ITMA*, the *Daily Mirror* critic Bernard Buckham was less than impressed:

> The kind-hearted BBC seem to have adopted a new principle for their summer entertainments. Am I right in thinking that they desire to do nothing which would tempt us in from the open-air, or induce us to waste the precious hours of summer in listening to the radio?
>
> On no other basis do I find it possible to account for the quality of some of the new shows. Take for instance 'It's That Man Again'. Yes, take it, and I could tell you an appropriate destination for it, but we have to make at least some effort to be polite in print, even if BBC comedians no longer trouble to be so on the air.
>
> Perhaps they feel there are only a few people listening at the start and more at the finish, so that a little crude vulgarity, honest or otherwise, doesn't matter one way or the other. I had an impression that radio shows were carefully written and rehearsed, but 'It's That Man Again' showed little sign of either process. It had one good idea, and one only – the 'dog bites man' series of topsy-turvy interviews. But it is one thing to strike a good idea and another to work it out successfully.
>
> Neither Mr Sam Heppner nor his barber appeared to have any acquaintance with histrionic technique, and, as a result, their dialogue – even if it had been good dialogue – was bound to be flat and characterless. The turn got plenty of studio laughs, so evidently something funny was going on, but listeners could only guess what it was.
>
> The hair-cut could have been an air cut and we at home would have lost nothing … Tommy Handley had to make it a one-man show so far as humour went, for it is difficult to find anything very exciting in a young lady who slavishly

> imitates Gracie Allen [the American internationally known as the scatterbrain partner of fellow actor and comedian George Burns] without saying so; neither am I, for one, any longer thrilled by the comic (?) foreigner who makes silly mistakes with his English.
>
> Even our own inexhaustible Tommy seemed to find the situation desperate at times … though I must say that he and the band between them would probably have given a better show had they been relieved of the assistance of the 'entire company'. 'It's That Man Again' is the first of a series. Let us hope for something better next time.

The show survived Buckham's withering review, and over the next ten years Handley went on to undertake a number of bizarre posts, fictional of course, such as Minister of Aggravation and Mysteries at the Office of Twerps; the major of a down-at-heel seaside resort called Foaming at the Mouth; and Governor of a South Sea island, Tomtopia. There were characters such as Colonel Humphrey Chinstrap, a permanently sozzled former Indian Army officer who, no matter what the question, assumed that he was being offered a drink and always replied: 'I don't mind if I do!' The character was played by Jack Train, who based it on someone he had known.

'I don't mind if I do!' became a catchphrase repeated in homes, shops, factories and pubs across the nation. Others caught on too: 'Can I do you now, sir?' spoken by Dorothy Summers' character, a cleaner called Mrs Mopp; 'Don't forget the diver,' spoken by Horace Percival who entered and exited as a diver; 'It's being so cheerful as keeps me going,' the words of Mona Lott, a depressed laundrywoman played by Joan Harben; 'This is Funf speaking,' a German spy also played by Jack Train. And, perhaps the most used of all – 'TTFN' ('Ta ta for now'). There was Ali Oop, a Middle Eastern character who sold saucy postcards and other dubious merchandise, and whose catchphrase was, 'I go … I come back.' And two over-polite workmen ('After you, Claude.' 'No, after you, Cecil'). The programme kept the nation entertained as it sat behind its blackout curtains, eking out that week's food ration, and wondering if this would be another night spent in the air-raid shelter.

ITMA would run for more than 300 episodes to January 1949. On 9 January that year, *The People* reported that *ITMA* producer Francis Worsley had arranged a 'high-spot comedy series' starring

Joyce Grenfell: 'With Tommy Handley on the one hand and Joyce Grenfell on the other, Worsley may end up with ITTA – It's Those Two Again.'

It was not to be. That afternoon, the irreplaceable Tommy Handley died a few days short of his 57th birthday, at Cleveland nursing home in Paddington after suffering a brain haemorrhage at his flat in Amersham Court on Craven Road, near Lancaster Gate. At 5.00 pm as usual the BBC began broadcasting a repeat of that week's *ITMA*. News of its star's death reached Broadcasting House barely five minutes before the show ended, and it was decided to allow it to continue.

Barely twenty-four hours later, *ITMA* had gone, too. Ted Kavanagh told a reporter,

> The show will definitely end. Tommy – 'That Man' – is dead, and the show could not possibly go on without him … Mr Jack Handley and his wife [Tommy's brother and sister-in-law] are here with Mr Francis Worsley, and we are trying make all arrangements. I can't quite grasp the fact even now. The whole cast is stunned … He was the greatest radio comedian we have had in this country. He was very easy to work with. His death is such a shock to me that it is difficult to frame words to express my admiration for him.

Tributes poured in from other members of the *ITMA* team. Jack Train: 'The news of Tommy's death is really staggering. Not only have I lost a great workmate, I have lost a very great friend.'

Diana Morrison: 'Tommy was the nicest person I have ever worked with. He was always amiable, a very sweet-tempered man.'

Joan Harben: 'Tommy was a wonderful personality and a charming person to work with. His death is a crushing blow to us all.'

Hugh Morton: 'He was always so full of life, a real human being, quiet, considerate and wonderfully easy to work with, and with all his success, completely unspoiled. I am one of the millions into whose lives he brought happiness and laughter. We shall miss him sorely.'

Fred Yule: 'I have known Tommy for over twenty-five years and there was never a grander fellow. He was exactly the same off the stage as on it. He was always ready to crack a gag, no matter how things were going. His death comes as a great shock. He was one of the grandest troupers ever.'

Great stars of the day also queued up to record their tributes. Jack Benny said, 'His death is a great blow. I am glad I got to see him when I was in London last year to renew our friendship that began when both of us were playing at the Palladium. He gave me much encouragement and help. He was a grand trouper.'

Danny Kaye said, 'I met him and heard his shows. It was one of the finest radio shows in any country. His passing is a terrible loss, not only for the British people who loved him, but for all the men and women and children he helped up the ladder.'

Charlie Chaplin was ill in bed, suffering influenza, but his family quoted him: 'I am terribly shocked. He was of the truly great ones.'

Tommy Handley had also appeared in two cinema films, *It's That Man Again* (1943) based on his radio series –the *Radio Times* called the film 'disappointing' – and *Times Flies* (1944), where he played a variety performer who, along with three others, accidentally travels back to Elizabethan times in a time machine. Handley was said to be the Royal Family's favourite comedian, and a letter writer to the *News Chronicle* demanded to know why he had never been knighted.

On the day after his death, the *Bradford Observer* captured the mood:

> Millions of listeners, young and old, will be the sadder this morning as they realise that, except for 'playbacks', they will never hear 'That Man' again. For five years during the war, and with a slight break each year since, this fellow of infinite jest led his great team of comic and fantastic mountebanks in a weekly verbal rough and tumble in which anything could happen – and usually did.

So great was the national affection *ITMA* aroused that thousands of people, six and seven deep, lined the route of Tommy Handley's funeral procession as it made its way along the six-mile route from a private chapel in Westbourne Grove to Golders Green Crematorium, just four days after his death. At points on the route where the traffic was stopped and the roar of London was stilled, bus drivers sat bareheaded in their cabs, their caps in their hands. Behind the hearse that carried Tommy Handley's coffin were three others laden with floral tributes from some of the millions who nationwide paid their respects to the man who, for ten years – six of them the most difficult of their lives – had made then laugh. That evening, instead of the usual *ITMA* broadcast, the BBC aired an appreciation of Tommy Handley, 'a programme of songs and music from *ITMA* which will be the radio memorial'.

On 27 January, a reported 4,000 people, including some bemedalled Chelsea Pensioners, attended a memorial service at St Paul's Cathedral. Many of the congregation had to stand and the service was relayed to a further 2,000 on the steps outside. Black-cloaked vergers went among the crowd, distributing printed copies of the service.

Tommy's wife had not been well enough to attend his funeral and now she sat at home listening to his memorial on the radio. She heard the Bishop of London, Dr William Wand, say of Tommy Handley, 'From the highest to the lowest in the land, men and women of every station have found in his programmes an escape from their troubles and anxieties into the realm of whimsical nonsense. His genius transmitted the copper of our common experience into the gold of exquisite foolery.'

Chapter 5

Mr Wu's an Air Raid Warden Now

> What George Formby has done for the fighting troops is beyond praise.
>
> Journalist N. W. Cutler, March 1945

In February 1944, Britain wondered when the Allied invasion of Europe would begin. However, the Rector of Cheltenham, Canon J. B. Goodliffe, had more pressing concerns. Writing in his parochial review, Canon Goodliffe confessed to being appalled by parishioners' behaviour in what most people had hitherto regarded as a genteel Gloucestershire spa town.

> Very soon another front will be opened. Gallant men will die. Is this the time for all this folly? I detest being considered the censor of morals. Here, however, are some facts which are disquieting. George Formby, in a sincere and brilliant broadcast reassured the womenfolk at home on two fundamental anxieties. In the whole of his tour in the East he had not seen a single drunken soldier, and in his humorous vein – and it was none the less effective because it was lightly stated – he also said that there was very little immorality with women. Had George Formby attended a recent dance at the Town Hall in connection with a well-deserved object in the town, he would have seen a disgraceful sight, and decent people left the hall. I do not wish to say more but I have given and will give facts that are shocking to any responsible person. Had George Formby walked through this town any evening during the blackout, or even visited the parish church porch, he would have seen disgraceful sights.

That Cannon Goodliffe had chosen George Formby to reinforce his point was yet another measure of the influence that the nation's number-one entertainer had on the general mood of wartime Britain.

Born George Hoy Booth in Wigan on 26 May 1904, the eldest of seven children, Formby had trained as a jockey before, in 1921, taking his late father's stage name to continue the family business as a music hall comedian, a northern working-class character of gormless disposition. Learning to play the ukulele not only broadened his act, it also became what might be described today as his unique selling point. Besides his sheer talent, though, it was Formby's warm, friendly personality coupled with the strong management of his wife, Beryl, that meant that by 1939 he was the highest-paid entertainer in Britain, earning a reported £100,000 a year, the equivalent of £8.36 million in 2023. Alongside live performances to sold-out theatres, film contracts with Associated Talking Pictures and then with Columbia made him the number-one box office star of the 1930s.

In February 1940, Formby took a pay cut when he signed up with ENSA, the organisation set up by producers and directors Leslie Henson and Basil Dean to provide entertainment for the British armed forces. Performers were paid £10 a week, members of the chorus £4. Still relatively generous wages at the time, but a massive drop for top stars like George Formby, although he remained under contract to Associated Talking Pictures.

Over the next six years, his ENSA journeys would take him to battlefronts halfway around the world. He was also enlisted to make morale-boosting films for the war effort. In the 1940 low-budget propaganda movie *Let George Do It!* he dreams of flying to Germany on a barrage balloon, landing in a Nazi rally, and punching Adolf Hitler.

Formby certainly knew how to connect with an audience suffering all the privations and inconveniences that the war was visiting upon them. In April 1941, he released a song entitled 'I Did What I Could With My Gas Mask'. The lyrics do not mention the war but contain such lines as, 'My sister has a lot of socks to mend, so she gave me a fat bouncing baby to tend. And when I felt it leaking at one end, well I did what I could with my gas mask.' His main purpose, of course, was to create laughter, perhaps poke fun at the madness of it all. But there was also the reminder that, wherever one went in those dark times, one should always carry one's gas mask.

There was also the wartime patriotism shown by his 'Mr Wu', who in 1932, after losing his heart to another, found his laundry business was going under, and so came the comic song 'Chinese Laundry Blues', written by Jack Cottrell.

In December 1939, George had Mr Wu change trades in 'Mr Wu's a Window Cleaner Now'. Then, in 1942, George recruited him for the ARP, patrolling the streets ensuring that the blackout was enforced in the song 'Mr Wu's an Air Raid Warden Now'. The song included the now politically incorrect line, 'So if you've got a chink in your window, you'll have another one at your door.'

On 12 February 1940, British newspapers reported:

> George Formby is to take a strong variety company to France next month to entertain the troops. He has offered to stay a month or even longer. A contract in pantomime has prevented George from going overseas before March, but he has already given shows to troops in Britain. Offers of professional engagements to follow his pantomime have all been declined so that he may go to France. By thus giving his services for NAAFI and ENSA troop shows, George has voluntarily sacrificed thousands of pounds.

That month, *The Sphere* carried a photograph of Formby giving an impromptu performance for members of the British Expeditionary Force who he had met by chance along the wayside in France.

Home and abroad, Formby appeared to be a workaholic. In January 1942, he undertook a three-week, seventy-two-show tour of Northern Ireland, including several in Belfast, one of which was at the Empire Theatre that had been placed at the disposal of ENSA for a special performance to an invited audience of HM Forces. Most of his shows were for the benefit of troops but he also did fundraising shows for local charities. One of these, at the Belfast Hippodrome, raised more than £500.

At an ENSA concert, at Wellington Hall in Belfast, he performed in front of an audience of 1,600 that included John Miller Andrews, Northern Ireland's second prime minister, and members of his Cabinet. The *Belfast Telegraph* reported:

> The famous comedian was given a foretaste of the welcome which awaits him at every centre in Ulster to which he will pay a visit during his stay. And he says he knows he is going to enjoy himself over here. In a brief

> speech at the conclusion of the show he told the crowded house that he is never happier than when entertaining the troops, and as long as the war lasted he would be found 'among the boys'. 'I am glad to be in Northern Ireland, and at least I'll get summat proper to eat,' he added, amidst laughter. George was bang on top of his form, and, as always, was generous with his encores which included a combination of 'Mr Wu' and 'Cleaning Windows,' and a side-splitting parody on 'Bless 'Em All'. A first-class supporting programme was provided by the Rialto Variety Company.

The following month he was taking an active role in the national campaign for waste paper salvage. Not satisfied with giving it his verbal support, he made rounds in his own car to collect paper in his native Lancashire.

Formby appeared almost everywhere. In March 1943 ,he visited the Empire, Southampton, for a concert in aid of the Southampton division of the British Red Cross Society Fund, and George Formby's Fund for Trawlermen's Widows and Orphans. *The Stage* reported: 'There was a full house to give a great welcome to Mr Formby who was in capital form, and it is expected that the net proceeds for equal division between the two worthy causes will be £500.' The summer was a chequerboard of concerts to troops, concerts to factory workers, and fundraisers (which he did for free) across Britain.

By now, ENSA performers carried the rank of commissioned officers. That autumn, the *Sunday Pictorial* told readers that, just like troopers going into battle, ENSA troupers also had to wear uniforms. The newspaper was not impressed:

> George Formby, too, has got his own natty uniform. It was actually rushed out by aeroplane to the Middle East, where he is playing to the boys. I know what they will think about it – and how popping mad they'll be. They have had enough of uniforms without meeting these chocolate soldiers from home. Fancy saluting an officer, only to find it was George Formby! I'll bet George will think the whole thing is 'daft'. And he'll be right. Can't ENSA think up something better to do with their money?

That month George and Beryl Formby gave the first ENSA show for the forces on Italian mainland. For ninety minutes, they entertained officers and men of the RAF, the army, and the navy at Reggio, the first city to be captured on the toe of Italy. Canadians and some Americans were also present.

George and Beryl played from a raised platform in a public garden used by the Italians for band performances. George, wearing a khaki shirt and shorts and a typically northern cloth cap, sang favourites such as 'Mr Wu', 'Little Stick of Blackpool Rock' and 'Bellbottom George'.

'This is the proudest moment of my life,' declared George at the end of the show. 'I'm glad and honoured to be the first British artiste to have played to you fighting lads in Italy. You've gone a long way and I've had a bit of a rush to catch you up.'

There was trouble ahead, however. On 16 October 1943, the Variety Artistes' Federation refuted Formby's claims that 'most of the stars are in the West End'. The executive of the Federation said that they were shocked at the suggestion that certain stage stars were reluctant to give their voluntary services for national service entertainment. They said that, when Formby returned, he would be asked the names of the artistes to whom he referred. They told the *Daily Mirror* that the majority of West End stage and screen stars volunteered their services for special tours. 'Many well-known stars have rung us today,' an official said, 'asking us to state that they are not guilty of Mr Formby's allegations. Next week will see an all-time peak in the number of well-known artistes going on tour for us. Two-hundred and sixty-one stars will be touring at the same time.'

Formby was unrepentant. Later that month, the *News Chronicle* reported:

> George Formby, who arrived home yesterday from an eight-weeks' tour giving ENSA shows to troops in North Africa and Italy, found that, back in England, he had created a war of his own. In an interview which appeared in a new forces paper published in Algiers, the 'Union Jack', he attacked stay-at-home stars. 'Most of the stars are in the West End where we left them.' he said. 'I had no idea that I was giving an interview,' Mr Formby explained last night. 'I was talking to a bunch of boys of the Eighth Army and among them happened to be the editor of a local paper. But

> my statements were perfectly true. Lots of stars are doing their share, and all I can say of the rest of them is – if the cap fits let 'em wear it!'

A few days later, it was reported in several British newspapers that Gracie Fields, the Rochdale-born actress, singer and comedienne who was a huge favourite with British forces, had been recalled from her visit to entertain troops in North Africa to fulfil a US radio contract worth $40,000 (about £8,000, which was the purchasing power equivalent to more than half a million pounds today, a staggering amount by any standard) a week.

ENSA's director Basil Dean put the blame squarely on the shoulders of Fields's husband, Italian-born Monty Banks. He said that on 30 September, when Gracie should have been back in the US, he had received a cable from Banks: 'Frantic. Lack of information regarding Gracie. American Tobacco Company purchased broadcasting facilities; weekly cost $40,000. We rely your positive guarantee she will return … I will hold you personally liable for all losses failure to return here. Please accomplish Gracie's return immediately.'

The Eighth Army newspaper *Crusader* published an open letter in which it made a bitter accusation against Gracie Fields – who even before the war, in the 1938 New Year Honours, had been awarded the CBE for her services to entertainment – and other named stars:

> You and the rest of the top-liners of the theatrical profession have let down the fighting soldiers. Blame it on ENSA if you like. Most of you do, but ENSA did not make Tommy Trinder, Max Miller, Leslie Sarony (who wrote a rather sickly song about us but did not come to sing it to us), Florence Desmond, the Crazy Gang, Stanley Holloway and the rest stay at home all these years to keep the spotlights burning.

The letter was signed by Sergeant D. H. Martin, who said,

> Dear Gracie, so you didn't stay with us very long. You told the *Crusader* you thought the Eighth Army saved England. You said if you had your way you would follow us to the end, entertaining whenever conditions permitted. Your

> wish reached the ears of army headquarters. They sent you a signal saying that all facilities would be given to you to stay with us. You received that signal. But you didn't stay. You had a contract to consider. Men whose lives you could brighten have had to break many more sacred contracts.

From Hollywood, Gracie Fields responded, 'I am now cancelling all future American engagements to return to the battlefields, possibly in January. The boys can be sure they will see me back sooner than they expect. I wanted to stay with them as my life is theirs.' According to Monty Banks, General Montgomery had wired inviting her to Italy. 'She wishes to accept,' said Banks.

Formby's criticism of some of his fellow performers produced a mixed reaction. Florence Desmond, who had co-starred with him in films, was indignant. She told the *Sunday Pictorial*, 'It's worth remembering that George Formby makes such fabulous sums of money that it doesn't matter to him whether he's earning or not. I have already given notice that as soon as this show is over I am volunteering for overseas.'

The Crazy Gang's Chesney Allen, speaking for Bud Flanagan and himself, said that they had both volunteered for overseas more than a year ago. Their offer was not accepted owing to the 'fluid situation then, but we're only too willing to go overseas as soon as our contract is fulfilled'. ENSA said that Tommy Trinder was 'going overseas soon'.

In December 1943, a letter appeared in the *Chelmsford Chronicle*:

> Sir, I and the undersigned officers and airmen of the unit under my command wish to express our wholehearted support for George Formby in the stand he is making for better entertainment for overseas troops. We had the pleasure of entertaining Mr and Mrs George Formby in our humble desert mess, when they were playing to troops in this area and on that occasion had the opportunity of discussing with them the absence of the top-line artistes in entertainments for the troops. They themselves were, in fact, the first well-known stage personalities we had seen during the whole of the desert campaign, and during two years in the desert we have seen only three ENSA concert parties.

After D-Day, performers followed the invasion force. On 24 July 1944, Reuters reported,

> George Formby paid tribute to the men of the minesweepers who have not been ashore for six weeks by giving the first ENSA concert in Normandy off the beaches this afternoon. Officers and ratings in the small cinema sang lustily, and cheered themselves hoarse with delight. Formby drove a duck [a DUKW, an amphibious truck] out to the ship but would not pull up alongside. He said to the driver, 'Eeh lad, tha'd better take over or we shall never get alongside – we shall go reight through.' The performance lasted two hours, with Formby singing almost continuously during the second-half. Later he repeated the whole show for those unlucky in the draw for seats. His new song 'Rolling On Through France' was given a great reception.

Often he would perform in the most improvised conditions, on farm carts or lorries, or in fields bearing the scars of war. In August, newspapers reported that ENSA artistes were following the advancing armies so closely that they frequently found their voices drowned by heavy gunfire. They ate only army rations, the men sleeping in tents, the women in vans, and after a three-week stint they returned to rest hostels for a short break. George Formby was reported to have crossed the River Orne in advance of the main troops and in three and a half hours gave six shows to groups of men gathered in dugouts only 100 yd (91.5 m) behind the frontline.

The Allies were making good progress in Europe, but there was still the war in Burma where the Fourteenth Army was being described as the 'Forgotten Army' because, in comparison to the Normandy and Italian campaigns, its operations there were often overlooked by the British press. In early January 1945, the lack of any kind of welcome back in England for some of those who returned from the fighting brought an angry reaction from loved ones.

One soldier's wife wrote to the *Liverpool Echo*:

> We read with great interest of the forces arriving in the north from the Far East, but there was bitterness in our hearts when we read that there were no celebrations for these men, no

> NAFFI girls acting as hostesses, not even a mobile canteen to give them a cup of tea on their arrival. What difference is there between the men from North-West Europe and those who have not only been fighting the common enemy, but have been struggling for years in a deadly climate? For a long time now, they have called themselves the 'Forgotten Army', but here, at last, is the proof that they are forgotten by all but their families and loved ones.

George Formby said that he certainly had not forgotten them. Before daylight on 18 January 1945, the Formbys left their home near Fleetwood at the start of their Far East tour. 'When you see us again,' George told the friends who had gathered to see them off, 'we shall have flown 30,000 miles and entertained close to one million lads.' Flying from London, they would make stops at Corsica, Cairo and Baghdad, and entertained troops stationed in Iraq and Iran. Then it was on to India and Burma. He and Beryl had been inoculated sixteen times for protection against various disease. 'Our arms look like a mass of red tattoo marks,' George said.

'I'm reckoning on being in Mandalay within a fortnight,' he said. 'Wherever the lads are, we are going. They'll be no forgotten Fourteenth Army with me.'

The couple returned in mid-March, six days after giving their final show in Mandalay. Newspapers reported that the couple had travelled 25,000 miles and entertained 200,000 troops, somewhat less than George's near-million prediction but still an impressive number. The largest audience saw them perform on a stage erected on a football pitch at the British Army transit camp at Deolali in India, where 12,000 watched in the afternoon and another 7,000 in the evening. 'Talk about high morale,' he told a *Sunday Dispatch* reporter. 'These boys of the Fourteenth Army are singing happy because they know they've got the Japs on the run.'

Despite George's assurance that no one would be forgotten, something seems to have gone wrong in Burma. In July 1945, writing in *The People*, Arthur Helliwell said that troops were 'bitterly disappointed' when George Formby wasn't able to do a promised show in Mandalay.

> You'd be surprised how much the boys take a thing like that to heart. They had been looking forward to hearing George

> and his ukulele for months. I really believe anticipation put an extra kick in their fighting during the closing stages of the battle for Fort Dufferin [Mandalay Palace that had been turned into a supply depot by Japanese troops], and when he didn't turn up they felt cheated.

It is estimated that during the Second World War, George Formby and Beryl entertained more than three million Allied troops. In the 1946 King's Birthday Honours list, he was awarded the OBE for his services during the war, his delight tinged with disappointment because Beryl, the driving force behind his career, was not recognised. He continued to tour and he appeared in the West End musical *Zip Goes a Million* before leaving the show in 1952 when his health broke down. After eighteen months, he eased himself back into work with one-night performances, seaside shows and pantomime.

In 1960, he recorded 'Happy Go Lucky Me'. It was the last of more than 230 records he cut. He appeared in twenty-one films and at two Royal Command Performances, and besides those hundreds of wartime shows he also made post-war tours to Canada, Australia and New Zealand, and South Africa, where he refused to play to racially segregated audiences.

In December 1960, he made his final television appearance, on the BBC's *The Friday Show*, during which he confessed that he could neither read nor write properly, and could not understand music. He had several ukuleles, he said, each one tuned to the key of the song he was singing. He was appearing in the pantomime *Aladdin* at Bristol when Beryl died, from cancer, on Christmas Eve 1960, in Blackpool. They had been married for forty – mostly unhappy, it was said – years.

On 6 March 1961, less than three months after Beryl's death, George Formby died at St Joseph's Hospital in Mount Street, Preston, shortly after becoming engaged to schoolteacher Pat Howson, who was twenty years his junior. Tens of thousands of people lined the route of his funeral cortege to the family grave at Warrington Cemetery. In the *Daily Mirror*, Donald Zec summed up the appeal of this 'old-fashioned, corny comic with a well-worn routine of japes, larks and homely jests – rounded off with funny songs and a ukulele ... you just couldn't help laughing – at George Formby'.

Chapter 6

More Than One Forces' Sweetheart

> On Wednesday a sergeant in The Buffs enthused, 'Did you hear Anne Shelton on the wireless yesterday? Great wasn't she? I can't think why the fellows fall for Vera Lynn.' … the fans deny that their particular idol has a rival. The idols deny it too. But the battle rages on.
>
> *Sunday Mirror* columnist Norah Alexander,
> September 1944

In August 1942, the English theatrical manager and impresario C. B. Cochrane took aim at the BBC's newly formed 'Committee of Seven' whose brief it was to eliminate over-sentimental songs and 'slush' from its programmes.

'I am fully in agreement that the anaemic and debilitated singing and music should be excluded from the fare set forth for the nation – but I would stress that I fail to see how seven gentlemen can agree on what is too sentimental and slushy,' Cochrane wrote. 'I believe it would be far better to have one man, as in the case of play censorship, to decide these things. The committee is bound to get entangled in argument and in differences of opinion among themselves.'

The BBC's concerns were driven by an increasingly vocal attack by some newspapers, politicians and even members of the public on sentimental songs and singers that they claimed demoralised members of the armed forces at a time of military setbacks in North Africa and South-East Asia.

Critics often cited the radio show *Sincerely Yours*, broadcast in a primetime spot immediately after the 9.00 pm Sunday news bulletin. Presented in the form of a letter from a sister or a sweetheart figure to the boys fighting at the front, the programme began with the song 'Wishing' and saw Vera Lynn as a sort of musical link between men at war and their girls back home. Lynn read out personal messages, and sang favourites like 'The White Cliffs of Dover' and 'Yours', before ending each programme with, 'You'll hear from me again next week. Good night, boys. Sincerely yours, Vera Lynn,' after which she sang 'We'll Meet Again'.

Cochrane wanted to reduce the number of dance bands, and have 'a man of catholic taste' to decide on the songs that could not be played. But he felt it difficult to draw the line between what was sentiment and what was not.

> I can give you an example. Take Vera Lynn, who is one of the biggest attractions on the air, on the music halls and on gramophone records. She may be called the apotheosis of sentimentality, and has built up a reputation in a few years by the depth of that sentimentality … Unlike Gracie Fields, she does not switch from sentiment to the comic. It may be asked, of course, but if we can win the war with slush, why not have slush?

Cochrane felt that 'it would be wiser to deprive the forces of their cigarettes than to deprive them of Vera Lynn'. That she was now receiving up to 2,000 letters a week reinforced his point.

Vera Lynn was born Vera Margaret Welch on 20 March 1917, in East Ham, eight miles east of Charing Cross. The daughter of a plumber and a dressmaker, she began performing publicly at the age of 7, and by the time she was 11 had adopted her mother's maiden name of Lynn as her stage name. When she was 16, she was spotted by bandleader Howard Baker and joined his band. A year later she toured with Billy Cotton's band before returning to Baker's. Her first record, the song 'It's Home', was made with Baker in February 1935, and in August that year she made her first radio broadcast, with the Joe Loss Orchestra. In 1937, she joined Ambrose and his Orchestra before, in 1940, making her first performance as a solo act away from Ambrose in a show called *Star Variety* at the New Hippodrome in Coventry. According to the Birmingham *Evening Despatch*, Lynn was 'a pleasing vocalist'. The *Coventry Standard* felt that her success 'is not due primarily to the quality of her voice but rather to the sincerity with which she sings'.

In April that year, just before the 'Phoney War' came to an abrupt end, members of the British Expeditionary Force serving in France voted Vera Lynn their favourite singer. They would soon be making their way to Dunkirk, and that autumn, as the Blitz started, Lynn began making regular appearances on the BBC's *Starlight*, a fifteen-minute programme produced by Cecil Madden and aimed at troops still serving overseas. To make sure that she never missed a show, Lynn would arrive early at the BBC's Overseas Entertainment Unit in the underground Criterion Theatre and sleep there until rehearsing for the 2.30 am broadcast. Late in 1941, *Sincerely Yours* began to build on her growing reputation as 'the Forces' Sweetheart'. Running, in two separate series, until April 1942, *Sincerely Yours* attracted listeners at home as well as those with the fighting forces, at its height 20 per cent of the population of Britain tuning in.

The weekly magazine *Melody Maker* reported that 'the bulk of requests sent in by soldiers of the Eighth Army to the Overseas Service were for sentimental tunes, with recordings by Miss Vera Lynn specifically and predominantly asked for'. However, just because she was popular did not mean that she was good for morale: that was the argument of those who wanted her off the air. The BBC's new Dance Band Policy Committee bowed to that view and although she was far too popular to ban altogether, it would be eighteen months before Vera Lynn was given another solo series.

In March 1941, the *West Ham and South Essex Mail* said that 'East Ham's own crooner holds her audience with a charming voice and a natural charm, and it is very easy to join in when she invites the audience to sing with her'.

Her place as a symbol of the wives and girlfriends, mothers and sisters of soldiers stationed overseas assured, Lynn, as part of ENSA, began visiting them, in Egypt, India and Burma. In March 1944, she went to Bengal to entertain troops before the Battle of Kohima, which would see the decisive defeat of the Japanese in their offensive upon India. Her three-month journey had begun in a Sunderland flying boat en route to Gibraltar. It ended on the road from Rangoon to Mandalay in a battered car.

There are so many instances of the impact she made on men so far from home. Corporal S. T. McCormack of India Command told his sister in Teddington:

> We had a surprise last week when we had a visit from Vera Lynn. She got a tremendous reception and worked like a slave to give the lads a good show. When you consider the

> heat and the general conditions in this country it makes you appreciate her all the more for coming out here to see us. Vera went around the hospitals during the day and gave shows for patients before going around the camps in the evening when she gave shows each night. She had to wear bush jacket and slacks as you are compelled to for malarial precautions at night. At each show Vera was soaked with perspiration which came right through her jacket – my word how that girl worked.

Lance Corporal P. Stead was visiting his hometown of Biggleswade after being abroad since a year before the war as a regular soldier. He said that he had had some remarkable experiences in the jungle, including marching 800 miles in fourteen days. He said that he saw a lot of wild animals in Ceylon but none in Burma. It did not matter, though, because he did see Vera Lynn, who sang for the troops and autographed captured Japanese banknotes.

Writing to his mother in Evesham that month, Fusilier Donald Brotherton, who was serving in Burma with the Welch Fusiliers, said, 'Tonight we are having another concert, this time featuring Vera Lynn. Having often heard her it's going to be alright seeing her too.'

That August, the *Mid-Sussex Times* reported:

> Vera Lynn, the Sweetheart of the Forces, fresh from her tour of India and the Middle East, where she was received with enthusiasm by the troops, has come to the [Brighton] Hippodrome at the head of a fine variety bill. Vera's career is one of the romances of the entertainment world. For an obscure singer with dance bands she has risen in a few years to be Britain's number-one crooner, a film star, a variety top-of-the -bill, and gramophone record bestseller.

Between 1942 and 1944, Lynn had appeared in three films: *We'll Meet Again*, *Rhythm Serenade* and *One Exciting Night*. Of *One Exciting Night*, *Kinematograph Weekly* said:

> Two striking features of this production are said to be the transformation of Vera Lynn – effected by the adept handling of director Walter Forde – and the especially good

> musical score of the picture … Vera has an opportunity to step out as a comedienne. The story, which is off the beaten track for her and which has a mystery flavour, tells of a girl's adventures when becoming involved in a plot to steal a valuable painting; how she frustrates the thieves and at the same time achieves fame as a singer.

After the war, Vera Lynn continued to broadcast, toured across Europe, and in 1952 her 'Auf Wiederseh'n Sweetheart', released by Decca Records, saw her become the first English artiste to reach number one in the American charts. Her contribution during the war and her charitable work after it saw her decorated many, many times, including the award of the Burma Star from grateful veterans.

Dame Vera Lynn died on 18 June 2020, aged 103. Her husband, Harry Lewis, a saxophonist with Ambrose and his Orchestra when they married in August 1941, went on to become her manager. He predeceased her in April 1998. Their only child, a daughter, Virginia, was born in March 1946.

Vera Lynn is still a huge symbol of Britain's wartime spirit, as enduring as Winston Churchill. Harry Secombe used to say, 'Churchill didn't beat the Nazis; Vera sang them to death!'

In May 1944, two seriously wounded soldiers of the Fourteenth Army occupied a ward to themselves in a forward casualty clearing station in Burma. All morning they had been looking forward to a visit from Vera Lynn, who they had first seen some weeks earlier when she visited troops on the Arakan Front. The first words of one of them on coming out of an anaesthetic were 'Are we too late for Vera?'

They were not. Gunner Fred Thomas of Peel Road, Bootle, and Private John Badger of Croft Lane, Sheffield were about to be treated to a unique performance. After sitting with them at their bedside in a small tent in the Burmese heat, drinking tea and chatting with them about their hometowns, she answered their request, a whispered, 'Will you please sing for us, Vera?'

Of course she would. She sang softly to what was almost certainly her smallest audience ever, and perhaps her most appreciative.

Before leaving, she presented each of them with a signed photograph and asked to be kept informed of their progress. Said their commanding officer, 'Vera Lynn has contributed enormously to the recovery of those two men.'

Vera Lynn, however, was not the only 'Forces' Sweetheart' of the Second World War. 'Crooners have been getting worse and worse lately,' wrote the *Daily Mirror*'s Bernard Buckham in May 1940. Buckham had, though, one piece of good news. He felt that Anne Shelton was a singer 'likely to lift the crooning art out of its rut'.

> She has a good and distinctive voice and can call easily on the emotion necessary to make a song something more than the mere humming of a tune. She is only 16 and so has plenty of time to develop a singing personality which she would be wise to make her own. I mean that there is too much imitation nowadays, and nearly all the girls who sing with the dance bands adopt a husky, adenoidal Americanised style which gets increasingly irritating. Anne should guard against any tendency to exaggerate, either in emotional expression or vocal mannerisms. Of course, it is impossible to gauge an artiste's quality from just one song, but I certainly thought Anne Shelton highly promising.

Although she did not quite achieve Vera Lynn's prominence, Anne Shelton, too, was to become an icon of the wartime years, another with that wholesome girl-next-door appeal that meant so much to servicemen far from home. Buckham had first heard her earlier that month when she appeared on the BBC talent show *Monday Night at Eight* in which she sang 'Let the Curtain Come Down'. He was a good judge. The girl born Patricia Anne Sibley in Dulwich in 1923 was on her way.

Another to hear her on that Forces Programme show was the dance band leader Bert Ambrose. He signed her up and a month later she was making her first broadcast with Ambrose and his Orchestra. Her first solo record – 'I Can't Love You Any More' backed by 'Fools Rush In' – soon followed, and in January 1941 Anne Shelton began regular broadcasts with Jack Payne and his Orchestra in a programme called *Moods Modernistic*.

She toured the provinces, her deep contralto billed as 'the golden voice of radio', and from the autumn of 1942 she had her own radio show, *Introducing Anne*, which was aimed at troops serving in North Africa. Her signature tune was 'Lilli Marlene', which she sang with English lyrics written by Tommie O'Connor, the lyricist who was also responsible for Gracie Fields's 1938 song 'The Biggest Aspidistra in the World'.

Anne Shelton oozed nostalgia and sentimentality and her popularity with the armed forces saw her given another show entitled *Calling Malta* which ran for five years and was the troops' only link with Britain during the latter part of the air bombardment and siege of the George Cross island in 1942.

When Glenn Miller arrived in England in 1944, he invited Anne Shelton to sign with his orchestra and she did six shows with him, but because of other commitments turned down an invitation to perform with Miller in France in December, the month that the American bandleader went missing over the English Channel. That autumn, she had appeared with Bing Crosby in the radio programme *Variety Bandbox*, a programme that would run until 1952.

Throughout the war, Anne Shelton performed at British military bases and she appeared in three comedy musical films: *King Arthur was a Gentleman* (1942), *Miss London Ltd* (1943) and *Bees in Paradise* (1943).

In the post-war years she continued to enjoy a good career, in 1956 topping the UK singles chart with 'Lay Down Your Arms', another song aimed at servicemen, the lyrics telling of a woman who is waiting for her soldier to return home.

In 1953, she married David Reid, a naval officer who she had first met at Crewe railway station in 1943. He later became her business manager. Lieutenant Commander Reid died in 1990, the year that she was appointed OBE for services to the Not Forgotten Association, a charity which provides care and support for disabled ex-service personnel. Anne Shelton died at Herstmonceux, East Sussex, on 31 July 1994.

In April 1941, several newspapers carried the headline 'Forces' Sweetheart to Marry'. Betty Astell was to marry the entertainer Cyril Fletcher. Astell, an actress best known for comedy productions, apparently had an act called 'Annette, the Forces' Sweetheart'. In August 1944, *The Sphere*, reviewing *Keep Going* that was playing at London's Palace Theatre, said:

> It would be pleasant to hand out to this production all the eulogy the pluck in risking it in these perilous times may possibly deserve. I fear that, on the whole, it is not a very good revue. Far too much of it indeed, is rather poor. But

> Miss Betty Astell, who has devised, written and composed most of it and who also sings her own songs in a pleasant voice, can be congratulated on having hit the bullseye occasionally.

Neither Vera Lynn nor Anne Shelton were Forces' Sweethearts damned with such faint praise.

Chapter 7

Sing As We Go and Let the World Go By

> Eventually one guest, uninvited, began to play the piano, with one finger, knocking out probably the only tune he knew. 'Wouldn't it be grand if Jerry dropped a bomb on him?' said another guest … Then everyone started singing, first 'South of the Border' and then 'The Last Roundup'.
>
> Journalist Ray Sprigle, reporting from an air-raid shelter in London, August 1940

> America has said that Mister Churchill is worth more than an army corps to Britain. Britain will say that there is no standard by which to measure what Gracie he did last night. We've had the first dose of the tonic. Let's mark the BBC bottle 'to be taken at regular intervals throughout the war'. Thanks Gracie!

So said the front page of the *Daily Mirror* on 12 October 1939 after a surprise performance from Gracie Fields, the Lancashire lass who had become a world-famous entertainer.

The war was less than two weeks old, but it was already clear that, if the nation were to be able to put everything into the war effort, such morale-boosting moments were going to prove vital. Of all the elements of the undeniable twenty-first-century nostalgia for the culture of the Second World War, it is the music that we revisit most often. So supremely affecting were the songs of that era that they still captivate us eight decades on.

The wartime music revival allows modern Britons to connect with the generation that kept calm and carried on. But for those who lived through the war, who tuned in their radios, attended concerts and dances, put records on the gramophone or gathered around the family piano, these songs were the soundtracks to their lives, providing moments of hope and encouragement, sentiment, humour, and distraction.

Whether they were jolly ditties to lift the spirits, wistfully sentimental tunes bringing thoughts of home or absent loved ones, or ballads of love to romance by, the songs of the Second World War played an essential role in maintaining the nation's morale.

Some songs of the period became perennial anthems of optimism. If ever a song were to perfectly encapsulate the overriding wartime experiences of the heartbreak of parting and the enduring hope of eventual reunion, it was 'We'll Meet Again'. Written by British songwriters Ross Parker and Hughie Charles at the outbreak of the war, it was first recorded, on 28 September 1939, by 22-year-old Vera Lynn and released on Decca Records. Lynn would record the song many times – the most familiar being fully orchestrated. The first version, however, features only the Novachord playing of Arthur Young. The song was so popular that, before the end of 1939, it had been recorded by at least four more artistes – Victor Sylvester and his Orchestra, Jay Wilbur and his Band (with a 'vocal chorus' by Sam Browne), Les Allen, and Joe Petersen and Dudley Beaven. In October 1939, the song had been one of eight of Lynn's recordings that Decca advertised as part of its 'Decca Keeps the Flag Flying … with Entertainment for the Troops and Home' promotion in British newspapers.

The song was perfect for communal singing – its simple melody and touching lyrics also became a standard for singers and dance orchestras across the nation. A song familiar to everyone in a crowd, but also personal to each of them.

In November 1940, the lyrics of the chorus were quoted in a coming-of-age message that appeared in the *Manchester Evening News*. Placed there by Lynda and Mona Woodward for their brother Thomas, a private in the Worcestershire Regiment, missing in action since early June. The following year the family would learn that Thomas had been killed in the chaos of Dunkirk.

'We'll Meet Again' is an enduring national favourite – a song as entrenched in British culture as any other, still drawn upon during times of national strife. In 2020, Her Majesty Queen Elizabeth II referenced it during her address to the nation at the height of the Coronavirus pandemic.

An entirely different type of song, 'There'll Always Be an England' was, nevertheless, another Parker and Charles piece written and distributed in the summer of 1939. Its bold patriotic lyrics, defiant tone and bright and breezy marching tune became popular once war broke out – by November that year, 200,000 copies of the sheet music had been sold. The lyrics focused on England's countryside and rural way of life, its towns and cities as well as its busy industries, and paid tribute to the support of the Empire.

The song first appeared in the 1939 Carroll Levis film *Discoveries* – effectively a filming of his regular radio talent show set into a fictional account of Levis's daily professional life, with skits and sketches but also featuring genuine previously undiscovered variety acts. It was sung by boy soprano Glyn Davies, 'a lad from Wales who has deserted us to defend his King and Country', according to Levis. The boy was dressed in a naval uniform and with a brass and choir accompaniment performed surrounded by dozens of extras dressed as the military of the Empire. Because he was the first famous artiste to record 'There'll Always Be an England', the song became synonymous with Billy Cotton and his Band, who for many years used it as the finale of their show. But it was equally as popular as a song for a singalong, and for times of trouble. An advertisement in the *Newark Herald* of 2 December 1939, read: 'Don't Worry – There'll always be an England – records of the stirring song on sale at Coynes! Sing it! Whistle it! It's a cure for the jitters!'

Vera Lynn's '(There'll Be Bluebirds Over) The White Cliffs of Dover' is widely considered to be the most 'British' of songs, yet it was written by two Americans – Walter Kent and Nat Burton – in 1941, when their native land was still an onlooker to the war in Europe. It had been inspired by the Battle of Britain and specifically the dog fights that had taken place in the skies over southern England. As most recorded versions would do, Lynn's left out the second and third verses of Kent's original. But what remained was still a song of hope and steadfastness, and of the belief that peace and tranquillity would one day be restored. The lyrics, of course, contain an interesting quirk in the inclusion of 'bluebirds'. Britons were used to hearing about 'happy little bluebirds' flying 'Somewhere Over the Rainbow' thanks to Judy Garland's hit song from *The Wizard of Oz*, but they would, surely, have been surprised to see them in flight above Dover's white cliffs, as Burton's lyrics would promise. Presumably neither Burton nor Kent knew that bluebirds were not indigenous to the United Kingdom, as they were in North America. For decades, American songwriters had alluded to them when they wanted to evoke something optimistic, free of fear and altogether joyous. When Kent wanted a lovely image to contrast with the picture of aerial warfare, it was the lovely bluebird to which he instinctively turned. It certainly did not prevent Britain's affection for the song. Nor did the fact that Kent had never set eyes on Dover or its iconic cliffs.

The song was also recorded by Glenn Miller in November 1941 and American singer Kate Smith – most famous for her rendition of 'God Bless America' – in 1942, when it reached the US top ten. It was regularly performed throughout the war by many bands and soloists, although it remained indelibly linked to Vera Lynn.

At the outbreak of war, it was not Vera Lynn but a lass from Rochdale – actress, singer, comedienne and impersonator Gracie Fields – who had become one of the world's most beloved stars. She had made her professional debut in 1910, aged just 12, filling in for a sick performer at Rochdale Hippodrome. She had toured the nation's music halls, appeared in the West End, and worked in the USA. She was Britain's top box office draw and possibly the best-paid entertainer in the world. In 1938, she was awarded a CBE. Despite this, she retained that attainable girl-next-door popularity. Vera Lynn might have been the Forces' Sweetheart, but Fields was simply 'Our Gracie'.

When, in 1939, Fields's fans learned that she was seriously ill – although they were not told that she had been diagnosed with cervical cancer – hundreds of thousands of them sent their good wishes to her hospital bedside. When the war began, she had been convalescing at her property in Capri but returned home and almost immediately joined the war effort. In October 1939, from a parish hall, 'somewhere in England' and in front of little more than 100 service personnel, but broadcast by the BBC to millions, she gave a concert that so impressed the *Daily Mirror*: 'Gracie Fields – the woman who only a few weeks ago was almost at the door of death. Yet last night, against doctors' orders, she made millions forget that there is a war on. Only Gracie could have done it. Only Gracie could have put it over.'

One of her best-loved, and most uplifting songs was 'Sing as We Go'. Written long before the war began, its lyrics and upbeat tune were perfectly suited to the war effort. It appeared on the soundtrack of the 1934 film of the same name. Set during the Depression, it had been written for Fields by novelist J. B. Priestley. In it she plays a laid-off millworker who moves to Blackpool seeking employment. The rousing song, which writer Harry Parr-Davies had originally written while a schoolboy for an end-of-term concert, comes at the end of the film as Fields leads the workers back into the reopened mill.

With its utterly uplifting lyrics and tune, it became something of an anthem during the war, especially when there was a particular need for cheerfulness. The *Manchester Evening News* of 2 September 1939 reported that, during the evacuation of twenty-seven trainloads of youngsters to places far from home, 'one true Lancashire woman shouted, "Come on girls – Sing as we go." And Gracie's famous song was taken up with feeling.' In October 1939, the *Northamptonshire Evening Telegraph* reported that 'Sing as We Go' was one of the songs sung by 'British Tommies in France' as they whiled away the days 'waiting for the war to begin'.

'Wish Me Luck as You Wave Me Goodbye' was, according to the *Hartlepool Northern Daily Mail*, 'the new *Tipperary*' and it did, indeed, have much in common with the music hall song that had proved so popular during the Great War. It was sweet and sentimental, yet cheerful and optimistic and, again, had not been written with a war in mind. In fact, it had been written for another Gracie Fields film – *Shipyard Sally*, in which her character sings it as she boards a train to plead the case of the local shipyard workers who face unemployment.

Gracie, still recuperating from her 'long illness', wanted, very much, to perform her new song to the nation. 'I do hope the boys will like it. When I'm a little better I want to sing it myself.' To tide over her fans, the newspaper printed the lyrics to the chorus. It was, Gracie said, her new 'national cheer-up song'. And so it proved. The song, which was written by Phil Park and Harry Parr-Davies, bounces along nicely. Its cheery melody and easy to sing along-to chorus made it an instant hit. For many in Britain, who were saying 'farewell' to loved ones, the song's sentimental lyrics certainly struck a chord. It became not only that 'cheer-up song', but a national song of parting and stoicism.

As popular as she was, Fields's image was not untarnished. In 1940, as Mussolini's Italy looked to join the war, her Italian second husband, Monty Banks, was threatened with internment as an enemy alien. The couple left for New York, and Fields was accused of abandoning her country in its hour of need. But her tireless work to entertain the troops and the public, and to raise money for charity, mitigated any concerns. She distanced herself from later accusations that many performers were avoiding working with ENSA to avoid the discomforts of the front line, by cancelling her North American contracts and travelling to entertain the troops wherever she was called.

Simple, sentimental, and jolly songs had become so dominant that, in February 1940, the *Manchester Evening News* voiced the opinion that the war might even 'kill jazz'. It did not, of course, and the likes of Glenn Miller and Joe Loss did much to popularise the new swing music, just as the Andrews Sisters brought jump blues to new audiences.

Most typical was 'Boogie Woogie Bugle Boy', released in September 1941. Written by Don Raye and Hughie Prince, the song debuted in the Abbott and Costello film *Rookies* (known as *Buck Privates* in the USA). The song tells the tale of a famed trumpeter who finds himself drafted to the US Army and is forced to play reveille every morning, before being permitted to play it in his own boogie woogie style. The song became more popular when the US entered the war, its vibrant rhythms a regular number at dances.

In 1943, Anne Shelton recorded her version of 'Comin' In On a Wing and a Prayer', by Americans Harold Adamson and Jimmy McHugh. Its catchy tune and lyrics about a damaged Allied plane returning from a raid over Germany had already been recorded in the US by the Song Spinners.

'Get in Your Shelter' is a song from 1940 that rarely gets an airing today. Its subject matter hardly seems to lend itself to such an upbeat ditty, and yet there it was, a jolly, light, catchy song about using your air-raid shelter. And recorded by one of the nation's favourite stars – 'Big-Hearted' Arthur Askey. The diminutive comedian, actor and all-around entertainer was possibly the only performer who could carry off such a playful song with lyrics like 'Bomb! Bomb! Get in your shelter. Bomb! Bomb! Don't helter skelter! Get yourself right underground, when those Nazis fly around,' yet still impart a vital message.

Askey had previously been associated with entirely lighthearted songs, often of the music hall variety, such as his 'The Bee Song' of 1938. And as much as wartime was a moment for seriousness, the period also saw many new fun songs, and Askey recorded one of the most popular. 'Kiss Me Goodnight Sergeant Major', written by Art Noel and Don Pelosi, was typical of the witty, playful songs of the period and also recorded by numerous artistes like Billy Cotton and his Band and Ambrose and his Orchestra. One advertisement for the release alluded to Askey's popularity and infectious personality. 'When he laughs, you laugh too – you just can't help it! … Now he's got the army singing.'

Bud Flanagan and Chesney Allen recorded many of the most popular tunes of the war. As part of the Crazy Gang, they participated in a number of theatrical revues. One – *The Little Dog Laughed* – featured the duo singing Noel Gay and Ralph Butler's 'Run Rabbit Run'. What seems to have begun as an amusing little song about a farmer hunting rabbits soon became a mocking allegory aimed squarely at Nazi Germany. In November 1939, the Luftwaffe attempted to attack British flying boats in the Shetlands. The bombs missed, leaving a huge crater where they landed, the only victims being a pair of rabbits. This has since been revealed as a propaganda stunt, with the rabbits brought in from the local butcher, but it allowed the song to become symbolic of the Luftwaffe's apparent ineptitude. Before long another version of the song saw the word 'rabbit' replaced by 'Adolf'. The recording featured another of their great wartime hits on the 'B' side – 'We're Gonna Hang Out the Washing on the Siegfried Line'.

In contrast, the song about Germany's fortified western border was written with ridicule absolutely in mind. The lyrics were the work of Irish songwriter Jimmy Kennedy – lyricist of many familiar songs including 'The Teddy Bear's Picnic', 'Harbour Lights' and 'Red Sails in the Sunset' – to a tune by Michael Carr with whom he had written 'South of the Border (Down Mexico Way)'. At the same time as Flanagan and Allen's version, Ambrose and his Orchestra released their own take, with a similarly-titled song – 'I'm Sending You the Siegfried Line (To Hang Your Washing On)' by Ross Parker, Hughie Charles and St John Cooper – on the other side.

Musical actress Binnie Hale had first performed A. P. Herbert's and Henry Sullivan's 'A Nice Cup of Tea' in 1937 in the musical revue *Home & Beauty.* Her recording, and that of Gracie Fields from the same year, proved extremely popular with tea-obsessed Britons, particularly after the nation's favourite beverage was rationed. Hale's use of different accents – from Cockney to middle class via her natural northern tones – adds to the song's very 'realness'. Ironically, on her version, Fields's familiar rolling Lancashire dialect is largely absent.

That is certainly not the case for Fields's recording of Gordon Thompson and David Heneker's 'The Thing-ummy-bob' – the 1942 song that celebrated the work of women on essential factory production lines. In Arthur Askey's version he pays tribute, in particular, to female munitions workers. As fun and lighthearted as the song was, the lyrics reminded the nation of the importance of every worker in the land – 'it's the girl that makes the thing that holds the oil that oils the ring that makes the thing-ummy bob that's going to win the war'.

Jolly songs were certainly not the sole preserve of singers like Fields and Hale; orchestra leaders could get in on the act, too. Both Billy Cotton and Joe Loss recorded versions of Gay and Butler's 'Hey Little Hen' – a plea by a chicken owner to their one remaining hen to 'lay me an egg for my tea' during rationing. A playful novelty song, 'Mairzy Doats and Dozy Doats', proved particularly popular with children. The Merry Macs made a very successful recording of the song in 1944. Despite its seemingly nonsensical lyrics, it is really a song about what animals eat – 'mares eat oats and does eat oats' … and so on. It was one of the most popular songs of the later war years and often used during audience participation singalongs.

Not every attempt at humour was appreciated. In July 1943, during his BBC broadcast, Noël Coward performed his latest song 'Don't Let's Be Beastly to the Germans'. Coward described it as 'a satire dedicated against [those who are] taking a too tolerant view of our enemies'. With lyrics such as 'Let's be meek to them, and turn the other cheek to them', some Britons overlooked the satire and interpreted it as encouraging Nazi support. There were countless letters of complaint and the BBC were forced to ban the song. Churchill, however, loved it and invited Coward to perform 'Don't Let's Be Beastly to the Germans' at seven different private events. But the controversy rumbled on. In October 1943, a mystified Coward argued that the song had been as 'vitriolic and bitter a satire as I could well make it'.

If humour was proving rather subjective, sentimental love songs were universal favourites. 'Good Night Sweetheart', written by Ray Noble, Jimmy Campbell and Reg Connelly, had first been published in 1931. A very romantic slow foxtrot, it had been recorded by a number of crooners of the day but it was the version by Al Bowly, recorded with Ray Noble's own orchestra, which became the wartime favourite. Bowly had been at the top of his profession for more than a decade when, in April 1941, he was killed during an air raid when a parachute mine detonated outside his central London flat.

'I'll Be Seeing You' was written by American duo Sammy Fain and Irving Kahal in 1938 for a short-lived musical. An early recording, in 1940, saw Tommy Dorsey and his Orchestra team up with young vocalist Frank Sinatra but the song did not become a hit until 1944 – the year a film of the same name was released. It was also the year in which Bing Crosby, Jo Stafford, Billie Holiday, Leslie Hutchinson ('Hutch'), Geraldo and Anne Shelton all recorded the song. The sheet music was advertised in *The Stage* as 'a smashing new Fox-trot ballad' that performers 'must have in your repertoire'. Shelton's lovely, heartfelt version, made with Stanley Black and his Orchestra, struck a particular chord in Britain.

A bittersweet love song, in the form of a letter from one lover to another, now far from home, 'That Lovely Weekend', was written by married couple Ted and Moira Heath in 1941. Recorded by many stars, one of the favourites was, inevitably, recorded by Vera Lynn. Its tremendously sentimental lyrics told a story all too familiar to married couples and sweethearts thinking back to a treasured time together.

Vera Lynn is believed to have been the first artiste to have recorded another wartime classic – 'A Nightingale Sang in Berkeley Square'. It was written by British lyricist Eric Maschwitz and American musician Manning Sherwin during the summer of 1939, in the French seaside community of Le Lavandou. Its lyrics speak of the frisson of excitement as people fall in love. It was recorded numerous times by artistes like Glenn Miller and Bing Crosby.

Several of the most sentimental songs looked forward to a peaceful future, and to a return to normal life.

'I'm Going to Get Lit Up (When the Lights Go Up in London)' was written by former BBC announcer, and sometime actor, Hubert Gregg in 1940. Often being performed with altered lyrics in which the lights go 'on' rather than 'up', it was the first of some 200 songs he would publish. The most famous was 'Maybe It's Because I'm a Londoner', inspired by the sight of V-1s over the capital. Gregg debuted it at an army show, but in 1943 it became part of George Black's revue *Strike a New Note* where it was sung by Gregg's wife, Zoe Gail. The song is about all the celebrations that will happen when the war ends and 'nations lose their war sense' and uses several euphemisms for drunkenness like 'lit-up', 'pickled', 'stinking', 'canned' and 'pie-eyed'. Gregg, who was fluent in German, worked for the BBC's German service. Reputedly, Joseph Goebbels assumed him to be a native German traitor. It was sweetly ironic, then, that in 1944, his song was broadcast to alert the French Resistance that the invasion of Europe was imminent.

It was hardly surprising, in a country that had been under strict blackout restrictions, that the idea of peace was very much associated with lights being switched back on. It was likely in the minds of Americans Bennie Benjamin, Sol Marcus and Eddie Seiler when they wrote 'When the Lights Go On Again (All Over the World)' in 1942. Popularised by

Vaughn Monroe and his Orchestra, and also by Vera Lynn, the song is about hope for the resumption of normal life when 'rain or snow is all that may fall from the skies above', and Britons would 'have time for things like wedding rings'.

On 17 May 1945, *The Cornishman* reported that the previous week the ban on coastal lighting had been lifted and that for that day, and the next two, all street lighting could be switched on again: 'Many young children saw lights in the streets for the first time in their lives. There was much celebration and a lot of singing. *When the Lights Go On Again (All Over the World)* was the popular tune in Penzance … everywhere one heard people singing it, or unconsciously humming it.'

There was some distance to go until the global war would be truly over, but already most people recognised that the songs, and the music, had played an important part in helping them to carry on.

Chapter 8

Great Symphonies and Concertos

> The season of Promenade Concerts ending this week has been so successful, despite early doubts, but the question arises whether the war's pressure and anxieties have caused more people than ever before to turn to great music for solace.
>
> *Western Mail*, August 1941

Beethoven's Second Piano Concerto was under way when Adolf Hitler invaded Poland, bringing an abrupt end to the forty-fourth Promenade Concert Season at the Queen's Hall in London's Langham Place. The BBC, now with other distractions, withdrew its support and Sir Henry Wood, who had conducted the Proms since their inception in 1895, needed to find a new way ahead.

The annual summer 'Proms' had been a popular diversion for the British people ever since they were first broadcast by the BBC in 1927 when the opening of the Daventry transmitter meant that 94 per cent of the population was now within reach of a broadcasting station and so almost everyone could hear a Prom for the first time – providing that they could afford to own a wireless set, of course.

The first item of the 1927 season was Elgar's *Cockaigne Overture*, conducted by Wood who, along with Robert Newman, was co-founder of the Proms. Newman, the manager of the Queen's Hall, had tempted Sir Henry with the idea of a series of nightly concerts that 'train the public by easy stages' until they had created 'a public for classical and modern music'.

Newman died in November 1926, leaving Wood to carry on organising the Proms alone. In 1939, Sir Henry suddenly needed a new backer. He quickly found private sponsorship and when the 1940 Proms season opened it was with the London Symphony Orchestra (LSO) replacing the BBC Symphony Orchestra. However, the Battle of Britain was raging overhead and there were still plenty of hurdles to overcome.

On 4 September 1940, the London correspondent of the *Bradford Observer* wrote:

> Putting forward by an hour and a half the start of last night's Promenade Concert, the management at the Queen's Hall hoped to finish the performance before the night raids began. That object was certainly achieved, but at the expense of a large proportion of the normal audience. Too much notice, however, should not be taken of that, for the long late afternoon raid ended only a few minutes before 6pm, so that large numbers of prospective patrons must have been unable to reach the concert in time, far less get their tea in comfort after leaving business. Consequently, my season ticket, which is normally for standing only, gave me a couple of seats in the 'smoking compartment', and altogether the sparse attendance made an unfamiliar scene to look down upon.

On 9 September, the *Liverpool Echo* reported:

> Owing to the traffic disturbance only a small number had reached Queen's Hall at the opening of the concert, but within half an hour or so the audience had grown to 1,300 or 1,400, which was more than might have been expected. The Promenaders are enthusiastic. The previous evening almost every one of them stayed after the interval to hear the new work, though the prospects of the journey home were not rosy.

The following day, a member of the LSO, approaching the Queen's Hall, heard anti-aircraft guns, looked up to the sky, and remarked, 'That man's made a mistake. We're not playing *1812* tonight.'

The same month, 'E. H.', writing in the *Birmingham Post*, said that he had received a letter from Sir Henry Wood concerning E. H.'s contention that the Promenade Concerts had always been too long. Wrote E. H.:

> He is kind enough to say that he thinks the complaint justified, as long as it is a question of regarding the Proms simply as part of the ordinary run of concerts … But the fact

> is one cannot fail to agree, whatever one's personal reaction may be, is that the Proms are not ordinary concerts … Many of the Promenaders, it was found years ago, in the days when the Queen's Hall concerts were managed by the late Robert Newman who had a very shrewd insight into musical audiences, are people who have nowhere to go after an evening out except home and to bed, and if the evening is too short that means an hour or two of depression after a short period of elation. The argument seems to be that it is better to tire people out with music and send them home sated.

As the Blitz began, the inevitable happened. On 26 August 1940, following a concert featuring the music of Wagner and Strauss, many of the audience were trapped in the Queen's Hall overnight by a bombing raid – the orchestra entertained them with the overture from Mozart's *The Marriage of Figaro* – and a few weeks later the season was abandoned. The *Belfast News-Letter* was one of several newspapers that broke the news:

> Owing to conditions created by the intensification of the air war the Queen's Hall Promenade Concerts have been suspended. An eight-week season was arranged and the concerts held during the first four weeks were very successful, for notwithstanding the difficulties arising from the blackout, the Queen's Hall was full nearly every night.

Yet despite public support, the series was brought to an early end.

Four days later, a regional newspapers' column, 'London Letters', commented:

> Music lovers will deeply regret that the season of Promenade Concerts at Queen's Hall has had to be suspended. It is ironical that this should be because the concerts have been too successful. Other concerts in town are able to continue, but in present circumstances it is considered unwise to allow the assembling of such large crowds as have flocked to the Proms at night. They have aroused exceptional interest – sentimental and musical. This was to be Sir Henry Wood's last season; he has conducted these concerts for forty-five years. Unfortunately for this farewell season it had been

> impossible to arrange for broadcasts. Music lovers just had to go to the Queen's Hall if they wished to hear the first performance of the many new works Sir Henry Wood has been introducing. That, too, contributed to record audiences.

The decision to close down during the Blitz proved to be a wise one. On 10 May 1941, the Queen's Hall, which stood next to Broadcasting House, was destroyed by an incendiary bomb, leaving the Promenade Concerts homeless. Undaunted, Sir Henry Wood soon found a new home – and it was still in London.

Less than a month after the Queen's Hall bomb, engineers were experimenting with the acoustics of the Royal Albert Hall. By bringing the orchestra forward and using other devices it was hoped that, before the Proms began, the Royal Albert Hall's 'notorious echo' would have been eliminated. With the assistance of the Department of Industrial and Scientific Research some success had been achieved, as an experiment had proved. For the concert season cloth coated with gypsum would be hung in front of the organ and over the concrete walls which were held largely responsible for the echo. Baffles had also been placed in the roof. These alterations together with police regulations would comfortably reduce the hall's capacity. Even so, with the centre of the floor as a promenade and the amphitheatre and three rows of boxes available there would still be more much more space for audiences than in the Queen's Hall.

The destruction of the Queen's Hall had been a heavy blow to Sir Henry Wood, for his association with the building had extended over a period of nearly fifty years, during which time he had conducted more than 5,000 concerts. Now he would conduct the LSO during the first half of each concert, while Keith Douglas or Basil Cameron would take the baton during the second half of each programme. It was also reported that the BBC had agreed to take twenty broadcasts of the new Proms series.

The Times music critic was impressed: 'The forty-seventh season of Promenade concerts conducted by Sir Henry Wood and the first to be given in the Albert Hall was begun on Saturday with every symptom of popular success.'

The *Weekly Dispatch* reported:

> There were two innovations at the opening of the forty-seventh season of Promenade Concerts last night. For the

> first time the Prom was held not in Queen's Hall (owing to bomb damage) but at the Royal Albert Hall. And for the first time Sir Henry Wood, now aged seventy-two, had the assistance of an associate conductor, Mr Basil Cameron. More than 4,000 attended. Nearly 1,000 stood in the arena. Music by Elgar, Walford Davis, Mozart, Handel, Rachmaninoff, Beethoven, Saint-Saëns and Wagner was played.

By the end of that month the *Yorkshire Post and Leeds Intelligencer* was able to tell readers:

> Attendances at the Albert Hall, the Proms' emergency address, have been beyond the organiser's dreams, I hear. The move west from the blitzed Queen's Hall has seemingly not deterred old enthusiasts, while it has attracted many new ones. The charred bust of Sir Henry Wood, rescued from the Queen's Hall ruins, has been renovated and installed in the vestibule of the new home.

In August, the Cardiff-based *Western Mail* commented:

> With the Queen's Hall a raid casualty the Proms this year had to brave the vast spaces of the Albert Hall, but the organisers' anxieties were soon soothed away by the throngs that crowded the famous floor. It may be questioned whether great music should be regarded as a means of solace but it cannot be denied that material worries seem very small and unimportant when the slow movement of the 'Emperor' concerto sweeps its assurance with nobility and purity into the mind and heart. It does seem as if more and more ordinary men and women, especially of the younger generation, are developing a liking for the accepted classics of music.

Never was this better illustrated than when, after the National Gallery was closed on the outbreak of war and its paintings moved to safe storage outside London, the celebrated pianist Myra Hess proposed that the Gallery be used as a venue for lunchtime classical concerts. The Gallery's director, Sir Kenneth Clarke, agreed. Government permission was granted for the Gallery to be converted to a concert venue and from 10 October 1939 there were daily performances from Monday to Friday. They ran every week of the war, even during the Blitz, a total of 1,698. Performers ranged from famous names to those unknown including musicians from the RAF. The final concert took place in April 1946 and over those six and a half years more than 800,000 people, many of them new to classical music, attended them. There was not a single cancellation and Hess, who in 1941 was created Dame Commander of the Order of the British Empire, could claim that, like the nearby Windmill Theatre, 'We never closed.'

The inevitability that London would become a major target for the Luftwaffe meant that the provinces began to enjoy more live classical music than would otherwise have been the case. Malcom Sargent, conductor and composer, toured with the London Philharmonic Orchestra (LPO) as well as conducting the Manchester-based Hallé Orchestra and the Liverpool Philharmonic, all for a modest fee. In July 1941, the visit of the LPO broke all attendance records at the Prince of Wales's Theatre in Cardiff.

In June 1941, it was announced that Lilian Stiles-Allen, a renowned concert soprano who had trained at the Guildhall School of Music and in Vienna, was to sing in Mendelssohn's *Elijah* at the centenary celebrations of Leeds Parish Church. She had been bombed out of her London home and was now living in Leeds. She said:

> My house was damaged three times before I moved, but when the front door was blown out with the rest of the windows, and the garden looks like a cat cemetery with tiles that ought to have been on the roof, and the doctor's house next door was no more, I saw the writing on the wall. So I came to Leeds. I left on the Wednesday and two days later, the back of the house was demolished. Now friends tell me there is nothing left.

Stiles-Allen went on to become the singing coach of Julie Andrews, who described her as 'a short, very stout woman, with thick ankles, an ample backside, and a heavy bosom … Always bejewelled, she dressed in long skirts to her ankles and sensible lace-up shoes on tiny feet … She walked with a strong cane and often donned in a wonderful velvet cloak and beret.'

On the trials of singing in the Blitz, Stiles-Allen once said that she had sung at a Promenade Concert 'while guns were firing' but that they did not deter her. Other reports suggest that she appeared at her last Proms in 1938.

As the war ground on, the popularity of classical music was ever growing. The *Western Mail*:

> It would be the finest thing that could happen to music in this country if it lost the appearance of ritual given to it by ranks of boiled shirts and an unintelligible jargon. Higher criticism must make use of technical terms but some of them are too easily used to impress the uninitiated, who are thus discouraged from finding out that the great simple symphonies and concertos contain straightforward melodies so good that they make the productions of Tin Pan Alley sound like the trash they all. In fact, the thumpers out of the latest smash-hits have shamelessly rifled the classics for tunes, and some of their more recent unacknowledged borrowings must have made Tchaikovsky and Chopin turn in their graves.

Sir Henry himself weighed in:

> Never in history of this country has the man-in-the-street taken such a vital interest in serious music as now. There is not the slightest doubt that this live public interest has come to stay because it is not merely a 'boom' or of mushroom growth. It is the logical outcome of a steady progressive policy pursued by certain management and music organisations during the past fifty years of the wireless, and of the more enlightened methods adopted in our schools … music can no longer be regarded as the toy of the favoured few, but as the healthy recreation of the people.

The *Nottingham Journal's* 'London Letter' columnist was convinced that music was helping to boost the nation's morale:

> Personally I find concerts far more satisfying than either stage or screen these days. If the music gets you, it absorbs you and you can forget everything. If it does not you are still left undisturbed with your own thoughts and do not have to concentrate on uninteresting banalities. There must be an enormous number of people in London who feel the same about entertainment just now, for on nearly every night they are turning people away from the Albert Hall, where the Proms accommodate a bigger audience than used to assemble at the Queen's Hall, and this in spite of the fact that most people have to get there too early to have had any refreshment since leaving work.

The *Yorkshire Post and Leeds Intelligencer*'s 'London Notes' columnist agreed:

> Last night's Promenade Concert at the Albert Hall marked the end of the first series of these concerts which it has been possible to complete for three years. In 1939 all entertainments were closed by the government when the war began, and in 1940 the air attacks on London brought the prom season to a hurried termination. This year there were preliminary doubts whether the music lovers would follow Sir Henry Wood to Kensington. In fact the season has been a tremendous success, far larger audience than ever went to the proms at Queen's Hall have assembled at the new home. There was any amount of traditional last-night enthusiasm and *Rule Britannia* was never sung in Langham Place with more zest or its rhythm stamped out more vigorously.

The Royal Albert Hall would now be the Proms' permanent home, although midway through thc 1944 series it was temporarily moved to Bedford. Four days after D-Day, Sir Henry conducted the first part of the opening Promenade Concert at the Royal Albert Hall but after three weeks the season there was abandoned as London again became the main target for German bombs, this time from the V-1 and V-2 'doodlebug' campaign.

The *Chichester Observer*'s 'Bognor Man's Diary' column had remained hopeful:

> In spite of the flying bomb, Sir Henry Wood's jubilee season of Promenade Concerts continues with all the vigour and colour that great music under a great interpreter can muster. This alone is proof that the work of great artistes can survive even the most sadistic and mathematical gods that a scientist can create and then bow down to worship … One more thing: we have the will to continue with such music, for in the midst of subversive moanings of a twentieth-century curse, the woman crooner, we find the men who are attaining great musical heights.

None the less, the renewed threat from the skies meant that the Royal Albert Hall was abandoned in favour of the BBC studios at Bedford Corn Exchange, which had been the home of the BBC Symphony Orchestra since 1941. The BBC had resumed its support for the Proms in 1942 and its symphony orchestra returned temporarily to London for the Proms season.

Earlier in the war, Bedford Corn Exchange had hosted Glenn Miller, Bing Crosby, Vera Lynn and Marlene Dietrich. From 29 June 1944, invited audiences listened to the remaining broadcast concerts of classical music.

On 28 July, Sir Henry conducted a performance of Beethoven's *Seventh Symphony*. It was his final Proms appearance. On 4 August, he was reported to be seriously ill at his hotel in Bedford, but was 'going along very nicely'. Five days later, the BBC reported that Sir Henry was suffering from an acute attack of jaundice and that Sir Adrian Boult would take his place as conductor of the fiftieth anniversary broadcast concert.

Sir Henry Wood died in a hospital in Hitchin on 19 August 1944. *The People* paid tribute to him:

> Sir Henry Wood, one of Britain's foremost conductors and the man who made the Proms … For over 50 years this burly man – with bristling black beard and carnation button hole – conducted concerts in England where he produced over 900 new British and foreign compositions for the

> first time ... He made good music flourish where it was never known before. Through these concerts he established a musical fashion in London which survived two world wars and he did more perhaps in any other man to raise our standard of musical appreciation.

On Saturday, 21 July 1945, just over three weeks before VJ Day, the Proms returned to the Royal Albert Hall where they have remained, now known as the Henry Wood Promenade Concerts.

Chapter 9

Soft Lights and Sweet Music

> Another dance organised by the local platoon of the Home Guard was held in St John's School last Friday, the event proving a big attraction. Reggie Stanworth's Band provided the music.
>
> *Nelson Leader*, November 1940

On 12 March 1942, Herbert Morrison told the House of Commons that the government was taking additional powers to control public entertainments where needed to avoid interference with the national war effort.

Horse racing would be restricted to a few courses with a view to economy in the use of public transport. Greyhound racing would be restricted to one day a week for each track and would take place only on Saturdays and public holidays. Professional boxing, already reduced to about 10 per cent of pre-war figures, would be further restricted, mainly in respect of 'large and spectacular events'. Professional football, cinemas, theatres and dancing, however, would suffer no further restrictions.

In the exercise of their new powers the government would not impose more restrictions than war requirements rendered expedient, but there would be no hesitation to impose such further restrictions as may be needed in the interests of the war effort.

'On the other hand,' said the Home Secretary, who was apparently a keen dancer, 'there is no intention of imposing needless hindrances to recreation or of carrying restrictions so far that total war unnecessarily becomes total misery.'

The issue had long been a contentious one. On 8 September 1939, *The Spectator* commented

> The closing of all theatres and other places of public entertainment at the beginning of the war was perhaps a necessary precautionary measure ... But it is as clear as

> can be that such a ban on entertainment could not possibly remain general without an incalculable loss to the good spirits and morale of the nation … It would be a grave mistake not to make all the use we can of actors, variety artistes and musicians who have the will and the skill to take our minds off the pressing disquietudes of the war.

One year before war was declared, Mass Observation had already concluded that dance halls formed a social centre that served to insulate the individual from the unpleasant realities of life: 'Under the soft lights and lured by the sweet music he can sink into a dreamland of wishful desire.'

A few days after war was declared, the polymath Tom Harrisson, who along with poet and journalist Charles Madge and painter and filmmaker Humphrey Jennings created Mass Observation, called the closing of places of entertainment 'bad for morale'. Three years later he was able to tell a North American audience in a BBC broadcast, 'In a number of our big cities the biggest dance halls are packed completely to capacity, and the other evening in Glasgow I simply couldn't get in when I arrived at ten o'clock hoping to see the local finals of a jitterbug competition. Hundreds were being turned away from the doors.'

The closure of entertainment venues had lasted for only a week. On 14 September 1939, the Dorchester was the first of the West End hotels to reopen for dancing after the resident band had returned from an engagement in the fashionable Normandy resort of Deauville. The Berkeley Hotel in Knightsbridge declared: 'We are starting dancing again in response to mass requests. After all, what is the use of sitting looking at each other during dinner? Dancing will make people forget their worries. We shall start at eight-thirty instead of ten o'clock, and so long as dancers are on the floor we shall carry on until a late hour.'

The following day, the *Manchester Evening News* reported, 'From today onwards Belle Vue Zoo and Gardens will be open from 10am to dusk with everything including the amusement park in full swing. Dancing in the Coronation Ballroom begins tonight and will continue each night onwards from 6pm to 9.45pm and on Saturdays will be continuous from 3pm to 9.45pm.'

There were, of course, special measures in place. The *Thanet Advertiser* reported that mandatory 'short frocks' had proved successful at the first wartime dance at Ramsgate's Coronation Ballroom in the Merrie England amusement park on the promenade:

> Attended by company numbering nearly 700 Ramsgate's first wartime dance, held the on Saturday, was huge success. Although the official edict had gone forth that no ladies wearing long dresses would be admitted – in view of possible danger on the stairs in the event of hurried exit – it was not necessary to turn anyone away on that account.
>
> As matter of fact, once inside the spacious, brightly lighted ballroom, there was very little to distinguish the dance from those held during the summer season. Only a half-dozen girls sported slacks, the majority wearing frocks that reached a few inches below the knee. Among the men there was larger proportion than usual in Service uniform. The only other reminder that times have changed was provided by an air raid rehearsal.
>
> As soon as the alarm had been sounded, Frederic Hargraves' Knights Swing struck up a quick march step, and under the direction of the MC, Mr A.L. Robinson, the dancers made in good order for the four exits. Within seconds the floor was completely cleared. The rehearsal proved so satisfactory that for the remainder of the evening dancing was continued without further interruption and at the close the general hope was expressed that it would be possible to hold similar dances regularly during the winter season. The next dance will be held on Saturday.

There was still the question of closing times, however. In November, the *Sheffield Evening Telegraph* asked, 'Can dancing go on till 11 o'clock?' It was a question, said the newspaper, on which Sheffield dance organisers urgently required a definite ruling.

> It was announced unequivocally, last night, that cinemas and theatres would be allowed to stay open until 11pm, but there was no mention of dancing. Is dancing included in the other places of entertainment to which the public is admitted on payment? Mystery surrounds the question, and

> while some dance organisers are taking it for granted that the extension applies to dancing, the police cannot say. 'It is impossible for us to say one way or the other,' a Sheffield police official informed *The Star*. 'We have had no official intimation yet even about the extension for theatres and cinemas, and only know what was heard on the wireless. I can't enlighten dance organisers. They know just as much about it as we do.'

Walter Collinson, a well-known Sheffield dance master, felt that an extension until 11.00 pm was better from the point of view of safety. Crowds on the streets would be 'staggered' with people leaving cinemas and pubs at 10.00 pm and dancers drifting away an hour later.

That December, the matter was resolved when the Home Secretary made an order under which it was decided that dances to which the public were admitted on payment no longer needed to be subject to the requirement that they must end at 11.00 pm, although police chiefs would have the power to prohibit or restrict dances where special risks would be involved in the event of an air raid.

Not every police chief or magistrate was sympathetic. In November 1940, it was reported that the income of the Skegness and District Cottage Hospital had fallen from £600 to £80 during the war, and the manager of Hildred's Hotel in the seaside resort wanted local magistrates to waive their policy of refusing extensions to music and drinking facilities on the occasion of dances. The hotel was holding a dance to raise funds for the hospital. The solicitor acting for the hotel pointed out that the government urged communities to 'carry on'. Surely this advice could not be put into effect if they were going to do away with all forms of public enjoyment, he asked the magistrates. The dance would materially assist in keeping the morale of the public high – and, besides, the function 'was not a sixpenny hop open to all comers but a high-class dance with strictly limited admission'.

The chairman of the bench suggested that 2.00 pm would be a very good time to start the dance. 'I am afraid that there would be very few there,' replied the solicitor.

'Well, I am sorry,' said the chairman, 'but the bench is adamant on the subject.'

It is likely that it was not the possibility of an air raid that bothered the Skegness magistrates. Sometimes trouble lay much closer to home.

In July 1944, the *Shields Daily Gazette* highlighted the problem of 'rowdyism' at a dance hall in Jarrow:

> Arising out of unseemly scenes at dance halls it is suggested that at Jarrow the remedy lies in closing the dance halls at 10pm. This, however, would curtail the enjoyment of many innocent people. Invariably the trouble is started by young men demanding admission about ten o'clock and then getting out of hand regardless of others' comfort. Some time ago, Jarrow Council made a rule in respect of the Baths Hall that anyone who left before ten o'clock should not be admitted again and newcomers after that hour should be refused admittance.

There were many instances of trouble at dance halls. In March 1940, army sergeant William Slater was fined £1 after assaulting a special constable during a brawl when a crowd of about 100 soldiers attempted to gain entrance to the Broadway Palace Dance Hall in Chester. It was after 11.00 pm and the hall was already full. 'It is a disgraceful way for a man in your position to behave,' said the presiding magistrates, Colonel F. J. Bonnalie. Slater apologised for his conduct, and said that he had mistaken the special constable for a civilian, who he thought was causing unrest.

In December 1941, a Polish sailor, Grzegorz Tarnowski, was found not guilty of murdering a Dundee soldier, Private David Reid, in a Dundee dance hall. After two witnesses swore that Private Reid was stabbed to death by a Polish soldier, the jury took only twenty minutes to acquit him. Reid's real killer had escaped justice.

In April 1943, two men, Edwin Albert Oatley and James Daniel Snow, were each fined £2 for obstructing the highway outside a Maesteg dance hall. Both were under the influence of drink and for ten minutes had persisted in trying to gain admission to the hall.

The Blitz inevitably saw critics questioning the wisdom of opening places of entertainment where hundreds, perhaps thousands, might gather. The morale-boosting effect weighed against the dangers, it was decided that dance halls could remain open, and it was up to the dancers themselves whether or not they made for the shelters when the alert sounded.

During the height of the Blitz, singer and instrumentalist Barry Gray, a familiar voice to BBC radio listeners since before the war, was conducting the orchestra at West End's 400 Club when he was blown off his stand when a bomb exploded nearby. Real name Eric Pountain, he was the younger brother of crooner Denny Dennis, who sang with Ambrose and Roy Fox and who had become known as 'Britain's Bing Crosby'. Eric was the resident singer at the 400 Club and had also sung with Roy Fox. In 1941, he joined the Merchant Navy and was a radio officer on SS *Stonepool* when the ship was torpedoed and sunk off Cape Farewell in the early hours of 11 September that year. The master, thirty-three crew members including 31-year-old Eric Pountain, and eight gunners were lost in the waters of the North Atlantic. Six crew members and one gunner were later picked up. Eric Pountain's name appears on the Tower Hill Memorial that commemorates men and women of the Merchant Navy and fishing fleets who died in both world wars and who have no known grave.

Back to the Blitz, even when precautions were taken to minimise the risks of injury and damage, very few venues proved absolutely bomb-proof. On Wednesday, 5 March 1941, *The Tatler* carried an advertisement for the Café de Paris where you could 'enjoy yourself in safety 20 feet below ground'. Entertainment included dancing to the house band, Ken 'Snakehips' Johnson and his West Indian Orchestra. The fashionable night club was in the basement of a building that also housed the Rialto Cinema on London's Coventry Street, between Piccadilly Circus and Leicester Square.

The Café de Paris had opened in 1924. With its luxurious interior modelled on the ill-fated White Star liner *Titanic*, it soon became popular with well-heeled Londoners but in 1941 prices had been lowered to attract a more diverse clientele including service personnel who could forget the horrors of the war, for few hours at least.

On Monday, 10 March, newspapers were reporting the death of 26-year-old 'Snakehips' Johnson, a doctor's son from British Guiana, 'who was killed on a recent air-raid in London'. He was one of the thirty-four people that lost their lives when the Rialto building was hit by two 50 kg (110 lb) high-explosive bombs at about 9.45 pm on the previous Saturday evening – just three days after revellers had been assured of their safety there.

One bomb failed to explode but the other went off above the band, on the gallery of the 'bomb-proof' venue that was crowded with dancers and diners and where the band had just begun playing the Andrews Sisters' hit, 'Johnny Oh! Johnny Oh!'

The *Leicester Evening Mail* reported:

> Women in evening dress and officers in uniform figured prominently among the couples crowding the dance floor, moving to the rhythm of Ken 'Snakehips' Johnson and his West Indian Orchestra. The number ended, the dancers made their way to their tables. Corks popped, glasses tinkled, and excitement increased. In a few minutes the cabaret would begin … The perfumed atmosphere was warm and friendly. The war was long way off. A second later it had crashed into their midst.
>
> A bomb, tearing through the roof, exploded with a terrific report on a balcony immediately above the orchestra. The gay throng, literally hurled to the floor by the blast, were lying everywhere – some dead, many more injured, and the more fortunate only dazed.
>
> 'Snakehips' Johnson, most of the orchestra, and Martinus Poulsen, a famous restaurateur, were killed. A staircase leading from balcony to dance floor was wrecked. Ceiling decorations had been ripped away to add to the avalanche of debris from which members of the band struggled to escape. Flying fragments of wine bottles and glasses were responsible for many injuries, and a number of victims staggered to the street, bleeding freely from cuts.

Albert Weaver, manager of the Mapleton Hotel opposite the Café de Paris, and a section commander in the Home Guard, told the newspaper, 'Everyone worked marvellously to help and all those still trapped in the building were released before midnight.' A young off-duty nurse, from Chelsea, was one of many who rushed to the scene. She had little to say about her work, except that while she was helping the injured someone ransacked her handbag, taking from it objects of sentimental value, including a fountain pen.

Two years later, the loss of life at a crowded dance hall in Putney saw people again question the wisdom of allowing such events to go ahead in areas most likely to be targeted by the Luftwaffe. On the evening of 7 November 1943, the Cinderella Dancing Club in Putney was packed when a bomber, probably aiming for Putney Bridge, dropped a 227 kg (500 lb) bomb directly on the building at 35 Putney High Street which also housed the Black and White Milk Bar below the dance club. The death toll was the area's single worst of the Second World War. Eighty-one – forty-six females and thirty-five males – perished. Eighteen of the dead were service personnel.

Five days later, the *Liverpool Echo* published a letter from someone signing themselves 'Cedor':

> While everyone's sympathies must go out to those who have lost loved ones in the recent raid on a London dance hall, one cannot but deplore the circumstances that made such a catastrophe possible. Surely in any locality that is liable to air raids, it should be the duty of the authorities to warn the public against (and if need be to forbid) any gatherings that are not absolutely essential, however much it might incommode the public or interfere with their pleasures. In any case, with the world still in a welter of blood, it is a pity that the minds of young people are not centred on more serious things than dancing. To say that recreation and pleasure are essential after the day's toil may be justifiable in normal times, but it would be a callous exercise for one in whose home a father or brother lay dying. It is not equally so when thousands are making the supreme sacrifice by laying down their lives in far-off lands in order that we may live in comparative peace at home?

Not every raid ended in tragedy and, such was most people's desire to keep smiling and carry on, those near misses often produced a humorous story.

Frank Budgeon of Manchester recalled:

> Although I worked as an electrical and magnetic instrument maker, in the evenings I played in a band. At the height of the Blitz, we were playing at a function in Altrincham, in a large hall that doubled up as the local ARP headquarters. On this particular evening, there was a big raid and many of the dancers left, either to go on ARP duty or just to get home to their loved ones.
>
> Suddenly there was a huge explosion, the building rocked around the clock, and the doors on all the emergency exits were blown open. I was ready to run off stage when

> I saw the pianist still tinkling away, so I stayed too, even though there was now nobody dancing. Eventually the All Clear sounded and we'd time to take stock. The first thing I noticed was a large switchboard for the lighting and telephone. Someone had pinned a notice to it: 'If the alarm bell goes once, raiders approaching; if the alarm bell goes twice, raiders in the vicinity; if the alarm bell goes three times – the bloody building has been hit.'
>
> Anyway, by now the pianist had joined me. I said, 'That was a brave thing to do, carrying on like that.' 'Carrying on?' he said. 'I couldn't stand up for fright.'

Dancing was so popular that attempts were made to avoid the laws governing them. In August 1942, the monthly meeting of Ballymena Borough Council was told of dances being held at the rear of premises in Suffolk Street in the town. A police inspector told the meeting that the hall was in a backyard and entrance was gained by ascending fourteen steps. The area of the hall was 40 ft by 20 ft (12 m by 6 m) and there was no exit except for the entrance door, and no sanitary facilities. Entrance fees were ninepence (4p) for men and sixpence (2.5p) for women. About thirty people were present when the police arrived. The organisers told them that it was a private dancing class. The town clerk was unhappy. Here there was obviously a dance but because it was arranged as a dance class to which it was claimed that the general public were not admitted, the council had no jurisdiction over it 'and anyone can go there and dance half the night'. One councillor said that the only thing that could be done was to draw the appropriate ministry's attention to it. Another said that, as they had a few boys and girls learning to dance there, the matter should be held in abeyance for another month. All agreed with that suggestion and the matter was dropped.

No one was ever going to stop people dancing. Even the Royal Opera House joined in. From 1939, it became a Mecca dance hall with up to 1,500 dancers each night filling the floor before, in 1946, the theatre returned to its original purpose. In October 1943, the 'London Letter' column in several regional newspapers reported that the Royal Opera House was one of several dance halls that were banning the jitterbug:

> I have never seen the jitterbug danced – excepting on the screen – but I hear it has got a very firm hold up on

> young people in this country … Its arrival here is, it seems, attributed as much to the films as to the influx to American serving men, if not more so. Indeed, two or three soldiers to whom I have spoken greatly disliked this substitute of gymnastics for dancing and are rather indignant that it should be regarded as anything really typical of their country.

The Royal Opera House dance was very popular with American servicemen and 'the organisation which controls this … states publicly that the dance will still be permitted at the Paramount in Tottenham Court Road which, I understand, has an even larger American patronage'.

Judy Warnock recalls letters written during the war by her Uncle John, a US Army sergeant stationed in England. Many of them touched on his love of dancing and they paint a vivid picture of wartime London's dancing scene. On 19 November 1942, he wrote: 'Thursday I went to a Charity Ball. It was a dreary night, one of those famous wet and foggy English nights and people were a little slow attending the affair.'

> 7 February 1943: 'Saturday I went to my usual … Was the same orchestra I heard last Saturday. I didn't stay to the end … 12 o'clock found me already in bed …'
>
> 14 March 1943: 'Saturday evening I went to a dance; somehow or other my round of good girl dancers is vanishing gradually; some have gone into the armed forces while others have defense jobs many miles away. I danced with one who was from Australia and now in service of the WAAFs. All in all, it was a fair evening although I did have better times than this one, many a time.'
>
> 6 September 1943: 'It was the most important week of my career – and the major rewarded me in praise for my effort – gave me a day and a half off this week – Tuesday noon to Thursday morning. Going to London – take in a few shows and then maybe a dance.'
>
> 8 October 1943: 'Had an enjoyable time on my leave – saw a movie in the afternoon … Then in the evening I spent my

> time dancing at the Hammersmith. I'm getting to be an old-timer there – and I can truthfully say there are some good dancers there.'

Throughout the country there was certainly an enormous choice of bands. In November 1942, the Grafton Rooms in West Derby Street, Liverpool, were featuring Johnny Claes and his Clae Pigeons. The son of a Belgian father and a Scottish mother, Johnny Claes, a trumpeter who had taken lessons from Nat Gonella, had formed his first band in 1941. He would have found an appreciative and very mixed audience at the Grafton Rooms. The following month, *Dancing Times* described the venue as the 'United Nations Ballroom of the North-West' where Royal Navy and merchant seamen, airmen and soldiers danced with WRENS, WAAFs and girls in the ATS, as well as girls from the 'Factory Front'.

During the Glasgow Blitz of March 1941, during which 1,200 people were killed, a Gaumont British News film showed the Barrowland Dance Hall packed for a jitterbug contest. The commentor said, 'It may surprise you to know that this dance is done in Great Britain.'

A black former GI, Cleother Hathcock, remembered, 'About that time the jitterbug was in and the blacks would get a buggin' and the English just love that. We would go into a dance hall and just take over the place because everybody wanted to learn how to do that American dance, the jitterbug. They went wild over that.' Unfortunately, while black servicemen were welcomed by their British hosts, there were a number of serious incidents between black and white GIs over Americans' policy of racial segregation in their forces. Dance halls saw their fair share of that.

During the Second World War, dancing was rivalled only by cinema and radio in terms of mass entertainment. Dancing helped to keep up morale, and factories engaged on war work organised dances for their employees. In September 1940, at the beginning of the Blitz, Mass Observation noted that even though morale among those sheltering from the bombs was low, it could be maintained in communal shelters 'by conscious efforts like singing, dancing etc'. One young woman said that she was going to the public shelter that night because 'they have singing and dancing there … it's no good sitting and moping'.

In October 1940, as the Blitz got under way in earnest, entertainment in air-raid shelters was a growing topic. A crowded meeting of the

Musicians' Union in London heard a proposal for officially organised entertainments in bomb-proof shelters as one way to help alleviate the critical situation faced by members of the profession.

Bermondsey was planning programmes that included entertainments but also occupational work, handicraft classes, dressmaking, and cookery courses. In Sevenoaks in Kent, a whist drive was held at the public shelter in Albion Road. It was arranged by the shelter marshals for the entertainment of the 'regular clientele'. Twelve tables were occupied and prizes were provided by friends. The sum of £2 4s (£2.20) in aid of the Twickenham Spitfire Fund was raised following four nights of entertainment at the 80-person capacity Twickenham Green shelter. Entertainment by Jessie and Danny Murphy, 'well-known club and cabaret artistes', was usually given between 8.00 pm to 11.00 pm.

Not everywhere enjoyed such facilities, though. In November 1940, Vernon Beste, secretary of the Unity Theatre Society, wrote to the *St Pancras Gazette*, urging St Pancras ARP Emergency Committee to organise a scheme of shelter entertainments 'which will adequately serve the needs of the shelterers in St Pancras'.

He said that he had been pressing for this since the war began, and with air raids now imminent, 'it was essential to organise a comprehensive scheme of entertainment for shelterers in order to allay panic ... the Society's experience of entertainment under all sorts of conditions would be enormously valuable to such a project'. The ARP controller replied that the ARP Emergency Committee 'did not consider that it would be desirable to organise such a scheme in view of the fact that many people might have serious objections if they wished to rest in the shelter'.

Mr Beste countered that the management committee of Unity Theatre Society 'are surprised to learn that the ARP Emergency Committee hold the opinion that an air-raid has no other psychological reaction on many people than a desire for rest, especially as, so far as they are aware, the committee has made no provision for this in the shelters in the borough'. He added that the ARP Emergency Committee had a duty, not only to preserve the bodies of the inhabitants of the borough from bombs, but their minds from shock. This could best be done by diverting the minds of the people from what was happening outside the shelter.

Undaunted, on 24 August 1940, the Unity Theatre Society had given its first show to shelterers, in Goldington Crescent. 'Since then,' said Mr Beste,

> hardly a night passes without Unity Theatre's players giving shows in various parts of London – in the Tubes, in reinforced basements, and even in the trenches. These little impromptu entertainments have been welcomed everywhere by marshals and the public, but it is obvious that we cannot cope with more than a fraction of the demand in London, nor can we single-handed, even see that the borough of St Pancras is supplied with this vital tonic for frayed nerves. This is a matter of public well-being which cannot and must not be allowed to shift for itself.

In the meantime, said Mr Beste, the Unity Theatre Society would continue giving performances in the shelters – but they needed more performers:

> The number and scope of those shows could be increased enormously had we more personnel. The type of entertainers which we require most are those who can play a portable musical instrument, sing, or do an individual turn. If any of your readers would care to help us in this work, which is truly of national importance, we should be very pleased to hear from them.

Air-raid shelters were not the only places where people were 'trapped' and in need of entertainment. In December 1942, the *Berwick Advertiser* carried an article from one of its pre-war reporters, now in the services, about the problem of boredom among troops stationed away from the battlefield.

'Many Berwick soldiers', he wrote,

> will spend their third winter in uniform. Some are in field units, stationed in isolated camps, visited occasionally by ENSA with the 'four artistes and a piano' mode of show. These calls of talented players are red-letter days, but all too few. The majority of our camps are entertained once

> fortnightly with ninety-minute programmes. It is only to be expected that commanding officers, with the danger light of previous winters glaring at them, send an SOS to ENSA – 'The maximum number of shows would be appreciated.'
>
> Take, for instance, a North-Eastern company stationed in the 'wilds' of the West Country. The nearest town, with a picture hall as the only source of amusement, six-mile distance. Buses pass by the camp gates twice day, at times which fail to cater for the servicemen. A lorry makes nightly trips, with journeys confined by Army Council Instructions to one weekly trip per man. The remaining six nights have to be spent in the desolation of a rural setting. The village offers a hall for entertainment. Dances are held twice week, to the alternate music of a military band and a radiogram. The villagers lack organising ability, the Army has taken over the entertainment aspect. A committee was formed. Ideas were soon to materialise into nightly programmes. Social events were mapped out. But the educational side – favoured by many in khaki – was not forgotten. Photography is the hobby of one. His name is noted for lectures and hints on how to obtain the best shots. Music, travel, shorthand – all are dealt with in the same way. As the Army plunges ahead, in ridding the scourge of boredom I should imagine that there will be a dwindling from 'Tommy' in his letters home of complaints of 'nothing to do'.

The writer described how, when ENSA failed to appear, soldiers were coaxed into performing their own shows – and after some initial reservations, fully enjoyed the experience.

> His peaked hat tilted at a dangerous angle, overalls splattered with grease, Bob, the corporal fitter from North of the Tweed, spends his working hours in the din of the unit workshops, coaxing life into Army cars. One night during the week, above the clatter of cups in the NAAFI canteen, he gave a pep talk. It was the evening before an impromptu concert. Interest in the venture had flagged. A sudden shyness had enveloped the boys over the forthcoming variety, which in the words of the entertainments officer

was 'for themselves, themselves'. Bob had ideas that the show must go on. It did go on, and was a hilarious success. The battle-dressed artistes, the majority making their debut, came back for curtain calls when the audience asked for more. It is with this spirit that the 'Tommy' you know best of all is entertaining himself this winter. Three years of war have taught the Army a lesson. The long nights breed boredom. Entertainment kills that bug. And the boys are doctoring themselves.

Chapter 10

In the Mood

> We didn't come here to set any fashions in music. We merely came to bring a much-needed touch of home to some lads who have been here a couple of years.
>
> Glenn Miller

On Sunday, 24 September 1944, there was a long queue outside the State Cinema on St Peter's Hill in Grantham. It had been forming for more than four hours but the residents of the Lincolnshire town were not waiting to see *Frenchman's Creek*, *Arsenic and Old Lace*, or any other film that was breaking box office records that year. They were there to see Major Glenn Miller and his American Band of the Allied Expeditionary Force give their first concert to civilians.

When the seats were full, more than 1,000 people stood outside listening to a broadcast of the concert that was held in aid of Grantham's 'Thank You Fund for the Forces'. In his opening remarks, the local MP, Denis Kendall, said that although the show was free, there would be a 'silver collection' so that local people could give a real thank you to the troops when they returned. It was not charity, he said, but a gift of thanks for the magnificent job they had done. The event raised £103 6s 8d (almost £103.40).

The AEF Band, which included former members of Benny Goodman's band, the Philadelphia Orchestra and the Boston Symphony Orchestra, had been in Britain for three months and had given more than ninety shows to Allied troops. Three weeks after appearing in the relatively quiet backwater of Grantham, Miller and the band were the star turn at the annual charity Jazz Jamboree at a packed Stoll Theatre in London's Kingsway. The Jazz Jamboree had started in March 1939, at the huge State Cinema in Kilburn, to raise money for the benevolent fund of the London branch of the Musicians' Union. It became so popular that all the tickets were sold within hours of them going on sale.

Reporting on the 1944 show, *The Stage* said:

> The high spot was the appearance of Glenn Miller and the Band of the AEF – even if you don't like jazz, you'll like Glenn's band. He was admirably introduced by Tommy Trinder [an English stage, screen and radio comedian whose catchphrase was 'You lucky people!'], who worked hard throughout the afternoon, with many a lively gag in announcing the various items.

It was no surprise that Glenn Miller was hugely popular in Britain. Thanks to the BBC, people were so familiar with the 'Glenn Miller Sound', numbers like 'Moonlight Serenade', 'Tuxedo Junction', 'Chattanooga Choo Choo', 'American Patrol', 'String of Pearls', 'Pennsylvania 6-5000', and, of course, 'In the Mood', first recorded by Miller in 1939. They had also seen his band in two wartime Hollywood films, *Sun Valley Serenade* and *Orchestra Wives*.

The bespectacled Miller, who looked more like a bank clerk than one of the biggest popular music stars of the 1930s, a man who had young bobbysoxers always in the mood for dancing, was at the peak of his career when, in October 1942, he joined the US Army, in the Army Specialist Corps, a uniformed branch of civilians considered unfit for military service – Miller was 38 and wore spectacles – but whose special skills would help the war effort in many different ways.

The authorities knew where Glenn Miller would give the most valuable service. A month after enlisting he was transferred to the Army Air Forces (AAF) where he screened musicians for service bands across the USA including recruiting for an elite unit that he would himself direct.

In May 1944, General Dwight D. Eisenhower cabled Washington, asking for Miller's AAF unit to be posted to Britain, where the Supreme Headquarters, Allied Expeditionary Force (SHAEF) was creating a combined Allied radio broadcasting service to help boost morale among troops waiting to take part in the invasion of Europe. Miller's organisation was the only one 'capable of performing the mission required', Eisenhower said.

Just after D-Day, Miller and his sixty-strong band were sent to Britain to entertain American troops waiting their turn to enter the Battle of Normandy and beyond. Miller flew to England on 18 June 1944, his band disembarking RMS *Queen Elizabeth* at Gourock on the south bank of the Firth of Clyde ten days later.

They were based at Bedford, thought to be safer than London during the Germans' V-1 and V-2 flying bomb campaign. The band's first performance on an active airfield was on 14 July 1944, at Thurleigh, five miles north of Bedford and then home to the 306th Bombardment Group – the 'Reich Wreckers' – who constructed a makeshift stage in an aircraft hangar where an estimated 3,500 enjoyed the music and, if they could find room, dancing.

The previous day the band's first British broadcast had come from Bedford Corn Exchange, or 'somewhere in England' as it was announced over the radio. On 27 August, they gave the only outdoor concert they performed at a base in Britain, at RAF Twinwood, close to Milton Ernest Hall, a Grade I-listed grand country house in Bedfordshire, which had been used as a base for the Special Operations Executive which carried out sabotage, espionage and reconnaissance operations. In 1944, the hall became the US Eighth Air Force's support command headquarters. The Miller band often enjoyed meals there, and the concert, in front of 1,600 officers and men, was in return for that hospitality.

Miller, though, was keen that his band should do more than perform to UK-based troops and through radio broadcasts. He wanted to directly support the men fighting in northern France, and he earmarked Christmas 1944 for a live performance in Paris. When the French capital was liberated in late August, Miller decided it was time to make good his promise, although he faced strong opposition from BBC producers Maurice Gorham and 'the GI's friend', Cecil Madden.

It was reluctantly agreed that the band would go, and to provide the BBC with plenty of the Glenn Miller Sound while they were away, they embarked on a gruelling recording schedule. In between twenty-three live broadcasts, they recorded eighty-eight programmes at the Abbey Road studio.

Miller, always in control of the detail, again decided to travel ahead of the band to make the final arrangements for the France trip. On 13–14 December, he waited in London, ready to fly on a scheduled service from USAAF Station 112 at Bovingdon, 7 miles west of Watford, but fog prevented any flights and he returned to Bedford.

The next morning, 15 December 1944, Miller was offered a flight from the grass runway at RAF Twinwood. Weather conditions were still inhospitable. From the Midlands down to the South Coast the fog still lingered, and the temperature was barely above freezing. But Miller's host, Lieutenant Colonel Norman F. Baessell, who made frequent trips to Paris this way, felt that the journey was possible.

That day, Baessell was scheduled to travel aboard a Noorduyn C-64A Norseman, a utility and cargo plane piloted by Flight Officer John R. S. 'Nipper' Morgan, the son of a Scottish coalminer who had emigrated to the USA. The 22-year-old pilot's experience was limited to ferrying and liaison work; according to a colleague, he had no operational experience.

The Norseman finally took off at 1.55 pm with Miller an unauthorised passenger. Its final destination was Bordeaux, but it would first deliver Miller and Baessell to a USAAF station at Villacoublay, south-west of Paris.

On Christmas Eve – nine days after Miller's aircraft took off from Twinwood – the news was broken during the *Forces Favourites* programme of records on the BBC Home Service: Glenn Miller had never arrived in France. The Norseman had disappeared over the Channel.

The Christmas Day newspapers carried an agency report: 'Major Glenn Miller, the American bandleader, is reported missing … It is thought that while he was arranging for a troops' concert he may have been captured.' The *Daily Record* reported that the Miller band was due to broadcast during the *AEF Christmas Show* on the Home Service that evening. Sergeant Jerry Gray would take up the baton in place of its missing leader. The *Daily Herald* complained that the BBC had issued a 'pathetic correction … it said, "delete Major Glenn Miller"'.

What had happened? The official verdict – that due to bad weather the Norseman had come down over the Channel – is the most obvious conclusion to be drawn, not least because the aircraft's pilot apparently had little experience of flying in such conditions and had probably become disoriented. There was also the likelihood that ice had led to equipment failure.

None the less, over the years conspiracy theorists have been busy, their claims ranging from Miller being captured and tortured before being executed, to him suffering a fatal heart attack in a Paris brothel. His brother, Herb, did not believe that Miller was even on the Norseman. He was convinced that the bandleader had died of cancer in a hospital bed, but the authorities wanted him to have had 'a hero's death'.

Another theory is that Miller died under 'friendly fire'. Many years after the war, amateur film emerged of an interview given by a former RAF navigator. Fred Shaw, then living in South Africa, said that on 15 December 1944 he was aboard one of more than 100 Lancaster bombers returning from an aborted raid on Germany when they dumped their bombs over the English Channel. Shaw said that, watching from the plane's observation blister, he looked down and saw a Noorduyn Norseman below them. It flipped over and disappeared under the port wing of the Lancaster. Did 'Nipper' Morgan stray into the designated jettison zone where bombers returning from an unsuccessful raid could unload their bombs before landing back at base? Shaw's account has been challenged many times as has the story that, in 1987, a trawlerman caught part of the wreckage of a Norseman in his nets before dropping it back into the world's busiest shipping lane.

The so-called Glenn Miller Mystery will probably never be solved. Eighty years later, the Glenn Miller Sound lives on.

Chapter 11

Over the Rainbow

> We are prepared for the safety of our patrons in every way. It is our intention to give the highest form of entertainment and to help in every way to keep the British tradition KEEP SMILING.
>
> Coliseum Super Cinema, Aberystwyth

Among cinema buffs, 1939 is regarded as the greatest year in the history of the industry. In Britain, the whole of the 1930s and 1940s is considered the 'golden age' of film. For just a few pence, cinemas offered a comfortable and warm place to spend time in relative elegance. The cushioned seating, the decadence of the velvet wall hangings and the grandeur of the fancy interiors of the nation's 'picture houses' offered a touch of luxury that, for most, was simply not available anywhere else. And, for those seeking a moment or two of privacy with someone special, the subdued lighting was just the ticket.

Little wonder, then, that by the beginning of the Second World War, cinema was, by some way, the most popular leisure activity in Britain. It afforded everyone a chance to escape from the often drab surroundings of their everyday lives. It was somewhere to spend small amounts of money. Something that could not be rationed. And somewhere which often offered a fantasy far removed from real life. There they could watch their favourite film stars like Ronald Colman, Cary Grant or Errol Flynn, Margaret Lockwood, Katharine Hepburn or Shirley Temple. And it was somewhere away from homes now often shared with lodgers, or feeling empty of loved ones now far away.

As clouds of war gathered over Europe, British cinema audiences had already been treated to several epic films.

Stagecoach had been released earlier in 1939 and was described in the pages of the *East Kent Times* as 'a story of breathless speed and excitement' set in 1880 'when America was young and overrun with Red Indians'. It had a varied cast of characters that included 'a lady of lax morals who has a large heart', 'a youthful renegade', and 'a timid whisky salesman'. It 'captures the imagination from beginning to end'. *Stagecoach*, which proved the breakout role for John Wayne, was one of the most popular westerns of the period.

At the end of August, as war seemed ever more likely, cinemas up and down the country announced their programmes for the rest of the week and the week ahead. On 1 September, the *Nottingham Evening Post* listed an almost bewildering choice for those wanting to go to 'the pictures'. In the city itself, the Ritz was showing radio's Syd Walker in *I Killed the Count* and George Sanders, and Wendy Barrie in *The Saint Strikes Back*. The Cavendish had Jane Withers in *Always in Trouble* and Joe E. Brown in *Flirting with Fate*. At the Elite was Nelson Eddy in *Let Freedom Ring*. Alistair Sim and Gordon Barker were appearing in *Inspector Hornleigh* at the Hippodrome. Scala was showing Mickey Rooney in *Huckleberry Finn* and Laurel and Hardy in 'one of their best comedies', *Blotto*. Judy Garland in *Listen Darling* was entertaining customers at the Bridgford Tudor alongside Gladys Swarthout and Lloyd Nolan in *Ambush*. The Roxy on Mansfield Road had Jessie Matthews and Michael Redgrave in *Climbing High*, while the Ritz-Carlton on Burton Road was showing *St Louis Blues* starring Dorothy Lamour. *Thanks for Everything* was 'on' at Beeston's Majestic and the Metropole in Sherwood offered *Peck's Bad Boy With the Circus* (also being shown at the Savoy on Derby Road) or *Lawless Valley*. And there were at least a dozen more cinemas from which to choose.

But then war was declared and everything came to a halt. Fearful of air raids and mass casualties, the government immediately closed all the nation's 'places of entertainment'. Patrons of the Plaza cinema in the Liverpool suburb of Waterloo, which opened on 2 September, became the cinema's first and last audiences as they watched Edna Best in *South Riding* before it closed on the same day.

Across the nation, more than 4,300 cinemas now lay idle. It was not long before rumblings of discontent were heard. On 5 September, playwright George Bernard Shaw wrote a letter of complaint to *The Times*. He was concerned that denying entertainment to soldiers and civilians at such a trying time was 'a masterstroke of unimaginative stupidity' and asked, 'What agent of Chancellor Hitler is it who has suggested we should all cower in darkness and terror?'

For their part, the government had public safety to consider. Most cinemas were in town centres and just one bomb falling on a packed cinema could mean massive casualties. Preventing unnecessary large gatherings did seem a sensible precaution but, once the initial panic was over, and there had been no bombing, thoughts turned to the importance of maintaining public morale. Restoring the nation's favourite pastime seemed the most obvious way and, on 12 September, the decision was made to allow all cinemas, including the Plaza in Liverpool, to reopen once local authorities deemed all necessary safety precautions had been put into place.

The return to normal opening was slow, however – unless you were fortunate enough to live near Aberystwyth, which was possibly as far from danger as a town could get at the start of the war. So unlikely a Nazi target was it deemed that many national treasures usually on display in British museums – treasures like Magna Carta, Shakespearean manuscripts and great works of art – were taken to Aberystwyth where they were stored in a so-called 'ARP Strong Room' in specially constructed tunnels cut beneath the National Library of Wales.

Cinemas in Aberystwyth reopened as early as 5 September 1939. The Chief Constable of Cardiganshire, Captain J. J. Lloyd Williams, decreed that all cinemas could reopen provided that each establishment had 'an operator on duty listening for air-raid warnings' and that all exits were kept perfectly clear with sufficient staff on duty to ensure no panic in the event of an air-raid. Also 'notices, in large type, indicating the position of the shelter and how to get there' were to be put in place. Guy Morgan, film critic of the *Daily Express*, noted that the long journey was well worth it when he watched James Stewart and Carole Lombard in *Made for Each Other* at the Coliseum Super Cinema in the town. The cinema assured its customers that it was now 'a perfectly safe place of entertainment'.

In London, where reopening was not imminent, a sense of black humour began to take hold. Outside the shuttered Embassy cinema in Notting Hill Gate was a blackboard with the helpful message, 'Nearest Cinema Open Aberystwyth, 239 Miles' with an arrow pointing the way to West Wales. Cinemas in the provinces were reopening by the middle of September, but it would be another month before those in the capital would join them. Outside the Trocadero Cinema at London's Elephant and Castle was displayed a large mocking drawing of Adolf Hitler exclaiming morosely, 'Blimey, that's torn it, the Troc's only been and 'gorn and opened again.'

Because of the nature of cinema in Britain at the time, the biggest cinemas in the largest population centres would have the most anticipated

Prime Minister Neville Chamberlain broadcasting from Downing Street the announcement that Britain is now at war with Germany. (*Alamy*)

It's That Man Again. From left to right are Leonard Sharpe, Tommy Handley Franklyn Bennett and Horace Percival, pictured in 1943. (*Alamy*)

George Formby entertains Londoners sheltering from Nazi bombs, deep underground at Aldwych Tube station. A makeshift stage has even been set up. (*Alamy*)

All eyes are on the Forces Sweetheart, Vera Lynn, as she entertains troops at a concert in September 1940. (*Alamy*)

Gracie Fields distributes tea to members of the British Expeditionary Force stationed in France during the 'Phoney War' in early 1940. Two monkeys have got in on the act. (*Alamy*)

German-born actress and singer Marlene Dietrich, one of several world-famous stars who appeared at Bedford Corn Exchange during the war. Her version of the song *Lili Marlene* was a favourite with soldiers from both sides of the conflict. (*Illustrated London News*)

Glenn Miller and his band recording at Abbey Road studios in September 1944, shortly before Miller's disappearance on his way to France. (*Alamy*)

They never closed. The Windmill Theatre, home of non-stop burlesque shows, pictured on 3 October 1941. (*Alamy*)

USAAF airmen take to the dance floor to relax between missions. (*Alamy*)

Above: On the set of the classic film *Goodbye Mr Chips*, which was released in 1939. Cinematographer Freddie Young is the man wearing spectacles and standing in front of the camera. Director Sam Wood is seated in front, wearing a hat. (*Alamy*)

Left: Private Charles Ford, one of three members of the Army Film Unit, who lost their lives during the filming of *Tunisian Victory*, which told the story of a memorable Allied victory that finally knocked Rommel out of Africa. (*Vicky Easton*)

Right: Crowds of shoppers throng London's Oxford Street just before Christmas 1944. The entrance to Selfridge's department store can be seen in the background. (*Alamy*)

Below: Soup, one penny. Roast beef, fourpence. No wonder there was a long queue of people waiting their turn to eat at this British Restaurant in the Midlands in 1943. (*Authors' collection*)

The game must go on. Welsh RAF personnel enjoy front-row seats at Wembley for the England-Wales football unofficial wartime international in April 1940. (*Authors' collection*)

Left to right: Winifred Shotter, McDonald Hobley and Jasmine Bligh during a rehearsal at Alexandra Palace for the return of the BBC's television service in 1946. (*Alamy*)

films first. It could take some months for a particular film to have been 'on' in every part of the country. At the end of September, the Embassy-Savoy in Fareham was showing *Stagecoach* for the first time, while at the Ambassador in Cosham, Merle Oberon, Laurence Olivier and David Niven were starring in a film which had been causing a sensation since its release in the early spring – *Wuthering Heights*, based on the classic Emily Brontë novel.

The *Sheerness Guardian and East Kent Advertiser*, in its review prior to a run at the Ritz, had declared *Wuthering Heights* 'an outstanding production'. The dramatic cinematic trailer declared the story 'The Greatest Love Story of Our Time … or Any Time!' It was to prove immensely popular, continuing to draw audiences to cinemas across the country for the rest of the war. Directed by William Wyler, the haunting tale of love, revenge and tragedy was dramatic, romantic, and sumptuous. It was nominated for eight Academy Awards, but won only one – for its stunning cinematography of the 'Yorkshire Moors', although it was actually filmed in Southern California.

In October, another adaptation of a classic British novel was released, this time an entirely British production, starring Charles Laughton and a debuting Maureen O'Hara. Directed by Alfred Hitchcock – it would be his final British film – *Jamaica Inn* was based on the Daphne du Maurier story. Its plot was described in the cinema review pages of the *Hampstead and St John's Wood News and Golders Green Gazette* thus: 'Charles Laughton's Sir Humphrey Pengallan is a jovial extravagant kindly squire with a roguish eye for a pretty girl and a connoisseur of all else that is beautiful. He is also the secret head of the wrecking gang and as justice begins to overtake him shows a streak of insane cruelty that brings him to a fittingly spectacular end.' Critics and cinema audiences were particularly impressed with the 'intensely realistic' wrecking and storm scenes.

The year 1939 saw the release of several more notable British films. Among them was another classic – *Goodbye Mr Chips*, which was released shortly after the declaration of war and instantly captivated audiences across Britain. Starring Robert Donat and Greer Garson, *Goodbye Mr Chips* was, according to an advertisement placed in the *Caerphilly Journal* – the film was playing at the White Palace in Pontypridd – 'Dramatic, Moving, Inspiring. Breathing the Spirit of Youth. Beating with the heart of England, reflecting the achievements of four generations.' Much of *Goodbye Mr Chips* had been made on location at Repton School in Derbyshire, and the film featured more than 300 of the students and staff as extras. Surprisingly, for a subject so quintessentially English – the tale of a classics master in a British public school – the film had already been released in the United States, where it had been a great success, earning several Oscar nominations and winning one – for Donat as Best Actor. Its UK release was highly anticipated, but not every critic was so easily convinced. Writing after a trade show preview screening in the summer, a critic for *The Era* newspaper complained:

> It was a pity that we heard so much about the success of *Goodbye Mr Chips* in America, because, if this film had come to us unheralded, we could have bestowed on it a little praise and not have had to bother our heads in wondering whether all the fuss had been justified. As it was, we went along expecting to see a super film and found, instead, a picture dealing with the unobtrusive history of a Shire schoolmaster which at times moved so slowly that there was a grave risk of it becoming a bore.

The general mood of the review was gently mocking, although it did rate the film's 'general appeal' as 'very good'. In contrast, the review appearing in the *Bradford Observer* could not have praised it more highly, highlighting Donat's 'sincere portrayal' of the lead character. *The Birmingham Mail* said the film 'has that illusive quality, charm', and the *Coventry Standard* that 'Greer Garson … illuminates every scene in which she appears'. The Odeon in Burnley assured its potential customers that the film was 'Entertainment for the Whole Family … the finest film of the year … It's a long time since you enjoyed a film as much as you'll enjoy this one … it's magnificent holiday entertainment.'

The Arsenal Stadium Mystery, which opened in the autumn of 1939, was also a very 'British' film – but this time a murder mystery set in the world of football. Filmed in part at the beautiful Art Deco Arsenal Stadium, Highbury, it also utilised images of the club's First Division game against Brentford – which would turn out to be their final Football League game before the outbreak of war cancelled the 1939–40 season. *Shipyard Sally* featured one of the nation's favourite performers, Gracie Fields, in what would be her final British film. She played a failed music hall performer who moved, with her father, to run a pub near a

Clydebank shipyard. When the yard is threatened with closure, Fields's character, Sally, leads a campaign to save it. *The Lambeth Walk* was the film version of the popular musical *Me and My Girl*, which had opened two years earlier. Filled with memorable songs, and a plot involving a clash of cultures between Mayfair society and working-class Londoners, it was just the sort of jolly entertainment that wartime cinemagoers craved. As was another of 1939's releases – Metro-Goldwyn-Mayer's fabulous *The Wizard of Oz*, which premiered in December.

Starring 16-year-old Judy Garland, the film was quite unlike anything that had come before it. Directed by Victor Fleming, it was an adaptation of L. Frank Baum's 1900 children's novel *The Wonderful Wizard of Oz*. Garland was third choice (after Shirley Temple and Deanna Durbin) for the role of Dorothy Gale. The musical fantasy with the iconic song 'Somewhere Over the Rainbow' transported audiences into another world entirely with its cast of extraordinary characters – the Scarecrow, Tin Man and Cowardly Lion – and soundtrack packed with memorable songs. The cinematography, which transitioned from a moody black and white real world for the scenes set in Kansas to full-on Technicolor for the fantasy land of Oz, was much lauded. Audiences and critics adored the film. In June 1940, the *Bucks Advertiser & Aylesbury News* noted its

> brilliant array of screen stars, glittering pageantry, lilting musical numbers, spectacular settings in Technicolor, gorgeous costumes, beautiful girls and elaborate dancing specialities … combined in a glorified extravaganza but far greater than any stage presentation could ever be … The galaxy of talent and its elaborate features make it one of the greatest musical spectacles Metro-Goldwyn-Mayer has ever produced.

The Wizard of Oz became nothing short of a sensation, running at cinemas across Britain for almost two years on its first run, with further runs throughout the war. Little wonder that it became one of the most-loved films of all time.

As successful as *The Wizard of Oz* was, it was certainly not the biggest film of the year. That honour would go to another huge Hollywood blockbuster, and one which was also released by Metro-Goldwyn-Mayer and directed by Victor Fleming. Released in April, *Gone With the Wind* became the most popular film of the era. Starring Clark Gable,

Vivien Leigh, Olivia de Havilland and Leslie Howard (the latter three all British actors), it ran at almost four hours and was often shown with an interval.

The epic romantic drama, set against the background of the American Civil War, would become a constant in the nation's cinemas, running at one Leicester Square cinema for four years through the so-called Phoney War, and the entire London Blitz, when queues reputedly formed early in the morning as fires from the previous night's bombing were still to be extinguished. The film did not finish its first run until after D-Day.

All that said, distribution of *Gone With the Wind* got off to a rocky start. In May, the *Nottingham Journal* revealed, 'Seven hundred British cinemas may not show the three hours forty minutes American film … unless the distributors bring down the rental price.' Gaumont-British and Odeon cinemas were concerned at the minimum prices that they were being asked to charge. Normally, a cinema ticket ranged in price between one and two shillings (5p and 10p) depending on the type of seat. For *Gone With the Wind*, they were asked to charge at least three shillings and sixpence (18p) which was quite a mark-up, given that average UK ticket prices would not reach that level until the mid-1960s.

Customers, warned well in advance of the increased prices, remained keen and many booked in advance; anticipation, it seemed, had served only to increase demand. Some cinemas did offer a number of unreserved front stall seats at a more reasonable two shillings (10p). The Capitol Cinema in Aberdeen was one of them and its advertisement declared, 'It's here today! The most eagerly awaited event in all entertainment history … David O Selznick's Technicolor Miracle … 3 hours 40 minutes of perfect entertainment … the longest film ever made which seems the shortest!'

In Dundee, Green's Playhouse called it 'the greatest picture and the greatest event in Dundee film history'.

A more considered, although no less enthusiastic, recommendation came from the pages of *Picturegoer & Film Weekly* which made a feature of readers' reviews and published the following from Miss Marian Gottlieb, London, SE11: 'A superb film throughout. Magnificent acting by entire cast … full of drama with touches of humour. The Technicolor and photography are perfect, especially that of Atlanta ablaze … full of life throughout every effort should be made to see this film.'

Gone With the Wind was not the only film to enchant British audiences. They also loved Walt Disney's *Pinocchio*, the company's second animated full-length feature film, after 1937's *Snow White and the Seven Dwarfs*. Based on Carlo Collodi's 1883 children's novel, *Pinocchio* had its UK release in May 1940.

Less family orientated, but equally as gripping, Anglo-American's *Gaslight* was a disturbing psychological thriller based on Patrick Hamilton's stage play *Gas Light*. It starred Anton Walbrook as a newlywed husband, having an affair with his maid, Nancy, and cruelly manipulating his wife Bella (Diana Wynard) into believing that she is losing her sanity. The audience discovers that not only is he using an assumed name, but he also murdered his aunt and now secretly searches the closed-off upper floors of the house for her valuable rubies. Four years later, Metro-Goldwyn-Mayer released their own version, starring Charles Boyer and Ingrid Bergman, who won an Oscar for her performance. The plots differ greatly, although the general premise is the same. But, while the earlier version adheres to the Hamilton original, the US film is more convoluted, its trailer proclaiming it 'the strange story of an international criminal's love for a great beauty'. The latter version, which features Angela Lansbury in her first film role, is now the more famous because MGM sought to destroy prints of its earlier rival. That survives only because director Thorold Dickinson kept a personal copy.

Alfred Hitchcock's first US film, *Rebecca*, was also released in 1940. Based on the 1938 novel by Daphne du Maurier, it starred Laurence Olivier and Joan Fontaine. Another popular film based on a book was John Ford's *The Grapes of Wrath*, about an Oklahoma family of sharecroppers during the Great Depression.

Grand epics aside, the majority of cinemagoers continued to watch films like *Destry Rides Again*, a Western comedy starring Marlene Dietrich and James Stewart. Another Stewart vehicle was *Mr Smith Goes to Washington*, named, in the pages of the *Bedfordshire Times & Standard* as '[Frank] Capra's greatest achievement … a film you must not miss … overwhelming in its universal appeal'. Indeed, that particular newspaper, in cooperation with Bedford's Plaza Cinema, devoted an entire page to a review of the film 'a comedy-drama richly embellished with human touches', biographies of the stars – 'Stewart is one of the finest actors on the screen' – and a competition for those who had seen the film to win further cinema tickets by correctly answering ten questions about the movie. Surrounding the articles were a series of advertisements for local businesses which attempted tie-ins with the film with slogans such as 'Mr Smith goes to Washington … thrifty housewives go to the Belfast Linen Warehouse' and 'Mrs Smith Goes to into Town … while Mrs Brown stays at home because she has to cook the family dinner'.

At some point, however, both Mrs Brown and Mrs Smith were likely to find time for a trip to the pictures. In 1943, the Wartime Social Survey revealed that 32 per cent of Britons went to the cinema at least once a week. Another 38 per cent attended once a fortnight and the remaining 30 per cent never visited the cinema at all. Men and women visited with equal regularity, but those on lower incomes were the keenest cinemagoers, and this may have been due to their type of job and relative free time, or simply that those on lower incomes had fewer affordable hobbies from which to choose. Predictably, location had a huge impact on cinemagoing. For example, half of those living in rural areas never visited the cinema, while three-quarters of those who lived in urban areas, where there were several choices of cinemas, were regular attendees. Age, though, was the biggest factor. Least likely to visit the cinemas were the oldest generation, 69 per cent of whom never attended, with only 5 per cent going once a week. They were, of course, the generation who had grown up before going to the pictures was even an option and so had simply not acquired the habit.

In contrast, 79 per cent of teenagers (to use the modern label) and 43 per cent of young adults were regular cinemagoers. They were also the demographic least likely to read newspapers and books. The government had been quick to see the potential in using cinemas to inform and influence young urban citizens. Together with radio, cinema was seen as the most effective way of providing the public with vital information, delivering propaganda and helping to shape public behaviour and maintain morale. By 1940, many new films were already themed around the war, such as Carol Reed's *Night Train to Munich*. The story of an inventor and his daughter who are kidnapped by the Gestapo after the Nazi invasion of Czechoslovakia, it starred Margaret Lockwood and Rex Harrison.

Throughout the war, cinema attendance continued to grow steadily, from a little under 20 million weekly admissions in 1939 to more than 30 million by 1944. Food was rationed and alcohol was in short supply: the cinema provided a relatively cheap, available alternative to those who would rather have spent their leisure hours in pubs or restaurants. In 1940 and 1941 probably the two hardest years of the war on the Home Front, cinema admissions stood at one billion for the year, rising to more than 1.5 billion in 1943, 1944 and 1945.

Even during the height of the Blitz, people still wanted to escape reality by going to the pictures. Although it had initially been feared that allowing citizens to gather in cinemas would be too risky, when the bombing began it was so widespread, caused so much devastation and seemed so random, that cinemas became regarded as no more dangerous places than anywhere else. None the less, as with all aspects of life on the Home Front, cinemas were sometimes the scene of near misses and of tragedies.

On 18 March 1941, the National Picture Theatre on Beverley Road in Hull was the site of miraculous survival. That night saw one of the worst bombardments of the entire war, in a city which had already experienced well over forty heavy air raids. The alert wailed over Hull at 9.15 pm and the all-clear was not sounded until 4.00 am the following day. At just before 8.00 pm, an audience of 150 had settled down at the National for a showing of Charlie Chaplin's latest film – his first 'talkie' – *The Great Dictator*. Chaplin played both a fascist dictator and a persecuted Jewish barber, and it became his most commercially successful film. An American anti-war political satire black comedy, it proved a great hit across Britain – particularly with its ridiculing of a thinly-disguised Adolf Hitler character. It contains a classic, brilliantly choreographed and performed, scene where Chaplin, as the dictator, toys with a globe of the world, tossing it up and catching it again, dancing this way and that. Not everyone, however, felt it was appropriate fodder for humour. Poppy Smith, of Brighton, wrote in her personal review that 'Hitler is not funny'.

No one recorded what cinemagoers in Hull thought of the concept. Due to the heavy bombardment outside the cinema, they had been trapped inside since the sirens sounded. Most had moved to the building's reinforced lobby, although a few patrons remained in their seats at the back of the stalls. At 9.50 pm, a 1,000 kg (2,204 lb) bomb exploded to the rear of the cinema. It destroyed the screen and the auditorium. Remarkably, all 150 patrons, plus members of staff, escaped injury.

The following day, the cinema's manager told the *Hull Daily Mail*:

> It was a miracle that we all escaped. It was impossible for people to go home, as bombs were whistling down … Then the crash came at the back, and it was remarkable how well everyone behaved. There was no panic and no one received a scratch; but it was sheer providence … the foreman had

> the narrowest squeak. He had been to the back to bank up the boiler, and had just returned to the stalls when the back wall and the screen were blown in.

It was even more of a miracle than newspapers reported: on busy nights the auditorium at the National Picture Theatre could seat 1,000 customers. Remarkably, what was not destroyed by the Luftwaffe that day – fragments of the lobby and vestibule as well as the entire façade – still stands, the only civilian Second World War bomb ruin remaining in Britain. After a long campaign to save it, in 2021 permission was secured to turn the remains of the National Picture Theatre into a memorial to Hull's civilian casualties, and an education centre.

Not all cinema patrons were to prove so fortunate. On 25 October 1940, an incendiary bomb fell onto the orchestra pit of the Balsall Heath Carlton Cinema in Birmingham, where Dorothy Lamour's *Typhoon* was playing to a packed audience. Nineteen were killed, and twenty injured. As was standard in cinemas, an air-raid warning had flashed up on the screen. Audience members were divided on whether to make for the shelters. In the event, there was no time. Just seconds after the warning, the bomb exploded. Many of those killed were found still sitting in their seats.

Among the dead was 15-year-old Irish lad Ted Byrne, who had been able to attend the screening only after his sister had given him the money from her bottle returns. He had already seen the film, but his friends managed to persuade him to join them anyway. After the raid Ted's father, serving in the Home Guard, helped carry the dead from the cinema. He was taken to see his mortally injured son at Selly Oak Hospital and was there comfort him as he died. Almost all of those who died at the cinema were teenagers or young adults.

Even worse was to come. Friday, 9 July 1943 was a wet and windy day in East Grinstead, West Sussex. Just after 5.00 pm, an audience of 184 – many of them schoolchildren – were settling down at the Whitehall Cinema on High Street to enjoy a *Hopalong Cassidy* supporting feature when the air-raid sirens sounded. As had become common by this point in the war, few people took notice of the warning that flashed up on the cinema screen in front of them. Although East Grinstead lay on a direct line between the South Coast and London, which was only 27 miles away, and although the alert had sounded many times, the town itself had yet to experience any bombs. Why would this time be any different?

Five minutes later, a single Dornier 217, part of a squadron headed towards London, became separated from the rest in cloud and its pilot began to look for a 'target of opportunity' to offload bombs before returning home. According to the *East Grinstead Courier*, the aircraft began circling. A train was approaching the railway station. The pilot opened fire and peppered the train with bullets before turning for the town's main streets.

Twice he went around before dropping at least eight bombs, hitting several businesses – an ironmonger's, a builder's yard, a ladies' outfitters, and a factory among them. There were countless injuries and many dead – shopkeepers, housewives, workers and children. But the greatest loss of life was at the Whitehall Cinema, which had taken a direct hit from two bombs, the first splitting the cinema roof in two.

Agricultural worker Robert Jack told the newspaper:

> The audience became restive, though not in any way panicky … It was all very orderly and the gangways were filled with people making their way casually to the street. I suppose about half the audience were on their feet and half had decided to remain. I had just reached the door and had my hand on it when there was an awful crash and I had a glimpse of the whole cinema filled with smoke and flames. Then something hit me on the head. When I came to, I was lying in a heap in a seat ten rows away from the door. My head was bleeding and I heard groans. I was able to drag myself away and collapsed in the arms of one of the rescue workers.

Thirteen-year-old John Parsons said:

> I was sitting in the front row – in the tenpennies. The first thing I knew was a sort of crackling which ran along the ceiling. The exit lights and the film went out at the same moment and the place was in complete darkness. Bits of debris started flying about. I got on the floor in less than a second. I crawled along in front of the seats, jumped up and ran to the exit. Just as I was going up the steps there was an explosion. Then I felt a pain in my face and found I had been cut.

It was a huge delayed-action bomb. Behind the schoolboy was a scene of utter devastation – the building had collapsed, burying dozens in the rubble. Only a very few had reached safety.

In 1993, projectionist, William Henn, gave his account:

> It was a terrible, terrible day. The auditorium of the cinema was the most awful sight I ever wish to see. It is still as vivid in my mind as ever. You never forget something like that. Everything was on the move, walls were collapsing around me. I remember standing there shaking myself and wondering what was happening. I was completely blinded by dust, but I could hear screams coming from the audience. People were crying and moans were coming from beneath the debris right under your feet. Bullets were ricocheting off the walls around me like something out of a Western film.

The Dornier pilot had taken another strafing run before flying on.

Mr Henn continued, 'I took cover in a hairdresser's shop and flung myself to the floor. The main shopping area along London Road was like a battlefield, half a dozen bodies were lying in the road.'

Help came almost immediately, from members of the ARP, police and National Fire Service, from locally stationed Canadian troops, Home Guard, and members of the public. Within five minutes, the first ambulances were on the scene.

In his 1946 booklet *Reminiscences of 1938–1945 by a Head Warden*, T. P. Peters, who was stationed at the town's Norton House post, described the tragedy:

> Hardly a body could be seen … I went … into the basement towards the stage as far as we could get, but rescue work from this point was impossible … The roof was still dangerous, or what was left of it, but nobody took any notice of that. This is where our training came in … even makers of tea knew their stuff. I never drank so much tea in all my life.

According to the *East Grinstead Courier* of 16 July:

> The combined services accomplished many feats of skill and daring, and worked feverishly throughout the late afternoon

> and night. There were many harrowing scenes as children and women were recovered from the debris … One by one, and two by two, pale-faced and lifeless children were brought out of the ruins. Some were found almost naked with their clothes blasted from them. It was a sickening scene, one which brought tears even to the stoutest hearts among the gallant lot of rescuers who toiled on through the night. One man was told it was time to rest. The rescuer looked up, inwardly moved, but not betraying a sign of emotion, replied, 'No, I work on. Under this rubble is my wife. I must find her.' And so he went on toiling. Also under the brick and dust was a worker's sister-in-law. He dug her out and went on looking for her child.

When the bomb detonated, Herbert Brackpool had been making jam tarts in his bakehouse in the basement of the cinema. The explosion left a hole in the ceiling through which had fallen the bodies of four women. The baker's son, Michael, was at the cinema and so Herbert joined the rescue workers. It was some time before one of his colleagues found the lad's body in the rubble.

Eighty of the 108 people who lost their lives that day were inside the cinema. This included thirteen children. Fifty more were badly injured. Among the dead were multiple members of several families who were there as a family treat, a toddler and an usherette.

There were lucky escapes, too. Young Eric Parsons was a regular Friday cinemagoer. That fateful day was the first he had missed in months because he was saving up to enter his two rabbits in the school rabbit show. Two nurses were there, but received only minor injuries because, instead of their usual seats in the centre of the cinema, they had chosen to sit at the back to eat the gooseberries they had just purchased.

While the fire service worked to extinguish the flames, which were spreading along the street, rescue workers continued to look for survivors. The last living casualty was brought out at 7.10 pm. The bodies were taken to a temporary mortuary at a local garage where the identification process could take place. Many of the victims were buried at Mount Noddy Cemetery, twenty-two of them in a communal grave.

With such graphic illustrations of real life's frailties, it was no surprise that films that showed Britain's successes, the nation in a good light, were among audience favourites. Some may have regarded films like 1941's *The 49th Parallel* as mere propaganda. After all, it had been the idea of the Ministry of Information, who approached the established filmmaking team of Michael Powell and Emeric Pressburger to make 'a film about mine-sweeping'. Powell, though, had other ideas and later said, 'I hoped it might scare the pants off the Americans.' Filming had begun on location in Canada in 1940 with the cooperation of the British and Canadian governments, and it was released in Britain the following year. It told the story of six Nazi U-boat sailors who try to escape from Canada across the border to the neutral USA, of their encounters with the brave Canadian people, and it warned of their threat to the USA. *The 49th Parallel* starred Laurence Olivier as a French-Canadian fur trapper, and Anton Walbrook as the leader of a Hutterite community. The film critic of the *Belfast News-Letter* thought that its propaganda value was limited, having convinced audiences 'that the Nazi is a dauntless, almost invincible animal, however ruthless – an effect which may not have been exactly the one aimed at by the Ministry of Information!'

A huge marketing campaign accompanied the film's British release with personal appearances by the stars and elaborate foyer displays featuring models of aeroplanes and submarines, maps, and globes. All this did the trick as *Kinematagraph Weekly* announced that it had been the biggest box office draw of the year. 'The best film of the year is British! This fact cannot be too forcibly stressed.' Perhaps that was the best propaganda of all.

Ironically, by the time the film, retitled *The Invaders* for its US release, was seen by American audiences in 1942, the country had been attacked by Japan and had already joined the war. Heavy-handed propaganda or not, audiences and critics loved *The 49th Parallel*, which was awarded an Oscar for Best Original Story.

The First of the Few, released in the summer of 1942, was a biography of Spitfire designer R. J. Mitchell and had a charity premiere in aid of the RAF Benevolent Fund. The film starred David Niven as a test pilot and Leslie Howard as Mitchell. Howard also directed and produced the film. It was Howard's last on-screen film appearance. Although there had previously been an unspoken agreement that commercial flights from neutral countries be left alone, on 1 June 1943 Howard's BOAC/KLM commercial flight from Lisbon to Bristol was shot down by the Luftwaffe over the Bay of Biscay. He had been attending a premiere for the film in neutral Portugal and had briefly visited Spain on behalf of the British Council.

Howard's death shocked Britain, for the actor was much loved. He was at the height of his success when in 1939 he returned to his homeland to join the war effort, having sacrificed royalties and bought himself out of several lucrative Hollywood contracts. He had worked tirelessly, appearing in propaganda and patriotic morale-boosting British films, making radio broadcasts intended to encourage America to join the war, and generally decrying Hitler. In 1942, Howard had appeared in an affecting Red Cross Appeal for British Movietone and Odeon Theatres. It opened with a clip of Howard and Niven in a hospital ward and continued as Howard spoke directly to the camera. In his broadcasts from Berlin, 'Lord Haw-Haw' had issued threats to Howard. 'We will make this pompous British actor repent his words. We will see to it that, after eating his own words, he will have the breath choked out of his body so that he will never be able to defame the Germans again!' went one. Another warned, 'We will see to it that Howard lives – or dies – to regret what he has done to the Germans!' A triumphal report of his death appeared in the Nazi Party newspaper *Völkischer Beobachter*, a vehicle for propaganda minister Joseph Goebbels.

This led to speculation and rumour. If the attack had not been, as the Germans claimed, an accident, then Howard might have been a realistic target. But so might his agent, Alfred Chenhalls, who bore a striking resemblance to Winston Churchill, who was due to return from Algiers any day. Even Churchill himself suggested that incompetent enemy agents might have made that error. Also on the flight were a mining engineer securing vital supplies of tungsten, and a Jewish Anglo-German businessman who had been negotiating the safe emigration of Jews from Spain and Portugal to Palestine. Howard himself, ostensibly every bit the English gentleman, was actually the son of a Hungarian Jewish father. But perhaps there was a more mundane explanation. First Oberleutnant Herbert Hintze stated that his squadron had not been informed of a scheduled flight in the area and so had interpreted the DC-3 as an enemy aircraft.

Many familiar faces from British comedy appeared in propaganda films. Tommy Trinder in *The Foreman Went to France*, Will Hay in *The Goose Steps Out* and George Formby, who appeared in so many morale-boosting films, did his own bit in *Let George Do It!*, *Spare a Copper*, *Get Cracking* and *Bell Bottom George*.

In Which We Serve, released in the autumn of 1942, was directed by Noël Coward and David Lean. It was written by Coward, who also composed the music for the film and starred in it as a naval captain, a character inspired by Louis Mountbatten. *In Which We Serve* – which also starred John Mills and Celia Johnson, and featured Richard Attenborough in his first screen role – was inspired by the sinking of HMS *Kelly* during the Battle of Crete in 1941. Following a preview at the Regal Cinema in Edinburgh, the reviewer of *The Scotsman* noted:

> Films sometimes fail to live up to the glowing appreciations which have preceded their arrival, but this is undoubtedly a great picture – one of the best films ever made, in any country. Without striking a single false note it gives a very realistic impression of life in the British destroyer service in wartime. Not only that but by connecting up the life of the ship with the lives of those who serve in her, and the lives of their dependents on shore, it builds up a comprehensive picture of service in the Royal Navy.

In contrast, *Went the Day Well?* was an entirely fictional tale, adapted from a Graham Greene story, about the fictitious Battle of Bramley End. The action takes place over Whitsun weekend in 1942. Royal Engineers billeted in a quiet English village are revealed as disguised German paratroopers serving as an advance party for the full-scale invasion. The local Home Guard corporal is revealed as their collaborator. Slowly the villagers become suspicious of the incomers – the use of a Continental '7' to keep score of a card game and the discovery of some German chocolate in the commander's belongings help to uncover the truth. The villagers are rounded up at the local church, the vicar is shot for attempting to sound the church bells to signal an invasion and numerous attempts at raising the alarm come to nothing. The villagers, and their enemies, often meet – surprisingly, for a film of that era – brutal ends. The Home Guard platoon are ambushed and killed, the postmistress kills a German with an axe, only to be violently dispatched herself while waiting for a gossiping switchboard operator to answer her call. The vicar's daughter discovers the collaborator and shoots him, and one of the villagers is killed when shielding local children from a hand-grenade blast. Eventually the alarm is raised, help arrives and during the final battle many more villagers are killed or wounded. It closes, as it began, with an elderly villager showing a visitor the graves of the German soldiers and 'the only bit of England they got'.

By the time *Went the Day Well?* was released in November 1942, the dangers of a Nazi invasion of Britain had diminished, but the film served as an inspiration to cinemagoers, and as reminder of the importance of remaining alert to the threat.

Giving a uniquely American perspective on Britain's Home Front was *Mrs Miniver*, a 1942 film starring Greer Garson in the title role. In Britain, many critics found it a rather unlikely portrayal of a middle-class English housewife and her family. It perhaps did not help that members of the Miniver family rather conveniently experienced just about all the wartime tropes. A family member died in an air raid, a son joined the RAF to fight in the Battle of Britain, and a husband took part in the rescue effort at Dunkirk. These events did, of course, happen to many people. Less common was the experience of Mrs Miniver herself, who discovers a wounded Nazi pilot in her garden, is briefly captured by him but, when he collapses, manages to disarm him and call the police. Despite the critics, the British public, particularly women, loved the film, apparently flattered that its calmly determined lead character and lovely star was deemed to represent them, and seeing it as what the *Montrose Review* called 'a gracious tribute from America to our country, our people and the British way of life'.

In 1944, Laurence Olivier starred in, and directed, the epic screen version of William Shakespeare's *Henry V*. Apparently under instruction from Churchill to produce an example of the best of British, Olivier left out some of the original's more brutal scenes. The film, which featured a score by William Walton, was largely shot in Ireland, using hundreds of locals as supporting artistes in the Agincourt scenes. It was partly funded by the government and went greatly over budget, and it would be the end of the decade before the film made any profit for Rank. Nevertheless, it is regarded as the first successful film of a Shakespeare play.

One of the biggest film stars of the wartime period was Humphrey Bogart. Two of his best-known films were romantic dramas and have become classics. In *Casablanca*, directed by Michael Curtiz and released in Britain in 1942, Bogart stars as the cynical nightclub owner, Rick, opposite Ingrid Bergman. It is, perhaps, the quintessential film of Hollywood's 'golden era'. Stylish, dramatic, romantic, filled with intrigue and tension. The plot, with its cast of resistance fighters, spies and Nazis is, it has to be said, rather similar to that of Bogart's other great film of the period, *To Have and To Have Not*, released the following year. This time, his co-star was Lauren Bacall, and the location is Martinique.

Although the big Hollywood movies were always popular with British audiences, they had a particular fondness for a good old British film. Particularly a sentimental one.

Director David Lean's classic British romantic drama *Brief Encounter* is regarded as one of the best wartime films ever made. Although not released until November 1945, three months after VJ Day, it was filmed between January and May 1945 with production pausing briefly to allow cast and crew to celebrate VE Day. Starring Celia Johnson and Trevor Howard, it was based on Noël Coward's play *Still Life* and tells the story of two ordinary people, Laura Jesson and Alec Harvey, each otherwise comfortably, if not entirely happily, married to others, who meet at a railway station refreshment room and 'accidentally' fall passionately in love. The pair continue to meet, spending entire days together, grasping the chance of freedom from their rather staid lives. Soon they realise their relationship cannot continue and they try to make the most of their last days of freedom. As they are about to part for the last time, they are interrupted by a chatty acquaintance of Laura's and the pair are denied their final moments together. The lead performances are utterly restrained, and perfect for the characters – a middle-class wife and mother, and a GP husband and father – and the worlds they usually inhabit. Unconventionally, no judgement is made of the lovers, and no punishment is handed out for their infidelities, save for the personal guilt each of them feels. The sympathy and understanding shown to two ordinary characters were much appreciated by audiences and critics alike.

The Thanet Advertiser said, 'This is a story in which the happenings are lifelike and not conventional film script.'

The Leicester Chronicle called it 'Noël Coward's best film'. However, Denis Myers of the *Sunday Pictorial* was not impressed, describing *Brief Encounter* as 'a rather dull film about a silly woman who ought to be spanked'. He did not offer an appropriate punishment for Howard's character. Myers also claimed that the film lacked appeal to 'ordinary' audiences. And that 'nothing really happens … just two kisses and a lot of running to catch trains'.

In response, *The Sketch*'s C. A. Lejeune wrote, 'What, you say, nothing happens? No stolen night together? No weekend in Paris? No convenient death for the superfluous partner? No, my eager friend. Nothing happens … the virtue of the film is that this decision is wholly in character, and is probably exactly what would happen in real life.'

Indeed, the characters' disquiet at their situation, their feelings of guilt, their decency, and, ultimately, their self-sacrifice was something that rang particularly true with British audiences, something it continues to do for modern film-lovers. In 1999, the British Film Institute named *Brief Encounter* second on a list of the Greatest British Films of All Time.

It truly was a golden era.

Chapter 12

Now Showing – Target for Tonight

> The Crown Film Unit is doing a fine job of work, and I for one hope something of their influence on film fashions will remain after this war.
>
> Everett Lawson, *Edinburgh Evening News*, March 1942

In early March 1941, British and Norwegian commandos carried out Operation Claymore, a raid on the Lofoten Islands of northern Norway. They captured the code books and a set of rotor wheels for the German Enigma cypher machine, a hugely significant event that enabled codebreakers at Bletchley Park to read German naval codes and helped Allied shipping to avoid U-boat packs.

Three weeks after the raid, the commandos were treated to a special preview before British cinemagoers were also able to view the action. An MOI (Ministry of Information) press statement read:

> Troops who took part in the thrilling raid on the Lofoten Islands will be the first to see on the screen the film story of their exploits. Cameramen of the Army Film Unit, it is officially announced, brought back from the raid dramatic film material which is now been made into a five-minute film in collaboration with the Crown Film Unit. Some shots have already been issued through the newsreel company. The film will be generally released on Monday, 24 March, but, meanwhile, special advance prints have been made and rushed out by the new Army mobile projection units for screening to the troops who took part.

The *Lichfield Mercury* reported:

> Selected British troops now go into battle armed with cameras instead of guns. They are members of the Army Film Unit

> [the RAF also had a film unit and both, together with the Crown Film Unit, were based at Pinewood Studios] and their job is to record for the screen our military operations. A detachment of the unit accompanied the successful Lofoten Islands raid and made a complete picture of the event. The finishing touches were applied in London in collaboration with the Crown Film Unit and in the national interest some of the material shot at Lofoten was released to the newsreels. The bulk of the picture has been made into an eyewitness account of the raid, commented on by Lieutenant Commander Anthony Kimmins, popular broadcaster on 'naval occasions'. *Lofoten*, as the film is titled, is an encouraging example of what can be done for the screen by co-operation between the Navy, the Army, and a government film enterprise.

During the Lofoten raid, according to Brigadier John Durnford Slater, who was credited with the establishing the first army commando unit, Kimmins, an actor, playwright, director and producer, became bored and went skiing on a nearby slope.

Newsreels and public information films might have allowed the government the means to control information being given to the wartime public, but most audiences valued being able to see for themselves, albeit briefly and often heavily edited, what was being reported in their newspapers.

In January 1941, *Kinematograph Weekly* had paid tribute to the British producers of short films

> which have produced featurettes comparable in every respect to those of their American competitors. Competition has, it will be observed, proved a great incentive. It has made the featurette a feature in miniature … Forced to improvise by war restrictions – little news trickles through from the Continent – editors and cameraman have not been slow in converting the newsreel into a veritable magazine.
>
> They have also made it a powerful weapon of propaganda. No wonder, then, that the short features can no longer be dismissed as fill-ups … they will remain if they are true to themselves and the public, the backbone of every kinema programme. 'Go to it!' we say to the manufacturers of British shorts and let 1941 be your finest hour.

Chief among the film producers mentioned in the article was the Crown Film Unit that could trace its story back to the Empire Marketing Board created in 1926 to persuade consumers to 'Buy Empire'. The following year, to further its aims, the Empire Marketing Board began producing promotional films, and when the organisation was closed down in 1933 its film unit moved to the General Post Office to make sponsored documentaries, perhaps the best remembered of which is the 1936 production *Night Mail*, a twenty-four-minute film about the nightly postal train operated by London, Midland and Scottish Railways. In 1940, the film unit was taken over by the MOI – which itself had been re-formed the day after war was declared – and rebranded as the Crown Film Unit.

The productions were not all about wartime action. In February 1941, the *South Yorkshire and Mexborough & Swinton Times*'s column 'From Me to You', which was aimed at young readers, told the 'Cornerites':

> Last week I said I would talk about films – so I will, for part of my space. I saw today what I thought was one of the grandest of the Crown Film Unit shorts – you know, the MOI features. It was called *Heart of Britain* and besides carrying a grand message, it also contained many beautiful shots. I think you will enjoy it too, if and when it comes your way.

There were many more adult films to come, however. In May 1941, *Kinematograph Weekly* reported on the twenty-minute film *Merchant Seamen*, which had a cast of real-life seamen:

> Here we have a profoundly interesting and suspenseful featurette, made by the Crown Film Unit, describing the hazards willingly accepted by those who go down to the sea in ships in wartime. The narrative opens with the torpedoing of a British merchant ship and the rescue of members of its crew. 'Nipper', a youngster is one of those saved and he takes a course in gunnery. Later, he and his colleagues sign-up again. Their ship is one of a convoy, but fog overtakes them.
>
> Suspense for a time is terrific but eventually they sail into clear weather. Suddenly a submarine is spotted. This

> is Nipper's big opportunity. Under the instruction of the gunnery officer he fires on the submarine, and it is hit. This ship and the rest of the convoy then proceeds serenely on their lawful occasions. The compilation, photography, commentary, characterisation, and dialogue are excellent. In fact, so real is the picture that those seeing it will never again waste a particle of food or a drop of petrol. Outstanding featurette.

Merchant Seamen featured one of the few film scores by classical composer and conductor Constant Lambert, a friend of William Walton.

In July 1941, the *Liverpool Daily Post*'s film critic declared:

> Perhaps the best war film yet made in Britain is *Target For Tonight*, produced by the Crown Film Unit with the co-operation of the RAF … It is the bomber's-eye view of a raid over Germany, the bomber itself beautiful in its functional precision, and the crew of jocose, informal young heroes make up a sort of complete personality which is the star of the film. We follow it with breathless excitement from the take-off, through the flight in the dark and the bursting flak to the target, the oil tanks where fires already raged to light the way. They swoop, they drop their bombs, they fly home through fog. They debate between baling out and trying for a landing, and safely they land. The sense of sharing in the risk and responsibility is wonderfully conveyed. Those of us who have friends among the bomber pilots of the RAF scarcely need after this film to badger them with any more questions as to 'what is it like?'

The film 'starred' Percy 'Pick' Pickford, the first RAF officer to be awarded the DSO three times. Pickford was 28 when he was killed in action in February 1944.

'It is in the incidentals,' said *The Times*, '… the markings on the blackboard for instance, an unexpected comment from the crew, that the film finds its strength. All through it realises the importance of understatement … Here is a record set down in something more than cinematic shorthand, and an inspiring record it is.'

King George VI, Queen Elizabeth and Princesses Elizabeth and Margaret attended the premiere. In 1941, the National Board of Review voted *Target for Tonight* Best Documentary, and in 1942 the film won an award from the Academy of Motion Picture Arts and Sciences. *Target for Tonight* was made with a budget of £6,000 (£360,000 at today's value), and by February 1942 the Treasury was reported to have made £50,000 (£3 million today) from ticket sales.

Not every Crown Film Unit effort was fully appreciated. In September 1941, the *International Woman Suffrage News* described *Words for Battle* as an 'over-ambitious effort of the Crown Film Unit'. *Words for Battle* (original title *In England Now*) was written and directed by Humphrey Jennings, one of the founders of the Mass Observation organisation that aimed to record everyday life through the diaries and answers to questionnaires of some 500 volunteers. The film contained images of urban and rural Britain, all overlaid with commentary by Laurence Olivier reading passages from English literary works and speeches. It was aimed at raising and maintaining morale during wartime, but the official organ of the International Woman Suffrage Alliance had reservations:

> *Words for Battle* ... serves only to emphasise the limitations of cinema. It is an attempt to give sound and visual image to the most memorable expressions of patriotism in our literature. Milton's 'Methinks I see an eagle,' read by Laurence Olivier, is associated with a squadron of Spitfires taking off, and Shakespeare, Blake, Browning and Kipling receive no more inspired treatment. Not until the end of the film, when, by unobtrusively emphasising its uniformed components, an everyday street-crowd is given a thrill and purposeful life of its own, is mediocrity outdistanced.

International Woman Suffrage News had more time for other releases such as *Airwomen*, *ATS*, and *Eating Out with Tommy Trinder*.

> The first two are effective demonstrations of the need for women in the auxiliary services, and make it quite clear that there are interesting and useful jobs for them to do. *Eating Out with Tommy Trinder* is an argument in favour of communal feeding with special reference to the British

> Restaurants. The economy in labour, fuel and foodstuffs, all, in their own way, munitions of war, is well brought out, and the housewife is urged help persuade her local authority to get on with the job.

The reviewer did not mention the final scene of *Eating Out with Tommy Trinder*, where the star picks up his food with fork in left hand and knife in right, but when he puts the food in his mouth, the fork is in his right hand.

In February 1942, the *Hampstead News* reported:

> Training secrets filmed by the Crown Film Unit and available only to members of the Home Guard and other defence services, were revealed at the Odeon Theatre, Swiss Cottage … 500 Home Guards and police units visited the cinema for a private show. The performance, on the War Office authority, was organised by No.14 company Hampstead Home Guard, with three other companies also on parade. Officers and men described it afterwards as one of the best shows they had seen and of the highest training value.

In late March 1942, *Kinematograph Weekly* was impressed by two films showing that week:

> Two outstanding items in this week's programme are sequences from the current newsreel showing the preparations on the Burma Front for resisting the Japanese drive; and a Crown Film Unit documentary, *Builders*, which is one of the best things this alert company has ever turned out. Short, simple, hard-hitting as a pneumatic drill, it brings to the screen the immediate actuality of the war effort as it is understood and practised by ordinary people in a way that has to be seen to be appreciated. … a welcome touch of individuality is shown … in which three builders discuss the value of their war effort …

In June 1942, the *Lincolnshire Echo* reported:

> Men and women of the Army, the Air Force, and the National Fire Service [NFS] are Britain's new film stars. At Pinewood

> Studios, in leafy Buckinghamshire, they are proving that they can act as well as any of the famous people whose names once appeared on Pinewood's dressing-room doors.
>
> Films with a purpose are being made at these great studios. Their purpose is threefold: to instruct the Services; to inspire the people of Britain and the Empire; and to record for posterity some of the noblest aspects of our struggle. Here, too, is a lesson in co-operation. Harmoniously working together at Pinewood are the Crown Film Unit, the Army Film Unit, and the newly constituted Royal Air Force Film Production Unit.
>
> All three of them rely almost exclusively for their acting personnel upon the men and women of the services, and other workers in Britain's war effort. All three co-operate by the interchange of ideas and materials and personnel, and by using in common many of the studios' facilities.
>
> Britain's new stars use the dressing-rooms formerly occupied by Michael Redgrave, Elisabeth Bergner, Jessie Matthews, Leslie Howard, Anna Neagle, and a host of other popular favourites.
>
> In production now at Pinewood is a 'blitz film' to be called *I Was a Fireman*. Mr Humphrey Jennings, who directed *Listen to Britain*, is bringing to life the very experiences through which his cast of real-life firemen lived during those perilous weeks which we all remember. Re-enacting the scenes they cannot forget, these men of the NFS play their parts with naturalness and sincerity. Before the war, one was a taxi driver, another a writer, a third a commercial artist, a fourth a waiter. Not one had any previous connection with the cinema or theatre. Now, like the men and women of the fighting forces who are working in the Army and RAF units, they receive nothing but their ordinary service pay while engaged on film work. Indeed, they say they are out of pocket because their expenses are higher.

In October 1942, *Kinematograph Weekly* reported:

> With her portable typewriter on her knees, squatting awkwardly wherever she could, Isobel Pargiter, continuity

> girl for the Crown Film Unit, spent over 200 hours in Sunderlands, Catalinas and Beauforts of Coastal Command, while cameras recorded the activities of their crews for *Coastal Command*. A lot of the action for the film takes place inside the huge aircraft whilst in the air. In spite of the roomy interior of a modern plane, by the time the crew were in their places and the cameras set up, the continuity girl had to fit in where she could while she recorded the dialogue and positions etc, which were later to be matched into scenes taken at the studio.

The film included scenes of an attack on a U-boat by a Catalina flying boat. *The News Chronicle*'s air correspondent, Ronald Walker, described it as the best flying film of the war:

> The ideal flying film was arrived at last. *Coastal Command*, produced by the Crown Film Unit, defies the Hollywood conventions of glamour and romance, and emerges as the finest film of Service flying ever made. It has no hero and no star. No bedraggled blondes stow away in the bombers. There is no story, at least not the usual story of love and friendship and broken hearts on the RAF command whose job it is to guard our shipping from enemy attack. The cast are officers, non-commissioned officers, airmen and Waafs of the Royal Air Force. Air Chief Marshal Sir Philip Joubert appears as himself in the operations room at Command HQ.

Reviewer Molly Hobman commented, 'Although the exploits of Coastal Command provide less obvious screen material than those of Bomber Command, the picture which the Crown Film Unit has made of this unspectacular branch of the service is in every respect a first-rate successor to the great *Target for Tonight*.'

In December 1942, the *Belfast Telegraph* reported:

> Film stars for a day. This was the experience of number of girl linen mill operators at Mossley this morning when a Crown Film Unit arrived to 'shoot' the works. It all came as a surprise to the girls and there was a last-minute rush for lipstick, powder, combs and mirrors when the camera crew

> arrived on the scene. All the 'act' the girls were called upon for was to 'act natural' as they perform their daily task of turning flax into linen, and this they did perfectly. The film unit was in the charge of Mr J.B. Holmes whose last picture, *Coastal Command*, was recently shown in Belfast. He spent the weekend – he arrived in Belfast on Friday – surveying the possibilities and decided that the manufacturer of Ulster linen best exemplified the province's war effort. He found an ideal location at Mossley where the unit spent a busy day. The unit is one of forty which is, in co-operation with Crown Films of London, engaged today shooting sequences in Australia, Canada, India, Great Britain and many other places irrespective of weather conditions. The result will be a unique screen record for day in the life of the Empire at war.

The official film and photographic record of the D-Day landings was undertaken not by the Crown Film Unit but by No. 5 Army Film and Photographic Unit (AFPU) which had been formed in 1943. They were embedded with the invasion force and ten of them went in on the initial assault. Several were injured and, six days in, 26-year-old Sergeant William Norman Clague of the AFPU was killed. Attached to No. 6 Commando, he was sheltering in a cookhouse at Le Plein during the 12th Parachute Division attack on Bréville when a shell scored a direct hit. He was laid to rest in Ranville war cemetery.

Filming in wartime has obviously always been a perilous occupation. During the Second World War, cameramen filming in the front line had to be prepared to turn their hands to anything. Those going into battle in a tank, hoping to capture footage through the tank periscope, might well have to discard their cameras and act as gunlayers. When flying with the RAF, in an emergency they would be expected to man a gun.

On 9 June 1944, the *Sheerness Times Guardian*, reporting on the film *Tunisian Victory*, touched on the subject:

> It is an unforgettable camera account of a memorable Allied triumph and it is a fine tribute to the British, American and Free French forces, who finally knocked Rommel out of Africa. Three of the cameramen who shot scenes for *Tunisian Victory* have since lost their lives. These are Flight Lieutenant [Donald] Gallai-Hatchard of the RAF Film

> Unit, who shot much of the flying material, and Captain Harry Rignold MC and Sergeant Colman [actually Serjeant Edward Arthur Coleman], both of the Army Film Unit. In addition, Driver [John Robert] Taylor, Driver [Malcolm] McGee and Private [Charles Oliver] Ford, all of the Army Film and Photographic Unit were killed during the filming of *Tunisian Victory*.

A week after D-Day, *Kinematograph Weekly* told the story of one of the war's most evocative songs, which had been made into a short film by the Crown Film Unit.

> The words of the song *Lili Marlene* were written in Hamburg in 1923 by Hans Leip, a poet and painter, who is well known in artistic circles. Fifteen years later, one of Goebbels's 'Tin Pan Alley' boys set the words to music and it was sung by Swedish cabaret girl, Lawler Anderson, in a Berlin nightclub. When the Germans marched into Belgrade their propaganda unit brought with them some records and all but one were broken in transit. The one was Lala Anderson singing *Lili Marlene*, the song of a sentry thinking of his girl waiting at the barrack gates. Throughout the time that *Lili Marlene* was on the air to the men of the Afrika Corps, our men of the Eighth Army listened too. Every night they used to sit in the dusk and quietly hum and whistle the song until it became so familiar with them that they adopted it as their own. It was when the Eighth Army paused before starting the assault on Sicily that somebody wrote new words for the song and turned it from a tango into a march and this became the battle song of the Eighth Army. Humphrey Jennings has produced and directed this interesting documentary for the Crown Film Unit, and Marius Goring and his wife, Lucie Mannheim, provide the narration and feature in the film.

The *Yorkshire Post and Leeds Intelligencer* said:

> One of the war's oddest stories of that sentimental German song *Lili Marlene*, which became the marching song of the

> Eighth Army in their sweep across North Africa, has been turned into a film by the Crown Film Unit. A friend who saw the preview tells me that he was captured, as he thinks most people must be, by the lilting, faintly wistful, little tune. The song became such a rage in Germany that more than a million marks were subscribed to a war relief fund named after Lala Anderson, the Swedish cabaret artiste who first sang it. That was in a Berlin nightclub. According to the film, a 'Lili Marlene' statue was erected by the Germans on the road to Smolensk. The Eighth Army heard the song in the desert and adopted it. The film ends with a suggestion that British barrel organs will be playing *Lili Marlene* after the war. Perhaps they will.

The work of the Crown Film Unit was certainly diverse. In June 1944, the Minister of Information, Brendan Bracken, told the House of Commons details of his ministry's film division. In the past year, 160 English language films had been made, and out of 96 of them no fewer than 338 foreign-language versions had been produced. A series of films for showing to liberated Europe was in preparation and the first batch of French language films had already been sent to France.

Most of the films, he said, belied their dreary designation – documentaries. It was worthwhile recording that the so-called documentary film was a peculiarly British development. Years before the war, members of some far-seeing government department encouraged the work of a handful of pioneers in the making of documentaries. The MOI took over that work in 1939 and now the country was beginning to see how important a contribution their work had been to the conceptions and techniques of commercial film production.

'I think that many people in the British film industry would agree,' Bracken said,

> that that in the past four and a half years, the Crown Film Unit has played an essential part in the development of a recognisably national style of filmmaking … The Ministry is ready to provide each country as it is liberated first with films which will show the part played by Britain in the war since Goebbels's blanket of darkness spread over their heads … I do not wish to give the House the impression

> that the ministry's filmmaking activities have been carried out in competition with the industry. That would be entirely wrong. On the contrary, with great goodwill, the British film industry have in the past year made four full-length films at our instigation. In return, we have done our best to help them in one way or another with the production of thirty-eight commercial films.

The same month, *John Bull* magazine let readers into a secret:

> You're in the cinema, let's say, and watching a newsreel or a documentary film about the war. Suddenly there bursts upon you a sequence showing Nazi generals in consultation, or Hitler talking to Rommel, or German soldiers leading an attack. And you instantly think, 'How in the world did they get those pictures?' When a bit of enemy film is captured, either at sea or in the field, the newsreel companies don't get hold of it at once. It is studied very carefully by official eyes … after War Office intelligence have viewed it, the film is sent to the MOI, where, providing it is considered likely to interest the public, it is put on the stocks for distribution and becomes available to all newsreel and film producing concerns. Enemy film is discovered in various ways. An ordinary soldier, picking up 4,000ft of abandoned film, might not even know what it was. The first time we captured Benghazi, some German film was picked up in a mobile cinema, and later, during Montgomery's advance, some more was founded in a deserted theatre in Matruh … Captured stuff like this can often be used as an excellent propaganda boomerang.

In November 1944, Sir Max Horton, commander-in-chief of the Western Approaches, the area of the Atlantic Ocean lying immediately to the west of the British Isles and absolutely vital to shipping, went to the Forum Cinema in Liverpool for a private preview of a new Crown Film Unit production entitled, appropriately, *Western Approaches*. It was the unit's first Technicolour production, and added dimensions to the sea that black and white could not capture. Along with everyone else, the film crew were under threat from U-boat attack, and the writer and director, Pat Jackson, said that three ships in the convoy that they filmed were sunk. Sir Max Horton gave the film a glowing review: 'I was very favourably impressed by the magnificent technical achievement of the film, from the seamen's point of view, and very accurate picture of what has happened on many occasions at sea.' He placed *Western Approaches* alongside the 1942 classic *In Which We Serve*, which was directed by Noël Coward and David Lean.

Kinematograph Weekly was also impressed with this 'magnificent all-Technicolour sea-war documentary' and although there was a 'slight tendency to dwell a little too long on technicalities during the opening sequences, it is directed with intelligence, authority, imagination and showmanship'.

> The technical camera work, too, is outstanding. Many of the shots are pictorially and dramatically breathtaking. And another thing is that its inspiring story and authentic drama strongly support the merchant seaman's that he should, following the cessation of hostilities, share with the men of the Armed Forces, the right to reinstatement in his pre-war job. It demands universal exhibition on the urgency and justice of its propaganda alone. Outstanding British documentary.

Western Approaches was banned in the US because of a 'mild profanity'. The MOI pointed out that as 'one of the finest sea pictures ever made, actually shot at sea with Merchant Navy men playing all the parts, it is an integral part of the reality of the film that they should use language which would hardly be in place in a drawing room'. 'It is on the grounds that these words are used in a war picture for dramatic purposes,' the statement continued, 'that the British Board of Film Censors passed *Western Approaches* for showing in this country.'

Liverpool audiences were also among the first to see the Crown Film Unit's production that showed the V-1 attacks on London and southern England during the eighty days before the Allies captured the launching sites in France. The *Liverpool Daily Post* said, 'The picture is vivid and expressive and is accompanied by a striking commentary written and spoken by Sergeant Fletcher Markle [a Canadian actor]. The film has been sent to America, where a wide distribution is expected.'

In July 1945, Royal Marine Anthony Sunnucks, who was serving with what he called the 'chairborne' forces in Ceylon (Sri Lanka), wrote to his local newspaper, the *Faversham News*, to tell them about an 'interesting job' that he had recently undertaken. His words gave a compelling account of the conditions in which the men of the 'Forgotten Army' fought, and they also illustrated the conditions in which filmmakers often had to operate in order to bring the war on the front line to those on the Home Front, albeit this particular unit was actually in Ceylon, not Burma.

Around the beginning of February that year, two members of the Crown Film Unit – a director who was a documentary expert, and a cameraman fresh from working on the epic *Western Approaches* – arrived at his camp. They announced that they had come to make a film about jungle warfare 'to show the folks at home what hardships jungle fighting imposed on the "Forgotten Armies" of Burma'.

Anthony Sunnucks was commissioned to assist with the drafting of a script, as well as looking after the accounts and all the other secretarial work. Alongside him were the two members of the Crown Film Unit together with a jungle instructor and an officer just returned from Royal Marine Commando patrols in Burma. After a fortnight's work, they had a rough shooting script ready, provisionally entitled *Jungle Mariners*.

> Sometime later, after the director had been out reconnoitring the jungle to find a suitable location, we embarked in car, amphibious jeep and truck to proceed to the chosen location. A shock awaited us. Arriving at the spot we were horrified to discover that an enterprising Ceylonese [sic] had cut down all the trees in sight to start a sawmill. However, after a little time spent in looking around, we chose a new spot and erected our shelter, above a river with a waterfall tumbling into a perfect natural swimming pool.

They began shooting the film the same day, working from 9.00 am to 6.00 pm every day, without a break for lunch – 'just a pretty solid breakfast and equally heavy supper' – and lived on army 'compo' tinned rations supplemented with pineapples, bananas and such birds as the cooks could shoot – 'some very weird birds found their way into the stew pot at times'.

Sunnucks was to keep a record of everything shot for the film, noting the length of film used in each take, the exposure given the particular subject, the names and positions of characters in the scenes. He also had to take all the still photographs. At each take, he said, they used up to something like 20 ft (61 m) of film.

He said, 'The seven marines and the corporal who were starring were a bit hammy and camera-conscious to start with, but soon settled down to working without looking at the camera.'

Working in the jungle had more than its fair share of thrills:

> One morning as the director was placing two chaps ready for a scene, a tic polonga, a deadly poisonous snake, slid over his boot. He had the presence of mind to stand quite still while the cameraman shot some 30ft [9m] of film of the reptile. Needless to say, it didn't live long after its film debut! Another day we found a huge tarantula spider sunning itself on a bush. The cameraman, who promptly christened it 'George', took yards of film of the deadly thing before it expired – apparently it couldn't stand the publicity!

The unit also took film of a crocodile, which crossed the river just above their bathing spot, and leeches – 'the most disgusting insects [sic] in the jungle' – and monkeys 'friendly but shy who sat up in the treetops and discussed the funny ways of those humans below'. A kabaragoya, a very large monitor lizard, lived close to their camp and was 'very partial to tinned cream cheese'.

Altogether the unit shot 18,000 ft (almost 5,500 m) of film. Sunnucks told the newspaper:

> The film was soon finished and is now in the process of being finished at Pinewood Studios, Bucks. You should be able to see it in the very near future, and, if it does what it was made to do, it shows you what the lads in Burma are going through every hour of every day of every week, month and year that they spend fighting up there. I shall be proud of my humble part in the job.

The Crown Film Unit continued through the austere early post-war years until the Conservative government closed it in 1952. There was opposition to the decision from Labour but the idea of a government-funded film unit was a difficult luxury to sell when independent companies could take on commissions from the Central Office of Information that had replaced the MOI in 1946. Its special place in wartime filmmaking lives on in films like *Target for Tonight* and *Western Approaches*.

Chapter 13

No Better National Service

> In the event of an air raid warning an announcement will be made by means of an illuminated box sign installed immediately in front of the footlights. Patrons are advised to remain in the theatre, but those wishing to leave will be directed to the nearest official shelter, after which the performance will be continued for so long as is practicable.
>
> Notice to patrons of the Playhouse Theatre, London

On 7 September 1939, *The Stage* reflected on the unenviable positions of theatre workers:

> The shadow of the war has fallen swiftly and with special heaviness on the arts and the industry of the stage … recently the West End managers resolved, at the meeting of their society, to carry on so long as they were permitted to do so; and in spite of the loss of business caused by increasing public tension as the crisis heightened, this spirited attitude was maintained not only in London but also in all other parts of the country. On Saturday the usual matinees took place in the West End and in the evening there were, with a few exceptions, performances at the unusually large number of central theatres open for this time of year. The blow fell on the announcement of hostilities with Germany.

The closure of Britain's theatres had forced hundreds of people out of work overnight. Not only did they face immediate unemployment, those working with touring productions were also in limbo far from home.

Noted actor, manager and producer Sir John Martin-Harvey, writing in *The Stage*, said that by shutting down theatres,

> we shall carry great suffering into the homes of an immense number of workers whose lot at the best of times is precarious enough … that is the terrible plight into which actors and actresses, variety artistes, concert party artistes, musicians, and the thousands of other workers in the course of public amusements are thrown. By a stroke of the pen they're utterly bereft of their means of livelihood. No special consideration seems to have been given as a corollary of the order, to this extremity into which the whole industry has been precipitated.

It was, indeed, a crisis for the families of every individual who relied upon the industry – actors, musicians, or backstage crew – and calls were made for theatres to reopen as soon as possible.

When it was announced that this would happen once appropriate safety measures had been put in place, actors' union British Equity urged that 'work in theatre in wartime should be regarded as national service for all artistes over military age or who are unfit for active service'. The government had certainly realised the importance of the industry to public morale. Not only the slightly cheap but cheerful entertainments that had filled theatres since the Great War, but also plays which had fallen out of fashion long ago. The Council for the Encouragement for Music and the Arts (CEMA) was set up to promote the 'high' arts of theatre, music and art. The 1943 Festival of English Comedy, held at the Arts Theatre Club in London's Great Newport Street, revived a number of rarely seen productions, including William Congreve's *Love for Love*, which proved a great success. And Victorian farce *The Magistrate* by Arthur Wing Pinero, which the *London Daily News* called 'a real knockabout comedy, deliciously "naughty"'.

Shakespearean plays had, in the inter-war years, become less popular with the public. Now they, too, experienced a revival. In 1942 alone, three new Shakespeare play productions opened in London. In 1940, Donald Wolfit and his touring company took a number of the Bard's plays to regional theatres across Britain. To suit the times, many productions were given a modern twist like the Old Vic's 1941 production of *King John*. In Sybil Thorndike's Old Vic company tour of Wales's regional theatres, she played Lady Macbeth opposite a title character, played by her husband Lewis Casson, who bore a striking resemblance to Hitler. As bomb damage during the Blitz necessitated the closure of more West

End theatres, so new touring companies sprang up, joining the existing regional repertories, and taking the biggest productions to the provinces.

The Stage stated: 'The artiste's lot is not a happy one at present. Artistes are confronted with unemployment, uncertain duration of engagement, personal risk, scarce and expensive lodgings, transit difficulties, and food-rationing difficulties.' The peripatetic nature of the work necessitated the issue of travelling ration cards that could constantly be transferred to a shopkeeper in the next town on a tour.

Restrictions on heating and lighting, food rationing and the risk of bombing brought about a change in audience habit, from taking in a show after dinner to opting for matinees or early-evening performances. As part of a campaign to remove restrictions and bring theatres in line with cinemas, stars like Noël Coward, Michael Redgrave and Ivor Novello formed the Campaign of Actors for Sunday Theatre. Rationing and shortages of materials brought unique challenges to set designers and wardrobe departments. The Theatrical Industry Clothes Rationing Committee was established in 1941 to consider all requests for coupons for new clothes to be used in theatres. Theatre bars had difficulty accessing a regular supply of alcohol, interval ice-creams were out of the question and even paper for playbills, scripts and programmes was difficult to acquire. Then there was the very significant issue of all the young male actors and production staff who were being conscripted.

During the Great War, theatres had remained open. Several had been bombed. And there had been no fatalities. The Blitz, however, was to do much more damage.

In October 1940, the Theatre Royal, Drury Lane, was hit by a high-explosive bomb. Debris fell from the circle onto the stalls, and a fire broke out. Fortunately, theatre workers sleeping in the building at the time all escaped injury and there was otherwise minimal damage to the building. London's Old Vic, which had closed its doors in September 1940 at the beginning of the Blitz, was also struck by a bomb in May 1941. In 1944, an attempt at restoration saw Laurence Olivier and Ralph Richardson, newly released from military service, serve as joint directors. Other London theatres fared much worse. In September 1940, the Queen's Theatre in Shaftesbury Avenue, on the corner of Wardour Street, took a direct hit which destroyed the façade and lobby. A raid that took place on 16–17 April 1941 destroyed both the original Shaftesbury Theatre, and the Little Theatre in the Strand.

Theatres across the country were damaged. In March 1941, *The Stage* reported that 'a theatre in a North-East town' had been hit by an incendiary bomb. Despite the tableaux curtains catching fire, the journal reported that the theatre, unnamed due to wartime reporting restrictions, opened the next evening, thanks to the emergency erection of a temporary stage across the orchestra pit and the first few rows of the stalls. The Argyle Theatre, Birkenhead, was severely damaged in September 1940 and, on the night of 15–16 April 1941, Sunderland's Victoria Hall Theatre was destroyed. The Manchester Palace Theatre and the Prince of Wales Theatre in Birmingham were among other major theatres to suffer bomb damage.

Unsurprisingly, some of the newer plays doing the rounds before the war remained popular. Some, like Arnold Ridley's *The Ghost Train*, were tweaked, with slight plot, setting or era changes, to make them more contemporary. *The Ghost Train* had first opened in 1925 and proved so popular that it ran in the West End for two years straight. Ridley, now better known as an actor for his portrayal of Private Godfrey in television's *Dad's Army*, had been inspired by being stranded overnight at Mangotsfield railway station in Gloucestershire and had written the play in only one week. Throughout the war it regularly featured in the repertoire of regional theatres. In 1941, it was made into a film, starring Arthur Askey, the communist villains now replaced with Nazi fifth columnists.

Rather than stifle new creativity, the war seemed to spur it on. Noël Coward managed to premiere three new plays. The first, *Blithe Spirit*, 'an improbable farce in three acts' according to Coward, opened in 1941 and concerned an author who invites an eccentric clairvoyant into his home to gather material for his latest book, but ends up tormented by a spirit from his past. The second and third, *Present Laughter* and *This Happy Breed*, both opened in 1942. The contrasting stories – one a tale of a glamorous playwright, the other of a middle-class family between the wars – shared a run, each play showing on alternate nights. Later, all three plays would share the rotation.

Terence Rattigan's *Flare Path* was initially rejected because of its wartime theme. But when it opened at London's Apollo Theatre in August 1942, it ran for 679 performances. The story, a love triangle between an RAF pilot, his wife and a famous actor, was often advertised as 'the famous RAF play'. However, it was not Rattigan's most successful West End play. That fell to *While the Sun Shines*, which was first staged in 1943 at the Globe Theatre (now the Gielgud), and ran for 1,154 performances. Essentially a farce, the play found little success in the US, but was one of only four West End productions to run for more than 1,000 performances during the war. Another was *Blithe Spirit*. *Perchance to Dream*, by Ivor Novello, opened in 1945 at the Hippodrome Theatre. A musical romance, it became famous for the song 'We'll Gather Lilacs', and consists of three acts, each set in a different era and telling the parallel plots of several inhabitants of the same house. The list is rounded out by Esther McCracken's *Quiet Weekend*, at Wyndham's in St Martin's Court. It concerns a weekend spent at a country cottage that proves anything but quiet. As a review in *The Tatler and Bystander* said, 'Unrest to the point of commotion'. A sequel to McCracken's *Quiet Wedding*, it proved even more popular. As the reviewer put it: 'It has true human touches and it is consistently commonplace', and, for the wartime audience, that proved just the ticket.

Chapter 14

Tonight and Every Night

> Congratulations to Vic Oliver … I liked his crack about being as hungry as a moth at the Windmill Theatre. The Windmill, if you didn't happen to know, is a revue house where the remarkable thing about the costumes is the absence of them.
>
> Bernard Buckham, *Daily Mirror*, November 1941

In January 1942, an airman who had been reported missing five months earlier walked into the Windmill Theatre in London's Soho and gave his actress fiancée 'a happy surprise'. Flight Lieutenant Archibald Winskill DFC, who had flown Spitfires during the Battle of Britain, had not been heard of since he left to escort bombers on a raid over Occupied France in August 1941. Now the mystery was solved: he had been shot down and had made his way back to Britain with the aid of the French Resistance. Early in the new year, he walked into the Windmill where he had learned that Doreen Moore was performing.

It was a romantic story but apparently not one with a fairy-tale ending because, in 1947, Winskill, who would go on to be knighted, rise to the rank of air commodore and become Captain of the Queen's Flight, would marry Christine Bailleux from the Pas de Calais. It was, however, yet another small chapter in the life of an entertainment venue that had already earned its place in the annals of the Second World War as one that exemplified Britain's 'keep calm and carry on regardless' attitude.

It was in 1931 that Laura Henderson, the wealthy widow of an East India Company merchant, purchased the building that had been the Palais de Luxe cinema in Great Windmill Street and, despite no previous experience in the business, had it remodelled into a 320-seat theatre. The small theatre lost money and was returned to screening films before Henderson hired a new manager, Vivian Van Damm. He reintroduced live performances, this time in the shape of *Revudeville*, a variety show featuring singers, dancers, showgirls and speciality acts and which ran continuously from 2.30 pm until 11.00 pm daily. The venture, though, continued to lose money – £20,000 in the first four years after it reopened in 1932 – before Van Damm hit on the masterstroke of incorporating glamorous naked females into the programme. He convinced Lord Cromer, the Lord Chamberlain, who alone made decisions on censorship – what he considered decent and what was not – that if the women remained still, then it was no more indecent than were the statues of nude figures that were accepted in museums, galleries and public buildings all over London.

Those who would become the legendary 'Windmill Girls' thus remained stock still as living statues or 'tableaux vivants', the rule being, 'If you move, it's rude.' Naked women could be hidden by fans, and then exposed when the fans were removed, provided that they themselves remained totally statuesque. Similarly, a nude girl could be twirled around on a rope provided she remained in pose even though she was moving through the air.

The shows proved hugely popular with men, and there was often an unseemly rush to occupy the seats nearest the stage as soon as they were vacated. By September 1939, the Windmill Theatre's *Revudeville* was well established and making money. The war saw it build on that, not least when after the government's compulsory thirteen-day closure of all theatres, from 4 to 16 September 1939, the Windmill could boast that 'we never closed', a claim sometimes humorously altered to 'we never clothed'. Performances continued defiantly, even at the height of the Blitz. When the warning sirens wailed out over London, the audience at the Windmill could choose whether to stay or go. Most often they stayed.

In October 1940, a bomb hit the café opposite the Windmill, badly injuring actress Joan Jay. She suffered eleven wounds, the most serious of which was in the thigh into which she put her fist to stop the bleeding. Four months later, Joan walked back into the theatre on the arm of Nugent Marshall, the juvenile lead at the theatre, who had cared for her while medical help arrived. She returned to dancing, her scars hidden by her costume, and in 1942 she appeared as a 'castaway' on the BBC radio programme *Desert Island Discs* when she was described as a 'glamour girl'. In 1946, she featured in a British Pathé newsreel story *Show Girl*. She named one of her two daughters Vivien, after Vivian Van Damm, who had arranged for the skin grafts to her legs following the bombing.

The popularity of *Revudeville* did not go unnoticed by other venues and in June 1941, the *Yorkshire Post and Leeds Intelligencer* reported on a rival to the Windmill:

> These very long light evenings and the lull in enemy bombing have made the West End a more lively place after business hours than it has been for some months. Streets which were almost literally deserted after about 6pm during the worst raiding periods are now thronged with people, and restaurants, cinemas and theatres are able to almost to recapture the illusion pre-bombing prosperity.
>
> These circumstances have brought a rival to the Windmill Theatre's policy of non-top variety, which has been the only continuously maintained entertainment in London since the Blitz began. Now there is another show of this kind at the nearby Prince of Wales's. These entertainments conform to strict traditions, some lending themselves to easy jokes on the current clothing shortage. They seldom aim at subtlety, but many people enjoy their flavour.

Windmill performers were able to cash in on the very fact that they had appeared there. In March 1941, at the reopening of Maidstone Zoo, the entire company of the Windmill's *Revudeville* made a guest appearance to welcome newcomers that included a Bengal tigress, a male drill (a primate related to the mandrill) and a pair of llamas. Visitors were invited to bring with them odd scraps of vegetable leaves and peelings to feed to the animals, and men and women of the armed forces were admitted at half price if in uniform. Most said they had come to see the cast from the Windmill. In January 1944, the Arcadia Theatre in Skegness put on a variety show called *Venus Adorned*. Among the acts was 'the glamorous blonde, Marlene D'Orsay, from the Windmill Theatre, who recites the confessions of fan dancer and suits her actions to her lines. In an exposition of a striptease she explains that she's a girl who knows how to get her man.'

In April 1941, the *Illustrated Sporting and Dramatic News* reviewer had something of a dilemma:

> It is difficult to know what to admire most in the entertainments at the little Windmill Theatre – their

> persistence in face of any number of difficulties (the theatre has carried on without a halt since the war began), that consistent excellence; or their variety. This last is sometimes amazing, as in the case of the present I-don't-know-how-manyeth edition of the revue. Here we have almost anything from glamour girls to readings from Byron, Keats and Tennyson, from imitations of stage favourites by Miss Maisie Weldon to a fencing display. In the old days of the theatre, a knowledge of fencing was part of the training of every actor with any claim to competence; it fitted him for fights and duels in Shakespeare and other classic dramas. How many of our modern actors can fence (or for that matter have any need to)? 'The Challenge' in this show is as good an exhibition as I have ever seen, with a lot of dancing thrown in. Male impersonation is cleverly undertaken by Miss Susie Ward, Miss Judy McCrea has other qualities in addition to beauty.

In October 1939, *The Sphere* had carried a photograph of Judy McCrea, 'a showgirl at the Windmill Theatre, London, who, when she is not on the stage is in an air-raid warden in Paddington. Here she is in her attractive wartime kit.'

In August 1942, *The Stage* reported, 'The Windmill Theatre in its latest edition of *Revudeville* again shows that a stage can be attractively set with the minimum of material. The Venetian scene, the slow-moving Grecian dance, and the ballet have delightfully decorative backgrounds, all excellent examples of an imaginative use of paintbrush and lighting.' It prompted Fred Barnett of Blackpool's Palace Theatre to write to the trade newspaper: 'It seems a pity that so little attention is paid to the lighting side of stagecraft. With many producers it is considered to be unimportant, which is probably the result of few stage electricians possessing any knowledge of the artistic side of stage electrics. Good lighting effects can be improved the simplest state set 100 per cent.'

That September, 2,000 men and women of the imperial and Allied forces, together with 2,000 men and women of London's fire service, watched the Windmill Theatre girls at a show in a London cinema. It was the fire forces welcome to the fighting forces, said the *Daily Mirror*. 'The guests spoke different languages, they wore different uniforms, these Czechs, Poles, Fighting French, Belgians, Yugoslavs, Dutch, Chinese and British and American fighters – but they laughed, clapped and cheered in the same way and with the same gusto.'

In March 1943, the *Daily Herald* thought that 'the Windmill Theatre's new continuous bill is the brightest for many months – and it is good to report an improvement on the sketches … Dancing of all kinds is on a very high level.' In June the following year, 'Sarge', in the *West Lothian Courier*'s 'Home Guard Commentary' column, reported:

> A pal, on a visit to London lately, was precocious enough, despite his advancing years, to visit the Windmill Theatre. Being amazed at the number of Services' personnel present, he naturally enough inquired as to the possible cause of the apparent spate. In reply, he was informed that they were there on a special map-reading course. Having recovered sufficiently, he asked what on earth a vaudeville show had to do with map reading, and was naively told that it greatly stimulated their interest in contours. Something phoney about it all methinks, what!

Laura Henderson died in November 1944. In her will she left £246,191 gross (almost £14 million at 2023's value). 'Old Mother Henderson', as she was known to the Windmill revue girls, left £100 (£5,673 in 2023) stock to the dancer Anton Dolan and £10 (£567 in 2023) to each employee of the Windmill Theatre.

A few weeks earlier, the *Daily Mirror*'s Hilde Marchant had described Mrs Henderson as 'a sedate little old lady with masses of white waved hair, neatly held in place with an invisible net, and an ankle-length black satin dress, plain to the point of boredom. So to meet her at the Windmill Theatre was rather like having an appointment with the Watch Committee in the Garden of Eden.' Mrs Henderson told Marchant that she had had an extremely Victorian upbringing – 'never allowed out alone with a gentleman'.

The *Daily Mirror*'s Dick Gordon wrote a moving tribute:

> The spark that burned to change a dusty echo-haunted building into a palace of glamorous Eves, where long-limb girls in wisps of costumes, beautiful near-nudes, danced and sang, went out recently.

> It died in the heart and mind of a little Victorian woman of 81, a wrinkled, tired widow whose memories drifted from her forever in a hospital bed. It died when Mrs Laura Henderson, owner of London's Windmill Theatre, as thirty of her pretty girls in their scanty costumes danced in a whirl of gaiety along the footlights. It was her last wish that the show should go on. She made it in the quietness of her hospital ward, where, away from people she knew, she had placed her spectacles and grey-white wig on a bedside table. 'I'm going to have an operation.' she told her producer. 'It may go wrong but, if I die, the show mustn't stop on my account.' So there was no difference at the Windmill. As the frail old lady lay dead, her 'godchildren' of the stage played on, in London's most undressed show.

In May 1942, a play about the Windmill Theatre – called *Heart of the City* – was enjoying a successful run in New York, and in 1945 the film *Tonight and Every Night* was based on what was now a legendary part of the London scene. The *Daily Mirror*'s Reg Whitley said of *Tonight and Every Night*: 'What better subject could there be for a story of this type and the career of our own little Windmill Theatre, the only West End showplace to brave the Blitz from start to finish? … Good entertainment and a striking tribute to the heroic troupers on the Home Front who carried on for the sake of the boys and girls on leave.'

Picturegoer thought that the film was a 'somewhat phoney romance with a background of London's theatre life during the blitz'.

> It has obviously taken the Windmill Theatre, which braved the blackout nights, as its prototype but has enlarged it to Colosseum proportions. Apart from this, it provides good entertainment and is beautifully photographed in Technicolour. Rita Hayworth as a star of the Music Box review is very attractive … Musical numbers are lavishly staged and the acting generally is on a high level.

That April, the Windmill Theatre was advertising in *The Stage* for 'Attractive Girls of 16 and 17 years of age looking for a real future in the profession … Must be capable dancers. Permanent engagement. Minimum salary £7 [worth £387 in 2023].'

Van Damm continued to run the Windmill until his death in December 1960. His daughter found it a struggle to keep it going in a now seedy Soho that was far removed from the cosy area of shops and restaurants run by local traders during the Windmill Theatre's heyday. *Revudeville* finally closed in 1964, along with the theatre itself. The building has since seen multiple changes of use. The days of 'We Never Closed' are now part of the folklore of wartime London.

Chapter 15

I'll Be Home for Christmas

> Presents this year will be limited and less money will be spent on toys, but as far as possible do see that Father Christmas visits the children. Their happiness will also give cheer to you.
>
> Suzanne Harrison, *Leicester Evening Mail*, November 1940

By December 1943, the lyrics of the new song recorded by Bing Crosby were particularly poignant on both sides of the Atlantic. As Britons prepared to spend their fifth Yuletide of the war separated from their loved ones, and Americans approached their third, Walter Kent, Kim Gannon and Buck Ram were inspired to write 'I'll Be Home for Christmas'.

Those at home in Britain once more turned their thoughts to buying gifts. Even in wartime, if possible Christmas is a time for joy. But in a time of shortages, whether that joy could be readily found in a bottle was debatable. Back in 1940, *The Scotsman* had reported a 'whisky famine in Glasgow'. The newspaper said that after several Glasgow pubs had exhausted their supply on the Saturday evening, 'customers were compelled to take other forms of refreshment'. The Scottish Licensed Trade Defence Association was going to approach the Customs and Excise Department to complain about restrictions of issues from bonded warehouses. If more supplies were not forthcoming than a reduction in licensing hours might have to be applied.

Now a secret MOI 'Home Intelligent Weekly Report' said that in Scotland in particular, racketeering of whisky 'is greatly incensing people'. George Bernard Shaw's 'liquid sunshine' certainly seemed in short supply by legitimate means at Christmas 1943. George Wilsher & Co. and W & S Strong of Dundee, producers of Black Bull and Real Mountain Dew whiskies respectively, made no attempt to suggest that their products would make ideal gifts that year. Instead – perhaps with a mind to future custom – they simply used an advertisement to wish readers of *The Arbroath Guide* 'all the very best'.

So, eyes turned to other advertisements on the same page but here too, local businesses exhibited an element of wishful thinking. Miller's manufacturing furriers of Reform Street, Dundee, noted that even 'Santa suggests furs' because they were 'a gift of sterling worth'. They promised 'flattering models designed in the styles of the moment … you are invited to see them … without delay for Christmas delivery'. A fur from Miller's would be 'admired and treasured for years'.

Alternatively, canny shoppers might turn to Jean Dougall Macdonald of Sauchiehall Street in Glasgow, which proposed the re-modelling and repairing of furs already in the wardrobe. Other businesses had a more realistic understanding of those looking for festive gifts. Dundee business Chalmers 'Civil, Military and Naval Bootmakers' suggested, because 'Christmas gifts may be in short supply' that 'Slippers … bear the genuine aureole [sic] of Christmas, as well as a definitely practical expression of your Good Wishes'. Alternatively, 'Token Cards … are a happy solution.'

Popular Dundee department store, Hunter's, could do little but sympathise with its customers: 'We cannot offer you our usual splendid selection of Gift Suggestions – we cannot even offer you our usual selection of everyday goods – we can, however, assure you that these days will come again. In the meantime, we promise to do our best towards making yours a Happy Christmas.'

For the practically minded, Shetland Industries of Whitehall Street, Dundee, suggested that parents might like to make their own children's toys 'Coupon Free'. Options included 'Golliwogs … John Rabbit … Dandy Dog … Daisy Duck … Dice Shaped Ball … full instructions how to make each toy with every article.'

If things were bad now, however, they were even worse when compared to the first Christmas of the conflict. Back in 1939, Christmas shoppers had endured little in the way of supply issues. The war had been under way for only a few weeks, France remained sovereign and much of everyday life remained unaffected. There was no food rationing, although it had been announced that, come January 1940, butter and bacon would be rationed. Rather than persuading Britons to be careful now, they seemed to be encouraged to splurge while they still could.

And there was plenty to splurge upon. Newspapers were filled with advertisements with suggestions of how to make your home more comfortable. The *Sunderland Echo*, for example, featured this from Wearside Furniture Stores Limited: 'This will be a Home Christmas more than ever this year. Let us help you to add to the comfort and utility of your home by providing those additional requirements you have had in mind for so long.' Palmers, who had two stores in Sunderland, suggested purchasing a new Bush Console radiogram. They were 'all the rage', although you had to have 15 guineas (equivalent to £1,300 today) to spare when the average male weekly wage was 35 shillings (£1.75).

In common with most Britons, what the people of Wearside really wanted to know in 1939 was what gifts to buy for loved ones. There was no shortage of ideas. Blacketts on High Street, Sunderland, had a huge variety of offers, from cushions, weekend cases and barometers to knitting bags, cutlery, and jewellery. For those preferring to purchase something practical – there was a war on, after all – Steel & Co. suggested their 'All-metal ... with Cream finish, round type' gas mask containers. That, and other items, could be selected 'at your own fireside, at your leisure' from a special eight-page catalogue to help shoppers 'Beat the Blackout'. Across the country, other useful wartime products included steel or Bakelite helmets and, for nights spent in the air-raid shelter, the 'Take Coverlet' – a cross between a sleeping bag and an overcoat.

The Stephenson Arcade Ltd in Chesterfield featured more typical gifts like the 'newest shapes in ladies' handbags', brush sets, dressing sets, cake stands and cake baskets.

National stores offered a surprisingly wide range of gifts. Shoppers at Boots the Chemist could choose from Old English Lavender Water and shaving kits to stationery sets and cake baskets. For those still unsure what to buy, there were Boots gift tokens, or even a subscription to Boots Booklovers' Library. For something more sentimental, there was always jewellery. H. Samuel, whose diamond rings and wrist watches were perennial favourites, placed advertisements assuring customers that their stores were 'lit brilliantly' behind the blackout.

Increasingly, children's presents were war themed. Among the most popular were miniature Red Cross, RAF and Naval uniforms, and card games such as *Blackout* and *Vacuation*. In the latter game, a spin on *Happy Families*, players had to get rid of every card in the hand they were dealt to achieve evacuation.

It seemed the streets were as busy as ever in the run-up to Christmas 1939. As the *Bedfordshire Times & Standard* reported:

> During this the pre-Christmas week the streets are crowded each day with shoppers, and it is gladdening to see such excellent trade in wartime. Every day Bedford's carnival of shopping grows. Industry given over to such a great extent to work of national importance has yet contrived to offer the public goods in adequate quantity and of high quality, whilst the shopper in search of 'something different' is not disappointed. We are reminded of peacetime Christmases in the afternoons, when shop windows lend light to the dull days, but then darkness begins to fall and blackout regulations have to be met.

Although shopkeepers did their best to keep festive window displays, many would be obscured by the diamond pattern of anti-blast tape.

'Phoney War', fancy gifts, and busy high streets aside, this year was going to be different. Many citizens were already displaced. Those serving in the British Expeditionary Force (BEF) were over in France, and thousands of children had been evacuated from the cities to the safety of the countryside and smaller towns.

Petrol had been rationed since September, and so missing from their chairs around the Christmas table were far-flung relatives who were very much discouraged from travelling long distances 'unnecessarily', either by train, or car. Although there were to be fewer settings at the dining table, if advertisements for grocers up and down the country were anything to judge by then there was to be no reduction in the size of the feast. In Eastbourne, the Scotch Bakery and Hammicks advertised Christmas cakes, plum puddings, mince pies, chocolates, crackers, table decorations and novelties which 'can be seen in abundance and variety' – not words that would be seen very often over the years that followed. For those with relatives on service 'allow us to pack your parcels for the troops at home and abroad, special care being taken that the goods may arrive in first-class condition'.

Duty on spirits had been increased by more than 100 per cent, yet Whiteway's Wines was still confident enough in its 'moderate prices' to encourage potential customers to stock up for the big day. Whether it was Port Style (Ruby & White), British Sherry or Ginger Wine, supplies seemed, for now at least, to be reliable. In 1939, most families were able to serve turkey or chicken and all the usual trimmings. But some, just as they had before the war, struggled. In Liverpool, Christmas morning saw volunteers from the League of Welldoers distribute some 250 hotpots and 250 grocery parcels to needy local families. Founded in 1893, in an empty cotton warehouse, the League had initially provided school meals to the poor and delivered food to the bedridden. And on Boxing Day they had provided 'the usual Christmas dinner' to 'ragpickers and sandwichmen', and 'an enjoyable entertainment was given by Madame Olive Lloyd and friends'.

Some servicemen, billeted far from their own homes, were cared for by families happy to welcome strangers for the day.

Blackout conditions meant no jolly illuminations in the street and no lighted Christmas trees peeking out from front-room windows to lift the evening gloom. Native holly remained plentiful, but mistletoe, usually imported from France, was inevitably in very short supply. And carol singing in the streets after dark was now impossible.

Many would head to the pub. According to a letter published in the *Bedfordshire Times & Standard*, a solicitor representing the licensed trade had argued for extended pub opening hours over the festive period. The writer, 'A.W', was annoyed at the solicitor's assertion that he 'didn't see why we should be miserable this season, even if we are at war', countering it thus: 'How much happiness will there be for the children and wives of the men who spend this season beer-drinking till 11pm, instead of around the home fires with their families. And how much of the Christmas season will there be for the publicans who will have to be in the bar until 11pm?'

The first festive season of the war also saw hundreds of thousands of child evacuees spending a first Christmas away from home. People in the towns and villages that lay in the reception areas for evacuation of children and adults did their best to soften the blow. Countless festive parties were held in their honour. In Bedford, to where some 17,000 evacuees were sent, mostly from London, children from Queen's Park, St John's, Whittington, Emanuel, Hanley and Yerbury Schools were entertained by the boys of Bedford Modern School who performed the Nativity Play *Glad Tidings*. Local children from the Mid-Bedfordshire constituency of Alan Tindal Lennox-Boyd were treated by the Conservative MP and his wife, Lady Patricia, to a motor coach trip to Hitchin to see the pantomime *Babes in the Wood* in celebration of the birth of their 'son and heir' Simon.

Some children, evacuated to Sussex from London, would have to wait for their presents. *The West Sussex County Times* reported that Father

Christmas, who planned to visit London children billeted in the county, would have to postpone his plans until early January. Across the country, cinemas controversially opened on Christmas Day. Traditionalists may have baulked at the arrangement, but there were long queues outside many picture houses. *The Birmingham Mail* reported that the city's Forum Cinema was showing 'a war picture with British brains outwitting the enemy spy upon our secrets … the ultimate overthrow of nefarious machinations, to a comedy in which love triumphs over all'.

Theatres, too, were thriving after the initial closures at the outbreak. In Newcastle alone, there was a choice of four different pantomimes, including *Robinson Crusoe*, which had 'a rousing first night' at the Theatre Royal where Man Friday 'stepped out of character to play tunes on a xylophone of jam jars'. For those who preferred to stay at home, there was always King George VI, who gave his now famous Christmas message quoting the words of poet Minnie Haskins: 'I said to the man who stood at the gate of the year…' There was also a NAAFI concert featuring Gracie Fields from 'somewhere in France'.

Communication between separated family members continued, as usual, by post. In Exeter, a new postal record of more than one million letters had been dealt with. On 23 December alone, a record number of 800 telegrams had been delivered in the city. Prime Minister Neville Chamberlain's own Christmas card was a rather plain affair featuring a Shakespearean quotation from *Henry VI, Part 2*: 'Now show yourselves men, 'tis for Liberty.'

The minutiae of British life carried on as normal. As the *Derby Evening Telegraph* of 27 December 1939 put it: 'It is hard to realise that there is a war on.'

That was about to change: 1940 would be one of the most testing years in Britain's history. Setback followed setback. Another 400,000 children were evacuated to the country. Holland, Belgium, Luxemburg and then France fell under Nazi control. The BEF was given a very bloody nose on mainland Europe, culminating on the beaches at Dunkirk. Any day now the Nazi invasion of Britain was expected and, as Christmas neared, the Blitz was at its height, leaving the centres of many of Britain's cities and towns in ruins. Civilians were now numbered among the casualties of war, and there was the constant threat of being caught up in air raids, both night and day. Even with the morale-boosting near-miracle rescue of 338,000 Allied troops from Dunkirk, and the remarkable successes of the heavily outnumbered RAF during that late summer's Battle of

Britain to draw upon, the situation on the Home Front was bleak. Britons had every reason not to feel 'festive'.

The Times urged readers not to dwell on their own difficulties, but to consider 'how trivial these deprivations should seem when the destiny of the world is at stake, how willingly our small sacrifices should be made and how unworthy are grumbles about them'.

Kathleen Pearcey, writing in the *Daily Mirror* of 16 December 1940, encouraged her readers to make as merry as was possible: 'The idea that giving or going to a party in wartime puts you in the Fifth Column Class is fast dying out … To have fun, to dress up, to laugh and play games is sense. It's Christmas and the only man who matters is coming home on leave.'

As determined as Britain might be to 'carry on', doing so would not be without its challenges – as was illustrated in a short film by the Crown Film Unit of the MOI. Ostensibly a propaganda piece intended for American audiences with the hope of encouraging US support, *Christmas Under Fire* remains a poignant and artistically skilled film and was nominated for the Best Documentary Short Subject at the Academy Awards of 1942. Scripted and narrated by American commentator Quentin Reynolds, it opens with the choir of King's College, Cambridge, singing 'Ding Dong Merrily on High'. Reynolds begins: 'It's not a very large Christmas tree. There's no demand for large trees this year – they wouldn't fit into the shelters or into the basements and cellars with their low ceilings. This year England celebrates Christmas underground.' Pictures of youngsters gathering holly and ivy from a rural hillside are played as Reynolds continues: 'The nation has made a resolve that, war or no war, the children of England will not be cheated out of the one day they look forward to all year.' He speaks of the family members not able to join the Christmas dinner because they are busy with the war effort 'driving ambulances, fighting fires, patrolling the streets … it will be a Christmas of contrasts. Holly and barbed wire, guns and tinsel', and commends the heroic shopkeepers who carry on even though 'they've had their windows blasted out, their goods ruined, their stocks reduced, their customers killed'. And then comes the point of the entire film:

> This is not the most cheerful Christmas that ever came to England, but everyone is determined to make it as cheerful as possible. Christmas here this year won't, perhaps, be

> the Christmas children in America will be lucky enough to enjoy – England is fighting for her life! And even the smallest child understands that it will be a strange Christmas, but in many ways it will be a very satisfactory one. England has much to be cheerful about. Her people, even the children, have shown in the past few months, that they are equal to their destiny … that first Christmas, the shepherds watched and guarded. Today in England even the shepherds are in some kind of uniform. And they're still watching and guarding.

The film, which was shown to British audiences in London from 28 December 1940 and across the country from 6 January 1941, closes to images of Londoners settling down to celebrate Christmas Eve in the safety of a Tube station decorated with a lovely Christmas tree, and of a young mother and her baby settling down to sleep.

Several films were made specifically for the benefit of the domestic audiences. *Christmas is Coming* was a Pathé News short which showed Christmas puddings being made for the troops, using 'real eggs', and one unlucky turkey being chosen as their dinner. There was an information film advising Britons to post early for Christmas. A Post Office service that now had fewer workers would struggle to deal with the same load of parcels, letters and cards as it had in years past. The extended blackout hours of the shorter winter days, and regular air raids, made deliveries and collections more hazardous. There was also the issue of the sudden relocation of thousands of householders. Newsreel films showed postal workers placing aside parcels, letters and packages intended for properties which now lay empty, abandoned or even in ruins, in special sections marked 'Correspondence for roped-off and bombed areas' where they would remain until new addresses for the recipients could be identified.

Across the United Kingdom, every effort was made to rise above these new difficulties and Christmas shopping was just as busy as in earlier years. At Lewis's department store in Manchester, both the first-floor Toy Fair and Father Christmas's Nursery Rhyme Grotto in the basement were very popular. Understandably, businesses did their best to use the war to promote their goods. Caley's Fortune chocolates ran advertisements showing a female ambulance driver 'who needs lots of pluck and nerves of steel'. 'Often, she has a pretty grim time but she hasn't lost her taste for nice things. Try her with a box of Fortune. She will love these best of all.'

'Bring slippers this year' advised the owners of Lupton Brooks, in Shipley. Teasel Brothers had plenty of stock available – the entire contents of its evacuated Eastbourne shop were now available to shoppers in Tonbridge and included handbags, scarves, handkerchiefs, books, umbrellas, coat-hanger sets, tea cosies, stationery and dolls and games. And Black and White whisky was keen to offer its liquor as ideal to keep in a flask to help cope with 'air-raid chills'.

Practical presents remained favourites and throughout the war one of the most popular Christmas gifts was a simple bar of soap. *The People* newspaper had one option to ease delivery issues – the ever-patriotic War Savings Certificates and National Savings Gift Tokens: 'They will save you and the postman trouble, give a lot of pleasure and help win the war!'

When it came to the Christmas dinner, as C. Patrick Thompson, author of the 1930 book *Cocktails*, wrote in *Britannia and Eve*, Christmas 1940 would 'not be a turkey and champagne Christmas, but a home-grown roast beef and beer Christmas'. That was assuming that the family had succeeded in saving up enough ration book coupons, and their registered butcher had managed to secure supplies. Strict rationing had been in place for almost a year and the only officially sanctioned Christmas treat came when the government doubled the tea ration for one week. There was a general suspicion that some people were making a great deal of money from wartime shortages, and Stuart Campbell, writing in the *Daily Mirror*, called for the Minister of Food, Lord Woolton, to 'start a clean-up drive on the people who are making us pay for the war through our stomachs', describing the food racketeers 'The Scrooges of 1940'. Nevertheless, the newspaper's Christmas Eve editorial declared: 'Nothing except the trump of Doomsday will ever prevent the English people from determining to be "merrie" at Christmas…'

In truth, the prospect of a lean festive feast was the least of many people's concerns. Never mind a shortage of fancy foods, this would be Christmas under attack. The decision by many to spend the nights leading up to Christmas in their shelters proved sensible – the Luftwaffe bombed several cities, particularly in the North-West, over Christmas week including, in the case of Manchester, on Christmas Eve itself. In London, nights spent in communal shelters had become so normalised that shelters organised proper Christmas parties with singing, dancing, and decorated trees, although those in London Underground stations bore no tinsel because each time a train arrived or departed it flew away. The station under Piccadilly Circus even boasted its own neon 'Happy Christmas' sign. For most, though, it was Christmas Day at home – a brief respite because for the first time in many decades, come Boxing Day, for so long a recognised holiday, it was back to work. Although, as *The Scotsman* reported, 'In London and the suburbs, many businesspeople and shopkeepers had decided to take the customary second day of rest.'

Many of those who were given the day off chose not to throng the streets, and 'were only too glad to have the opportunity of a rest at home without the distractions of sirens and shelters'.

The middle years of the war, 1941 and 1942, were little different. In December 1941, Rotherham Food Advisory Bureau produced for its citizens a booklet of 'off the ration' ideas to make meagre supplies go further. Inside was a Christmas section with specially adapted ration-book-friendly menus and recipes for festive favourites such as Christmas cake and mince pies. For Christmas dinner it suggested celery cream soup to start, a main course of steam-roasted chicken with wartime stuffing and bread sauce, roast potatoes, baked swede and brussels sprouts, all followed by Christmas pudding and hard sauce, or sweet white sauce. Other household cooks may have preferred to make 'Wartime Mock Goose' concocted from a mixture of stewed rabbit, sausage meat, oatmeal and mashed potato and shaped to 'resemble' the festive bird. By the following year, the recipe had been adjusted to a meat-free version with sliced layers of potato, apple and grated cheese.

For children there was the 'children's party' menu of sandwiches made from chocolate spread or egg and cress, fruit jelly (made without gelatine), 'Cinderella cakes', 'Merry-go-rounds', 'Rainbow Cake' and Christmas shortbreads 'cut in amusing shapes'.

The following year, the journal *Britannia and Eve* gave readers ideas for 'interesting' decorations that could be created from readily available household items such as disguising dried peas as holly berries by dropping them into melted sealing wax. One must wonder, though, just how many were really tempted to fashion a table decoration of a 'very realistic' barrage balloon made from material stuffed with cotton wool and tethered with tinsel guy ropes. It is hard to imagine that, in a country standing ready for a Nazi invasion, with areas of dozens of industrial towns and cities lying in ruins following air raid after air raid, and which had suffered a catastrophic loss of civilian life, anyone could really be persuaded to the charms of a model barrage balloon.

In the nine months from September 1940 to May 1941, more than 43,000 civilians had been killed, half of them in London. And, although not with the same intensity – because much of the Luftwaffe was now diverted to target Russia – air raids had continued through the year. Then the Japanese attack on the USA naval fleet at Pearl Harbor changed things dramatically. The US declared war on Japan on 8 December 1941. Three days later, they joined the fight against Nazi Germany. Britain no longer stood alone.

Rationing and shortages still governed everything. With so little of its product available in the shops, a Chivers Jelly advertisement asked that 'when your grocer has some, please let children and invalids have first choice. There will be plenty of jellies once again for everybody when victory is won.'

Eric Rudsdale, curator of Colchester Museum, kept a journal throughout the war, and noted that, in his hometown at least, there was some opportunity for celebration. On Christmas Eve 1941 he wrote:

> The streets were packed with howling mobs of soldiers and ATS girls. Everywhere one saw drunken soldiers sprawling on the pavements, or reeling along, singing. Army lorries were going slowly up the High Street, collecting those men who were quite incapable. The inert bodies were being heaved over tail boards, respirators and tin-helmets following with a metallic crash. I noticed the civil police kept well in the background.

Dance halls in most towns and cities had a thriving scene. In Christmas week 1942, Leas Cliff Hall in Folkestone featured the Hallmark Dance Band, led by Ivy Read, with Arthur Kingdom at the organ and vocalist Sylvia performing at dances every evening, and even a 'Sunday Social' on the 20th and a tea dance on Boxing Day. Nearby Bobby's Restaurant, run by the Bobby & Company department store, warned customers to 'book your tables early' for dinner-dancing on Christmas Eve, Boxing Day and New Year's Eve.

By the early winter of 1944, five years' separation had given those lyrics to Bing Crosby's 1943 hit even more poignancy. While relatively few loved ones would 'be home for Christmas', following the invasion of mainland Europe and the Allied successes, even the most cautious Britons were openly discussing whether the war might really be over by next Christmas. By mid-December, however, as the Germans began their Ardennes Offensive and resumed their doodlebug attacks on England, it was clear that there was still more to endure.

A short editorial in the pages of the *Lynn Advertiser* of 22 December attempted to sum up the national mood:

> It would be mere affectation to write of the Christmas of 1944 as recalling and renewing old-time associations of the great Christian festival. The state of the world and the scars on many a hamlet and home are too tragic for that. Nor are the people as a whole in the mood for the merrymaking and the feasting … if under present conditions these were possible. Nevertheless, children remain with us and to them there is no substitute for the expectancy and joy of the Christmas season. Family reunions and social contacts still bring happiness to the dwellings where guests have been long-awaited. And the soldier or airman, if lucky enough to be on leave, relaxes in an atmosphere of domestic affection.

The editorial had also mentioned 'the dearth of seasonal presents'. Despite this seemingly perennial problem, businesses throughout the nation did their best to both keep trading and provide good gifting items for all the family. Curry's in King's Lynn High Street declared itself 'the leading local house for value' and boasted stocks of 'new radio sets, cycles and prams at prices to suit all'. The store's toy bazaar offered a variety which was 'still the best in town'.

In Derby, shoppers had no choice but to follow the suggestion of department store Thurman & Malin of St Peter's Street, which advised customers to concentrate on 'pleasing and practical' and 'sensible and suitable' gifts like underwear, table mats, handbags, gloves, scarves, shopping baskets and coat hangers. Just across the road stood Central Educational which had a beloved book department and offered 'books for the kiddies', like recent publications Ursula Moray Williams's *The Good Little Christmas Tree*, Eileen Mayo's *Nature's ABC*, and *The Paper Boat* by Edgar Primrose Dickie. The town's Co-op, with its 'dividend on all purchases' offered 'best value for money and coupons' on its fashionable winter coats 'in a good selection of warm, serviceable materials, smart colours and attractive styles'. Around the corner, Sydney Bradley – 'the Man's Shop' – had good stocks of ties, pyjamas, dressing gowns, and 'Yankee shirts' with attached collars.

When it came to the pleasures of festive eating, the Ministry of Food had delivered some good news. Special Christmas rations of extra sugar, margarine and meat were made available. Vegetarians were granted extra cheese, children extra sweets and the over-70s extra tea. The entire country was to be given a quarter of a pound (142 g) of nuts, although finding them would not be easy. Most shopkeepers did simply not receive enough nuts to supply every customer, and demand far outweighed supply. The *Newcastle Chronicle* even featured a joke about keeping on the right side of their registered grocer, so that 'there is every prospect of him letting us have at least three peanuts'.

As a timely reminder that Hitler was not yet defeated, on Christmas Eve 1944, an area across the North of England was targeted with more than thirty V-2 rockets. Areas from Epworth in Lincolnshire to Spennymoor in County Durham and Newport in Shropshire were hit, but the majority of the damage was done in Greater Manchester. Come Christmas Day, though, most families were able to settle down to a meal uninterrupted by explosive presents from Nazi dictators.

For many the day meant settling down to listen to the radio which, after an address by the new Minister of Food, Colonel John Llewellin (Lord Woolton was now Minister of Reconstruction), was generally lighthearted on both services. From Christmas Eve to Boxing Day there was a mixture of orchestras and dance bands, concerts by brass bands, comedian Will Hay and an episode of the popular *In Town Tonight* (an early example of a chat show) as well as a 'narrated radio version' of the original musical comedy *Sunny* starring Jack Buchanan and Elsie Randolph. Children were not left out, and there was also an ENSA show. At 2.00 pm on Christmas Day there aired *The Journey Home*, described thus in the *Radio Times*: 'the peoples of the British Commonwealth and their Allies are linked again by radio to greet the men and women everywhere fighting in the cause of freedom, and to send special greetings to the families of Europe who are home again this Christmas Day.'

At 3.00 pm, the king made what would prove to be his final Christmas Day broadcast of the war. His wife and daughters at his side, the monarch spoke of the successes of the year gone by and of his hope that the Allies would finally prevail. Already, he said, some of the lamps which the Germans had put out all over Europe were being rekindled and were beginning to shine through the fog of war: 'At this Christmas time we think proudly and gratefully of our fighting men wherever they may be. May God bless and protect them and bring them victory.' He sent his good wishes to the sick and wounded in hospitals and to the medical staff caring for them, to prisoners-of-war and the relatives waiting at home for their return – 'families rent apart by the call of service, people sundered from people by the calamities that have overwhelmed some' – and for those people of the Empire who had helped bring victory so near and whose aim was 'a world of free men, untouched by tyranny'.

During the war the two princesses, Elizabeth and Margaret Rose, had organised and performed their own pantomimes, the fourth of which – *Old Mother Red-Riding Boots* – played for three performances in Windsor Castle's Waterloo Chamber and featured fifteen local schoolchildren, as well as some of the princesses' friends. Moneys raised were donated to the Royal Household Wool Fund, which supplied yarns with which to knit comforts for the troops.

Pantomimes had really been the mainstay of family-friendly theatre during wartime festive seasons. Jimmy Clitheroe was the star of Derby's Grand Theatre production of *Humpty Dumpty*. Popular sand-dancers Wilson, Keppel and Betty were three of the stars at Bristol Hippodrome's production of *Aladdin*. And music hall favourite Duggie Wakefield co-starred as Widow Twankey. Wakefield was the brother-in-law of Gracie Fields with whom he had performed in the film *This Week of Grace* (1933). A review, complimenting a production of *Jack and the Beanstalk*, a few miles up the road, at the Theatre Royal in Bath, noted: 'some very attractive numbers and beautiful staging and dressing'.

At the Liverpool Empire, comedy duo Ethel Revnell and Gracie West – whose act made much of their 12-inch height difference – were starring as *Babes in the Wood*, while the Croydon Empire featured the famous Kirby Flying Ballet in their version of *Robinson Crusoe*.

A significant improvement for Christmas 1944 saw blackout restrictions eased with carol singers once more permitted to carry lanterns as they walked through Britain's streets and lanes. And churches, which were finally permitted to light-up, were also able to ring their bells without causing an invasion panic. Up and down the country there were joyous reunions too, as thousands of troops were able to get home to their families for twenty-eight days' leave. There was still an element of chaos, though, and many of those on leave arrived with little, or no, advance warning, while others arrived earlier than expected. No one much minded, especially the many evacuees who were returned to their families for a first home Christmas in many years, for these were happy days.

The typically unreliable British weather did its best to scupper plans. While the RAF Film Production Unit captured jolly snow scenes of grounded Spitfire pilots throwing snowballs and tobogganing, a 90 mph gale swept the south of the country, sending 60 ft (18.2 m) waves crashing on to South Coast beaches. This was followed by a dense fog which cast more doubt on many festivities. However, remarkably, as Christmas Day dawned, bright sunshine shone across much of the country. All in all, Christmas 1944 was good enough for the *Western Mail and South West News* to declare it 'the best' of the war. By New Year 1945, many felt confident that it would also prove to be its last.

Chapter 16

Smiling Through Coupon Monday

> Grandma Buggins on The Kitchen Front remarked this morning: 'Well, if you don't care about the nice recipes I bring you, I might as well go to Russia and fish for surgeons in the vodka.'
>
> Extract from the diary of Miss C. M. Edwards, Lincolnshire, January 1942

Food, glorious food. For many people, one of the great comforts in life is a hearty meal. It is a distraction, cheers them, helps them forget, for a brief while at least, their troubles. The Second World War was going to challenge even that pleasure, but somehow, often thanks to a great deal of inventiveness, folk still managed to smile through it all.

On 8 January 1940, the government introduced food rationing. The newly established Ministry of Food had already issued every person in Britain with a ration book, and the holders of those books – most often the housewife on behalf of her entire family – had to register with nominated retailers. The Ministry explained its reasons for the introduction of rationing: half the nation's meat and most of its bacon, butter and sugar came from overseas and it was unreasonable to ask sailors to risk their lives to bring in unnecessary cargoes. Now more ships would be released to supply the war effort with vital raw materials. Also, if divided equitably, then rationing would ensure ample food for over 44 million people.

On the first day of food rationing, the *Lancashire Evening Post* announced: 'Today will be known as "Coupon Monday".' The *Daily Mirror* assured the nation that 'The king, too, is on rations,' and the Windsor food controller said that, when the royals were stopping at Windsor Castle, their travelling ration cards would come down with all the Royal Household cards.

Seven days before rationing was introduced, the Ministry of Food issued this advice:

> Do make certain that you have registered with your supplier for bacon, ham, sugar and butter. If you have left it till now, do it at once.
>
> Do use lots of potatoes and as much fish as you can get.
>
> Do notice that eggs are getting cheaper, and that plenty of home-produced poultry is now available.
>
> Do remember that the small discomfort entailed in rationing is nothing compared with the national service it involves.

Rationing, the Ministry said, prevented uncertainty and meant that there would be no need to queue as people did in the First World War, when rationing was not introduced until 1918. But, as shortages increased, so long queues for unrationed goods became commonplace. Word would spread: 'Mr Brown has had a delivery of onions.' And housewives would rush to his shop. Sometimes they joined a queue without knowing what reward would be at the end of it.

At first it was only bacon and ham, butter and sugar that were restricted. At the onset, each person's weekly allowance was 12 oz (340 g) of sugar, 4 oz (113 g) of butter, and 4 oz of bacon or ham – you could not have both. Meat was rationed from 11 March 1940 but, unlike all other rationed foodstuffs, allowances were measured by cost not weight. Initially the ration per person per week was 1s 10d-worth (9p) of meat. This would be reduced to 1s 2d (6p) in July 1941 and would remain at that for the rest of the war. From May, cheese (1 oz [28 g] per week) and, from 9 July, tea (2 oz [56 g] per week) were added to the list. The inclusion of tea meant that many workers would now have to use their own precious ration to enjoy a mid-shift break. On 24 July, a sympathetic government announced: 'The Ministry of Food has authorised Food Control Committees to issue special permits for industrial, business and clerical workers in cases where they cannot obtain tea from the registered canteens. This will enable them to have tea during working hours without drawing on domestic rations.'

Cooking fats were also rationed in July 1940 and more items would follow in 1941, although bread, potatoes and other vegetables together with fruit, fish and coffee would never be rationed. Children did not receive the tea ration but could have extra fruit juice, and people with special needs, such as diabetics, were catered for. Children and expectant or nursing mothers would be allocated extra milk and eggs. As early as 1937, vegetarians had lobbied the government for recognition, but it would be 1942 before they secured more eggs, cheese and nuts in exchange for the meat that they did not claim.

In January 1940, a letter writer to the *Nottingham Evening Post* reminded people: 'Turning to a good way of helping our indomitable seafaring men, remember that good slogan "Dig For Victory". Why not dig up half your lawn for the duration of the war? If everyone who could did that it would make a great contribution to the food production of the nation.' The slogan had come into official use in October 1939 shortly after the government launched a drive to increase the number of allotments in England and Wales by half a million. In a broadcast to the nation, the Minister of Agriculture, Sir Reginald Dorman-Smith, said: 'Let "Dig For Victory" be the motto of everyone with a garden and of every able-bodied man and woman capable of digging an allotment in their spare time.' In fact, the words had first been publicly used at least a fortnight earlier, in a headline in the *Bedfordshire Times and Independent*.

Even before war began, the government had produced its 'Food Defence Plans' that allowed for an increased consumption of potatoes, oatmeal, cheese, carrots and green vegetables. Vitamins A and D that occurred naturally in butter would be added to margarine, and additional calcium would be added to 'National Bread'.

The *Daily Express* had always been against food rationing, running what almost amounted to a campaign against its introduction. In January 1940, the newspaper said that food rationing had been brought in only because a 'vast organisation' was already in being and rationing simply gave its staff something to do: 'The Ministry of Food employ nearly 11,000 persons. If they were disbanded we could buy 100,000 cows for the same money.'

Polls taken by Mass Observation and the British Institute of Public Opinion (BIPO) showed that the public did not agree. The BIPO poll showed that 60 per cent of those questioned thought that rationing was necessary; 28 per cent were against it being introduced; 12 per cent said: 'Don't know'. A Liverpool housewife told Mass Observation: 'I wish to goodness they would introduce rationing. At least I would be able to go into a shop and get what I was allowed.'

Far from introducing a job creation scheme, the problem that the government foresaw was that Britain relied heavily on imports for its food, especially meat and fruit. An enemy would obviously target merchant shipping, countries from where some foods came from might be occupied, and bombing might destroy warehouses where food was stored. Within a week of the outbreak of war, the Ministry of Food was operational, with Lord Woolton now the nation's Minister of Food. Generally, in times of shortages, price increases were the most effective form of control, but in these now extreme times that would leave the better-off to eat well and the poor to go hungry. There was a war on. It had to be fair shares all round. The working class would be entitled to the same amounts as the middle class and the rich. In 1940, though, there was already limited choice and availability. While rationing was seen as fair, sometimes it was the inability to buy unrationed goods that caused friction. A customer with limited means might be told: 'Sorry, we're out of stock.' But when a 'best customer' asked for the same, the item would miraculously appear from under the counter or from 'out the back'.

There were some spectacular examples. In March 1940, Mrs Yvonne Reekie of Bovingdon in Hertfordshire was fined £50 for obtaining sugar – equivalent to the weekly ration for 140 people – in excess of the amount prescribed in the Rationing Order, and £25 for obtaining it without a coupon, from John Kay Ltd in Watford. A summons against the shop for supplying the sugar was adjourned. The court was told that on 24 February an employee of the Food Control Committee saw a Rolls-Royce car drive up to Kay's shop. A chauffeur was seen leaving the shop carrying a large cardboard box that contained blue bags. The box was placed in the car, and it was driven away with Mrs Reekie inside.

'I admit the whole thing,' said Mrs Reekie. 'I paid Kay's manager two guineas. I did not get a receipt. Why should one shop have so much sugar by them and so tempt people? I realise that what I did was wrong but, at the same time, I was only doing what any housewife would have done.'

Not many housewives did their shopping by chauffeur-driven Rolls-Royce and most began to prepare for a long war. The *Derby Evening Telegraph* joined forces with the Derby Gas, Light and Coke Company to arrange a series of lectures entitled 'Economic Wartime Cookery' given by Beryl Abbey at the Temperance Hall in Curzon Street.

More advice came from the monthly magazine *Britannia and Eve*, which had news of a gadget for making one's butter ration go twice as far. A 'clean and workmanlike churn' made two pounds of merged butter from a pound of butter and a pint of milk. The butter was cut into slices and put into the churn with the milk. This was then stood in a pan of hot water, then the top screwed on and the mixer brought into action. After the mixture had hardened, 'you will like the result ... sweet, wholesome and nourishing'. The churn cost from 8s (40p) to 21s (£1.5). No clue was given as to what refinements were missing from the cheapest version. The same magazine asked readers how they were helping the morale of the nation. Because of rationing, did they go around with a face like Cleopatra's Needle? It suggested that housewives could get together and collect peelings, scraps of bread, bones and so on: 'Perhaps there is a farmer in the country just beyond your suburb who would be willing to call for pig fodder two or three times a week.' In the meantime, 'housewives should form their menus from whatever happens to be flush on the market at the time of shopping. Don't grumble if one particular thing is unobtainable ... Explore every economic possibility...'

No one was ever short of official advice. In association with the Ministry of Food, the BBC produced a series of cookery programmes broadcast six days a week after the early morning news on the Home Service. *The Kitchen Front* – there were also regular newspaper columns of the same name – presented well-known cooks offering advice on how to provide cheap but sustaining recipes. 'Woolton Pie', a vegetable mixture thickened with oatmeal and topped with pastry, became a familiar wartime family meal.

If anyone could afford to dine out, then those meals were 'off-ration' – and expensive. West End restaurants continued to enjoy patronage from rich customers. This did not go down well. On 8 July 1940, Lord Woolton broadcast to the nation: 'I have told you already that when restrictions are necessary I shall impose them without hesitation and without apology. I am stopping luxurious feeding and I have arranged for the consumption of food in hotels and restaurants to be reduced.' The introduction, in 1942, of a 5 shilling (25p) top limit on what could be charged for a meal finally put an end to the most ostentatious – many felt unseemly – examples.

There were, however, many restaurants, cafés and teashops that continued to provide the occasional and sensibly priced treat. For working people in particular, the 'British Restaurants' that were run by local authorities in premises as diverse as church halls, schools and empty shops, offered a welcoming and moderately priced three-course lunch.

The scheme had grown out of London County Council's Londoners' Meals Service introduced in September 1940 during the Blitz. In March 1941, Lord Woolton announced the rebranding of the communal feeding centres, adding that he hoped that 'locally they will be given a domestic name as well, something bright and jolly'.

Kingston Corporation in Surrey was one local authority quick off the mark, converting a local swimming baths canteen into a British Restaurant that could feed 500 people in one sitting. It began operating in May 1941 – the official opening was performed some weeks later by Freddie Grisewood, presenter of the BBC's *The Kitchen Front* – and for one shilling (5p) workers could enjoy a three-course midday meal of soup, followed by roast beef, Yorkshire pudding and vegetables, a choice of pudding and a cup of tea. Those on a tighter budget could miss out the main course and pay just sixpence (2.5p).

There were, of course, still tragedies. On 10 February 1943, twenty-nine of the forty-one people killed during an air raid on Reading were inside a British Restaurant known as the 'People's Pantry'. It received direct hit when a lone Dornier 217 dropped four bombs on the Berkshire town. 'It was early-closing day,' said an official. 'The restaurant would normally have been well filled. It seated more than 200. As it was, there were not many taking tea at the time, but nearly all the casualties occurred there.' One woman who lost her life had returned to the restaurant for the handbag that she had forgotten.

British Restaurants continued to serve their purpose for the remainder of the war and into peacetime until, on 1 April 1947, the government's Civic Restaurants Act came into law, empowering local authorities to take over their running. The move angered many local business owners. At the annual meeting of the Independent Traders' Alliance at Chester, held in Manchester just a week after the law came into being, one delegate called 'any form of rate subsidised and licensed restaurant abhorrent to the independent trader'. A resolution opposing the Act was carried by a large majority. In fact, the restaurants were not a charge on the rates. Some were profitable, and if a loss occurred over three successive years, the Minister of Food could terminate the service. Food rationing ended in 1954, but it would be a few years before the last Civic Restaurant stacked its chairs for the final time.

Chapter 17

Holidaying at Home

> The holiday-at-home idea requires a little mental readjustment. One would miss the preliminary excitement of packing, that annual taxi ride to the station and then the train journey to Blackpool or Scarborough or Llandudno.
>
> *Daily Mirror* reporter, July 1941

On 9 September 1939, reporting on the marriage of Vera Coulter and Leslie Daw at Northolt, the *West Middlesex Gazette* said, 'An intended honeymoon at Ventnor was prudently cancelled in view of the threat of war.' The same day the *Middlesex County Times* carried an advertisement urging holidaymakers to go to Ventnor, 'the safest place and an ideal spot for your vacation'. Such was the dilemma facing anyone who had been planning a late summer break when Hitler invaded Poland.

There was a solution, though. Why not make better use of the amenities on your doorstep? Two hundred miles north, the *Halifax Evening Courier* said that while the residents of Hebden Bridge 'would likely to remember their September holiday Monday for 1939' because 'it was neither desirable nor convenient for people to travel far afield', many local residents had found enjoyment on Calder Holmes Park close to the town centre.

Between the wars, if holidays abroad were the province of only the well-off, by the late 1930s most working people could look forward to a few days by the seaside or in the countryside. But now the government feared that at peak holiday times – most industrial towns and cities in Britain had specific holiday periods such as the Wakes Weeks particularly celebrated in the North-West – trainlines needed for the movement of troops and materials would be clogged up with people going on their holidays. In 1940, the Railway Executive Committee published a poster asking the nation, 'Is Your Journey Really Necessary?'

Petrol rationing also hindered 'unnecessary' travel. Petrol had been rationed since 22 September 1939 but most people did not own a motor vehicle. Only when it was decided to ban pleasure motoring was there an outcry, not just from the middle and upper classes who could afford a car but also from shopkeepers and guesthouse proprietors who relied on day-trippers for a living.

On 18 June 1940, the issue of 'joyriding' was raised in the House of Commons after Geoffrey Lloyd, the Conservative MP for Birmingham Ladywood, and the minister in charge of the Petroleum Warfare Department, told members:

> The House will be glad to know that, as a result of action taken by the government before and since the war, our supplies of petrol are at present very satisfactory. Substantial economies in the civil consumption of petrol have already been made by rationing, and this automatically secures a corresponding economy in lubricating oil. I have recently issued a new Rationing Order, designed to check abuses in the use of petrol, and I am proceeding with the appointment of inspectors to aid in this purpose. In view of these facts, I do not propose at this moment to make a further general reduction in petrol allowances, but I would emphasise that it is vital that all petrol users should cooperate to the full in the strict observance of the Rationing Order.

William Leach (Labour, Bradford Central) asked:

> What does the Minister mean by the abuse of petrol? Is joyriding an abuse; is going to a racecourse, in the circumstances of the day, an abuse; is taking your best girl out an abuse? Is the Minister satisfied that he has adequate power at this moment to deal with wasteful expenditure of petrol by private users?

Mr Lloyd replied:

> It is not an abuse to use the limited amount of petrol allowed in the basic ration for purposes of reasonable recreation, but it is an abuse to use petrol given on a supplementary allowance for purposes for which it is not given. In regard to that, I have powers, and I intend to use them. Prosecutions

> will be taken in proper cases, and I am appointing inspectors for that work.

Thomas Levy (Conservative, Elland) said:

> Is my honourable friend aware that a number of manufacturers engaged on national work who are using motor transport find that they have absolutely insufficient to do this work of national importance, and that they still see this colossal amount of joyriding and the wastage of petrol, which ought to be controlled in some manner? If there is ample petrol, give this transport that is used for national service sufficient quantities.'

Mr Lloyd assured him that 'no issue of petrol for domestic purposes in the basic ration in any way prejudices the issue for national purposes'.

The authorities came down very hard on the 'abuse' of petrol. A man from Derby was fined for wasting it because he was caught driving to watch Derby County. Another Derby supporter got round this by taking his friends to the football in a furniture van. They all crowded inside around a piano. His plan was that, if the police stopped him, he would say that his journey was essential because he was delivering the piano to the NAAFI. He was never stopped and the piano went back and forth, from his house to the football ground, a round-trip of some 20 miles, for about two years.

In 1940, the government approved a Defence Regulation cancelling that year's August Bank Holiday because it felt that 'in the present circumstances the normal activities of the country should continue on 5 August as on ordinary days'.

Meanwhile, the question was continually being asked: 'Is Your Journey Really Necessary?' Slogans alone were not going to keep people at home during their summer break, however, and whatever difficulties were placed before those seeking a few days away were generally overcome. In the hope that the rest of the nation would follow the early example of the residents of Hebden Bridge, the government launched its 'Holiday at Home' campaign and instructed local authorities to do all they could to provide sufficient attractions locally to keep people occupied during their holiday from work.

The *Bedfordshire Times and Independent* reported:

> The finance and general purposes committee [of Bedford Town Council] reported receipt of a letter from the commissioner for the Eastern Region which stated that, while holidays in the old sense were not possible this year, it was most essential that workers should have a break during the summer months and their holidays should be as beneficial as possible under existing circumstances. Travelling even short distances was discouraged by the Ministry of Transport and therefore local authorities would be in asked to provide as many attractions as possible for holidays at home.

The newspaper's columnist 'Bedfordian' was unconvinced:

> For the good of our souls, our pockets, and the national transport we are advised to spend our snatched holidays at home. Very well then, according to the amount of pleasure we can extract from simple things, or the qualities of imagination or ingenuity that the fairies gave us at our birth, we shall be hopelessly bored or we shall enjoy a few days each fit to be marked with a white stone of real refreshment, rest, refreshment, recreation, ruminations or retrospection ... At any rate, even if you have mental reserves and the capacity for amusing yourself, you will want to get out of Bedford, with all its attractions annoyances, for a little space.

It was certainly an initiative not universally received, neither by the local authorities themselves – they were given no additional funding to implement the scheme – nor by the workers of Britain.

A government weekly intelligence report dated 23 June 1942 read:

> There appears to be a persistent feeling in some quarters that 'the government should have done more than request people to take holidays at home', and that 'the rich, the idle, the selfish' and 'the professional classes' will not comply. Reports from two Regions mention appreciation for the efforts that some local authorities are making 'to brighten

> up towns' so as to 'enable workers to have enjoyable holidays', and open-air dancing in Princes Street Gardens [in Edinburgh] is said to be 'a huge success'. In spite of this, however, the Scottish report says that 'a special enquiry shows that workers are arranging to holiday away from home as far as possible'. A movement to withdraw savings, which is reported from one of the largest factories in the South-Western Region, is believed to be accounted for by the arrival of the holiday season.

One week later:

> Reports from four Regions indicate that 'the government holiday-at-home campaign appears to be having little practical effect'. According to the Scottish report, for example, 'long queues at stations for Clyde coast resorts are commonplace, and accommodation at holiday resorts throughout Scotland is impossible to find'. The government is blamed for 'failure to produce a definite plan to meet holiday needs'. Apart from the feeling which many people have that 'they have denied themselves real holidays for two years and are now entitled to a complete change', three influences are quoted as 'operating against stay-at-home holidays':
>
> Newspaper announcements of extra trains to the seaside are mentioned in three Reports as being responsible for people disregarding the government's appeal, and for confirming the impression that 'those who obey government requests are mugs'. It is asked, 'What is the use of broadcasting appeals to people not to travel – or at least only for short distances – when the newspapers are publishing stories about special trains being run from Lancashire towns to the seaside, and the railways announce that it may be possible to arrange short distance holiday trips?'
>
> Reports that seaside resorts are well stocked with goods which are in short supply in industrial areas: People returning from Blackpool, for example, report that 'shops there are packed with food – cakes, sweets, chocolates, cigarettes, etc'. The Ministry of Food has been criticised

> for 'failing to curtail supplies of food at coastal resorts and for not providing extra food in connection with holidays-at-home schemes'.
>
> Increased earnings: Many people are said to feel that they can afford to go to the seaside, in spite of the high prices being charged. According to the report from the South Eastern Region, 'It is openly stated by some of the holidaymakers, including war workers, that they don't see why they shouldn't spend the money instead of saving it for a government which has, or will, let them down'. The case is mentioned of a 'working-class woman, unable to board the last train, offering a taxi-man £3 10s 0d (£3.50) if only he would drive her from Weston to Bristol'.
>
> Inconvenience to business travellers: Reports from three Regions stress the great inconvenience to workers and business people caused by holiday travellers, and particularly by day trippers on buses and coaches. It is suggested that 'the only solution which will give everyone a sense of fair play is the rationing of all kinds of transport services by the issue of passes for essential travel, whether for work or recreation'.

In fact, some towns had already provided facilities to keep people at home. In July 1941, a *Daily Mirror* reporter said that they were 'enjoying my holiday at Huddersfield with 20,000 other work people who are obeying Mr Bevin's appeal to holiday at home'.

'Huddersfield,' they wrote,

> is the first town in the country to put the government suggestion into practice and has provided hundreds of diversions for all sorts and sizes of people … It is proving that it is possible to be happy in a holiday at home … the freedom of the parks has been conferred on them. Pitches had been marked out for cricket, rounders, stool-ball, rugby touch and netball. There is racing, jumping and folk dancing. The quiet ones could go to a tent and read books supplied by the libraries and the schools. I have never seen so complete a free programme of entertainment for children. There was even a miniature railway with a tiny engine driven by steam.

The previous month, the *Halifax Evening Courier* had reported:

> How far municipalities will feel able to implement the Minister of Health's suggestion for improving the workers' holidays without travel, which are this year in the national interest, is at the moment largely a matter of conjecture. In many towns in the West Riding, however, it would doubtless be thought that there is room for increased amenities for recreation and entertainment to add to the pleasures of stay-at-home holidays. Among other things it is officially suggested that there should be encouragement of entertainments – bands in parks and other public places, visits by concert parties and theatrical and variety companies to factories and other places not normally used for entertainment, dancing in parks and other public places, special morning performances at cinemas, and more extensive visits of fairs. Attention is drawn also to the encouragement of personal activities – walking and, in co-operation with local authorities and clubs, cycling, tennis, golf, swimming and athletic meetings and gardening and the improvement of facilities for more restful recreation more extensive – provisions of popular novels at public and subscription libraries.

The *Yorkshire Post and Leeds Intelligencer* told readers:

> A red-letter day for hundreds of Huddersfield children whom the war has robbed of their annual holiday by the sea. In Greenhead Park organised games of every description will be held, and there will be plenty to attract girls and boys of all ages. A rest corner has been provided in the park for children who become tired by their exertions, while another corner has been reserved for the very young who will be able to spend some happy hours playing with fascinating toys and games. Parents may rest assured that their children will be well looked after, and in case they are needed, a doctor and nurses of the St John's Ambulance Brigade will be in attendance.

The *Newcastle Journal* suggested that

> those who want a more active holiday will be able to help with the harvest, travelling held each day from the towns to the fields. The Ministries of Labour, Health, Agriculture, Transport, Information and Education have formed a committee to advise on the manner in which local holidays may be organised so that workers may get the maximum benefit from the sunshine, fresh air and open-air entertainment.

Plenty tried to do as best they could. To make holidays at home seem like those at the seaside, Middlesbrough Town Council bought fourteen donkeys for children to ride in the parks. In Keighley, West Yorkshire, a £200 grant by the town council enabled the parks committee 'to give the town a real holiday atmosphere'. Young and old were catered for, with Punch and Judy shows, sports, a fair with roundabouts and other features, and in both the afternoons and evenings there was open-air dancing, while the Market Theatre Company, which was run in connection with the Council for the Encouragement of Music and the Arts, performed in the assembly hall of the Keighley Girls' Grammar School.

In Liverpool, one secondary school opened its playing fields on three mornings and two afternoons every week during the summer holiday and its tennis courts on the other mornings and afternoons. It also organised swimming classes and art classes and allowed 'the generous use of books from its own library to the students'.

But then there was the concern that local authorities were making their towns and cities too attractive. In June 1942, the *Liverpool Echo* commented:

> The difficulty is not to discover or invent sources of entertainment for holidaymakers whom it is desired to keep at home, but so to balance the attraction that they will not bring into the city people from outside which would, of course, defeat the purpose of the scheme. Liverpool could – incredible though it might seem – be made too bright and it requires almost the judgement of a Solomon to decide how bright it is safe to be.

Yet, despite its successes, there were also complaints that many people were still ignoring the Holiday at Home initiative – and that this was putting pressure on traditional holiday destinations. Although workers were advised to enjoy their leisure time at home, many demanded a change and invaded towns that were already full. During Wakes Weeks complaints about food queues at holiday resorts were growing, and resorts that were accommodating evacuees, civil servants and members of the forces were experiencing shortages of both rationed and unrationed foods.

Llandudno Food Control Committee drew up its own food suggestions for visitors. If they possessed any jam they should bring it with them 'as this toothsome commodity is not supplied on emergency cards'. The Llandudno committee urged visitors to refrain from queuing for scarce commodities. Residents had to get through their work and could not compete with visitors who had nothing better to do than sunbathe or stroll along the promenade. When visitors took home food from holiday resorts, they deprived a local resident or another visitor of their share. As a general rule those who spent their holidays at home fared better as regards food, and holiday resorts were hanging out warnings to prevent what they feared would be mass invasions.

In September 1943, in Staffordshire, the Newcastle under Lyme Trades and Labour Council debated the success – or otherwise – of the Holidays at Home scheme and suggested staggering holiday periods. Mr W. Horton moved that 'the council directs the attention of the TUC and the Ministers of Labour and of Transport to the essential need for workers to enjoy annual holidays away from their home surroundings'.

> Whilst appreciating the need for conservation of transport required in the progress of the national effort for victory, we believe that such holidays could be made possible by the separation of the country into defined holiday period areas and that arrangements by counties to allocate special periods for holidays could be organised to which surplus transport could be made available to provide reasonable transport for such holidays in each defined county area.

Mr Horton said that it was no change to have a holiday at home. The 'higher-ups' could have their holidays without discomfort. The holidays-at-home programmes, despite the boosting, were a complete flop. Every worker was entitled to have a holiday away from home after working for a year. Extra trains were put on despite what was said about 'Don't travel'. The workers were as much entitled to an annual leave as other members of the country. Members of Parliament had their holidays despite the pressure of the present time. Mr C. Bearne said the difficulty of staggered holidays was that opposition to them came from the workers themselves. Mr H. Matthews said that he did not think the resolution was opportune at the present time. The motion was referred back for further consideration.

The *Yorkshire Post and Leeds Intelligencer* agreed that 'the government fully recognises the need for refreshing holidays for all workers and for the colour and gaiety which means so much to the jaded mind', but 'to provide this with scrupulous economy of means is the problem facing the local authorities at this time'.

> In seeking to solve this problem they are no doubt wise to do what they can to produce a seaside atmosphere. Blackpool, Scarborough and Bridlington are not popular for nothing. But the chance should also be seized to widen appreciation of what the district itself has to offer in interest and natural beauty.

The newspaper had one final point that should not be overlooked:

> The one person who is apt to get no holiday when holidays at home are arranged is the housewife, particularly if she is the mother of a young family. Yet no one needs or deserves a holiday more. Special care should be taken to lift the burden of family cares from the shoulders of the mothers during the holiday weeks by providing both entertainment and efficient supervision for the town's children.

In 1945, a study by the National Council of Social Service said that the success of Holidays at Home 'has nothing to do with them being a substitute for proper holidays; everyone who could … has had a proper holiday as well'.

In September that year, the *Daily Dispatch*'s 'London Letter' columnist looked forward to better times:

> People who may be indulging in pleasant dreams of being able to spend a holiday abroad next year can continue doing so without much risk of being disappointed. Much to my surprise, I learned in a very good quarter that the government realises that holidays on the Continent or pleasure cruises were much in demand after several years of enforced holidays at home, and facilities for such holidays will not be discouraged. That is not to say that any guarantee of complete removal of restrictions by next year can be given at this stage. It may be necessary, for example, to discourage pleasure travelling by limiting the amount of money or credit to be taken out of the country, but, broadly speaking, such restrictions will be the exceptions to the rule.

A wartime holiday at home meant different things to different people, especially children. Len Johnson of London remembered:

> I always think I was lucky because during the war we lived in Kent, right under the Battle of Britain. That might sound strange if it came from an adult but were just kids. I suppose we spent more time searching around bombsites, and places where aircraft had crashed, than anywhere else. In the long summer holidays, it was great fun. We used to collect shrapnel and anything else we could find and swap it for other things like sweets – which were obviously in short supply – or perhaps even a football, if you had enough 'currency'. Because that is what all these spoils of war were – currency. Sometimes, you'd just swap what you had for a 'better' bit of shrapnel to build up your collection.
>
> Anyway, one day my brother was setting off for work and I was still in bed, and he called up to me that a German plane had been damaged that night and that part of its engine was lying in our front garden. I'd never moved so fast. I got dressed as quickly as I could and raced downstairs. There was no sign of anything in our garden, though. He was pulling my leg. That was the thing, though – we lived right in the thick of it and we just made a joke of it all. It was just part of our lives. The holidays always seemed such fun.

For those who eschewed the easily accessible delights of the local park, there was always a newspaper to read or a good book to take to bed. But even that delight was threatened. Paper went on ration. On 8 February 1940, the Ministry of Supply announced that newspapers would be restricted to 60 per cent of their immediate pre-war tonnage, an allocation that decreased throughout the war. Newspaper sizes dropped by more than half, which meant less space for advertising, although that was compensated by a steep rise in sales as people eagerly devoured the latest war news. Eighty per cent of British families read at least one of the mass circulation dailies such as the *Daily Express*, *Daily Mail*, *Daily Mirror*, *Daily Sketch*, *News Chronicle* and *Daily Herald*. Middle-class families favoured *The Times*, *Daily Telegraph*, *Manchester Guardian* or *The Scotsman*.

Book publishing also faced difficulties. Publishing was not an occupation exempt from national service, and air raids destroyed premises and stock. Paternoster Row was the centre of the London publishing industry and in the fierce raid over the night of 29–30 December 1940 – the so-called 'Second Great Fire of London' – Longman's available titles were reduced from more than 5,000 titles to just twelve. Altogether more than 5 million books were lost in the inferno.

Then came what seemed a bizarre suggestion: in July 1941, it was reported that words in books might be 'weighed'. To adjust the increasing sales of books to the intensifying shortage of paper, a scheme was afoot for the production of books in which the number of words would be measured in ounces. The technical advisory committee of the Publishers' Association was considering a plan whereby each book must contain 6,000 words for every ounce of its weight when bound. Possibly there might be a lower ratio for educational, technical and juvenile books, which might require provisions for illustrations or diagrams. The scheme did not deal with the price of books. If adopted, it would provide more books for the same weight of paper and volumes of lighter and handier form and would save storage space. It was also suggested that 'the proposal might bring home to authors the desirability of writing more concisely'.

Chapter 18

A Sporting Life

> Sports like football have an absolute effect on the morale of the people and one Saturday afternoon of league matches could probably do more to affect people's spirits than the recent £50,000 government poster campaign urging cheerfulness.
>
> Mass Observation, 1940

There should have been plenty to talk about as football supporters all over Britain headed for the exits on 2 September 1939. On the second Saturday of the new season, Blackpool had beaten Wolves 2-1 at Bloomfield Road to lead the First Division with maximum points. Ted Drake had scored four times in Arsenal's 5-2 win over Sunderland at Highbury. In the Second Division, Newcastle United had put eight goals past Swansea Town. In the Third Division South, Bournemouth and Boscombe Athletic had scored ten against Northampton Town. The Glasgow giants, Celtic and Rangers, had both won, but in Edinburgh there was a surprise when Albion Rovers, relative newcomers to Scotland's top division, beat Hibernian 5-3 at Easter Road. Yet on the trams and buses taking fans home for their tea on that stifling, brooding afternoon, no one said very much.

At The Valley, the game between Charlton Athletic and Manchester United had been a tedious affair, the players' apparent lack of interest mirroring that of the 8,608 supporters who had bothered to turn up to a ground which the previous year had seen 75,000 packed in. Even a 2-0 home win had failed to spark any celebrations. The mood of the Manchester City players who had beaten Chesterfield was not helped by the sight of barrage balloons on the skyline around Maine Road.

At Highbury, where the kick-off had been put back for two hours due to traffic congestion as the first of London's children were evacuated from the capital, the atmosphere was especially subdued. Even Ted Drake, never short of a few wisecracks, had little to say despite his four goals. The previous day, Germany had invaded Poland. For once, the result of a football match seemed unimportant.

Football's first reaction to the declaration of war was not to make the same mistake as in 1914 when the Football League and the FA Cup had been allowed to continue for a whole season before being suspended and everyone connected with the game had been denounced as both unpatriotic and unproductive. *The Times* had carried a letter from the historian A. H. Pollard: 'Every club that employs a professional football player is bribing a much-needed recruit away from enlistment and every spectator who pays his gate money is contributing so much towards a German victory.'

The First World War had been fought largely by volunteer soldiers. Conscription, introduced in 1939, prevented a repeat of that. And now there was also the imminent threat of air attack. Almost every family in Britain was touched by the First World War, but largely through their menfolk away fighting on the front line. By 1939, the prospect of German air raids on British cities had been in the public mind for several years. Thus, one of the government's first reactions after the declaration of war was to ban the assembly of crowds. That meant that all forms of public entertainment had to be suspended immediately, especially football, where tens of thousands might gather in one relatively small area. An air raid could see a catastrophic loss of life.

However, a few days after war had been declared, the government lifted its ban on sporting activities outside highly populated areas such as London, Birmingham and Manchester, and on 9 September 1939 the first wartime football match took place behind closed doors, at Loftus Road, when Queen's Park Rangers put ten goals past a hastily recruited army team.

On 25 September, the stipulation that matches could be played only between clubs no more than fifty miles apart was altered to allow games where the away team could be 'there and back in a day'. Three days earlier, attendances of up to 8,000 in evacuation areas and up to 15,000 in safer centres were allowed. There were stipulations, however. The limit of 8,000 could be no more than half the capacity of the stadium. The bigger grounds in the non-evacuation areas could admit up to 15,000 provided that tickets were sold in advance, an arrangement which soon proved impractical. Nevertheless, football supporters began to see their local grounds quickly reopened, although had the local chief constable had his way, Birmingham (a club that added 'City' to its title in 1943) would never have played a home match during the Second World War.

When football was allowed to resume, Cecil Moriarty was having none of it. In his opinion, the area around St Andrew's was a likely target for the Luftwaffe – as it turned out, he was right – and there would be the risk of serious loss of life if thousands of people were allowed to gather to watch football. The club did everything in their power to overturn his ruling and on 12 March 1940, Birmingham City Council passed a resolution asking the chief constable to reconsider. They argued that people who spent long hours working in munitions factories deserved some recreation, and that included watching football at Birmingham. The matter was raised in the House of Commons, but Home Secretary Sir John Anderson – after whom the cheap domestic air-raid shelter had been named – declared that he could not intervene in such a local issue. A letter to the local *Sports Argus* accused Moriarty of 'killing people's Saturday afternoons', adding: 'He would change his views if he had to work in a factory for fifty or sixty hours a week.'

Eventually, when it was pointed out that St Andrew's was the only football ground in Britain still closed, Chief Constable Moriarty and the eight Birmingham councillors who had backed him had no case. On 23 March 1940, the ground reopened and there was an attendance of 13,241 to see Birmingham play Walsall in a Midland Division game, for by then the wartime regional competitions were well under way.

The joint FA-League War Emergency Committee had announced its plans towards the end of September. There were to be eight regional competitions: two would be styled 'South', with divisions 'A' and 'B', and would comprise clubs from London and elsewhere in the south of England. The other sections would be East Midlands, Midlands, North-West, North-East, Western and South-Western. Six clubs decided not to take part: Aston Villa, Derby County, Exeter City, Gateshead, Ipswich Town and Sunderland. In Scotland there would be two divisions, East and West. As in England, six clubs declined: Brechin City, Edinburgh City, East Stirling, Forfar Athletic, Montrose and Leith Athletic. The Irish League – basically the Ulster League – decided to carry on as normal; the League of Ireland was unaffected because the Free State would remain neutral throughout the war.

Players would be paid thirty shillings (£1.50) a match in England – where the maximum pre-war weekly wage had been £8 – and £2 in Scotland. Guest players would be allowed provided the player's original club granted permission. Such a rearrangement of the Football League was bound to cause disaffection. Newcastle United found themselves in what was effectively a Yorkshire division with only lowly Hartlepool United for company from the north-east of the country. Preston North End and Bolton Wanderers in the North-West Division had to play against Carlisle United and Barrow, while the Merseyside and Manchester clubs were put in the Western Division, which no doubt pleased the likes of New Brighton, Crewe Alexandra and Chester who joined them there. Luton Town might have hoped for a place in one of the southern sections but instead lined up with Wolves, West Brom and Birmingham in the Midland Division. Some divisions were so small that the clubs would have to play each other four times over the season instead of the normal two.

Even so, in the first few weeks of the war, Mass Observation noted that the banning of competitive sports – and therefore the breaking of well-established routines – might have 'deep repercussions'. The organisation could not find one pre-war football supporter who thought that the game should be suspended for the duration of the war. Perhaps more significantly, they found that only 2 per cent of people not interested in football in peacetime were against sport being played in time of war. In 1940, Mass Observation also found that 65 per cent of supporters who attended pre-war matches could not now get to football because of Saturday shift work in factories, travel restrictions and family obligations.

The Phoney War ended in May 1940, but what amounted to phoney football carried on throughout the war with guest players, competitions based more on geography than on merit, and some bizarre situations.

On 20 January 1940, Swindon Town found themselves with only ten men at the Aero Engines Company Ground at Kingswood for their match against Bristol City. Swindon's manager, Neil Harris, 43 years old, his previous competitive match over nine years earlier, was forced to turn out in borrowed boots too small for him. Swindon lost 5-2 and Harris lost two toenails.

In November 1942, Ken Teasdale was working as a postman when Bradford City asked him to play in goal for them. For the next three seasons he was their regular goalkeeper, often having to change his shifts in order to play. 'For home games I'd work from five in the morning until one o'clock. For away matches I switched to nights, which often meant arriving back just in time to go back to work. In the beginning I played as an amateur but after I was established, City paid me.'

The Tranmere Rovers player Harold Atkinson recalled, 'You never knew which team was which because blokes were coming home on leave and then couldn't get … I've been at Goodison and it's come over the Tannoy: "Any footballers in the crowd?" Some fans used to go to take their boots to games, just in case.'

On 31 August 1940, the *Manchester Guardian* commented:

> When the time comes to write the history of this war, it may not pass unnoticed by the chronicler that, as the Battle of Britain developed, the Football League launched a season of competitive football. It is, at all events, no small act of temerity on the part of sixty-eight of the League's flock of eighty-eight to embark in this new wartime enterprise in circumstances obviously more difficult than those last winter and early spring.

One month earlier, at the annual meeting of the Football League, plans for the 1940–41 season had been agreed. The competition would carry on with whatever clubs were prepared to play. They would be split into two large regional groups, north and south, and would arrange their own fixtures, although each club from the First and Second Divisions would have play at least two from the Third Division. There would be no points awarded; positions would be decided on goal-average, by dividing the number of goals scored by the number of goals conceded.

It was going to be an unusual sort of football season. At The Dell, the League South game between Southampton and Brighton was held up for thirty minutes after an air-raid warning. The attendance of just over 1,000 reflected people's caution at attending football matches on the South Coast when the Luftwaffe was likely to appear at any time. The biggest attendances of the day were in the north of England, with crowds of 5,000 at Liverpool and Newcastle, and 4,000 at Manchester City. In the south, no club rivalled that kind of support on the first day of a season which no one could guarantee would progress very far.

The following Saturday, with only sixty seconds remaining at The Valley and the visitors, Millwall, leading Charlton Athletic 4-2, the air-raid warning siren sounded. The raid was a heavy one with shrapnel from nearby anti-aircraft guns falling on the stadium. The 1,500 spectators took cover and when the all-clear sounded, the game resumed and the final minute played out. A week later, Charlton's match at Brentford was interrupted after sixty-five minutes. Again the players resumed the game, this time before the remnants of a crowd which had numbered only 600 at kick-off.

Playing football as the Battle of Britain raged overhead was a precarious – and sometimes tiresome – occupation. The Home Office had ruled that play must be stopped whenever the air-raid alert sounded. Clubs attempted to counter this with a system of 'spotters'; even after the alert sounded, play would continue until the spotter on the roof of the stadium signalled the actual presence of enemy aircraft. The government considered this too risky and refused its implementation, although eventually it was adopted. In the meantime, matches continued to be interrupted, occasionally for up to an hour. The players passed their time in various ways. Card games, singsongs, games of housey-housey, they all played their part in keeping footballers occupied while they waited for the all-clear. Some, however, got fed up and went home. When the referee went to round up everyone for a restart, often the teams could not be completed so the game was abandoned. Not unnaturally, many supporters decided not to waste their Saturday afternoons hanging around in air-raid shelters waiting for the football to resume.

The Scotland–England game at Hampden Park in May 1940 was staged against the background of the Dunkirk evacuation and a German propaganda broadcast threatening that the Luftwaffe would attack the ground before half-time. Scotland's national football stadium was only half full – that still meant an attendance of around 70,000, of course – and the barrage balloons hovering silently over Clydebank provided those who still needed it with a grim reminder of the times.

Football had already returned to Wembley, on 13 April 1940, when Wales celebrated their first ever visit by beating England 1-0 before a crowd restricted to 40,000. Wartime 'caps' did not count, even though many of the teams could be considered some of the strongest in the history of the game.

As the intensity of Blitz eased, so football found it easier to continue for the next few wartime seasons. Wembley began to host cup finals again, although the stadium's capacity was of only academic interest to many supporters, especially those in the north. The principle adopted by the government for transport in wartime was very simple: the needs of the war must come first. That meant absolute priority first for service personnel, then for vital workers and materials. By 1943, hundreds more trains each day were needed. Drastic travel restrictions, including the withdrawal of cheap day tickets and tickets for various kinds of pleasure travel, became effective from September 1942. Jolly days out to Wembley were not easy to arrange. When the poster campaign asked, 'Is Your Journey Really Necessary?' football fans might have argued that it was; the government did not agree. Supporters from northern clubs mostly tuned in to the wireless instead of descending on the capital, while the crowds for matches at Wembley were also drawn largely from the London area.

Towards the end of the war, the attendance limit was ended and in April 1945, the *Sunday Times* reported increased police activity before the South Cup final between Chelsea and Millwall at Wembley, when uniformed and plain-clothes officers carried out an extensive petrol check. Particular attention was paid to vehicles coming from South London garages, which were just outside the ten-mile limit for Hackney carriages. Whatever underhand means supporters were using to reach Wembley in those times of petrol rationing, this was a Wembley final which had so irked Frank Butler of the *Sunday Express*, with its undignified scramble for star guest players and its poor football for all that. Chelsea won 2-0, in front of 90,000 spectators.

Wembley contributed much throughout the war. In 1942, a 'pageant of youth' was staged in the arena. The Fitness for Service movement had encouraged reservists and civilians to take part in physical training and organised sport. American troops had played baseball on the hallowed turf, both teams comprising professional players. When 5,000 members of the Civil Defence were stood down at the war's end, Wembley staged the show. In 1946, the Empire Stadium was still being used as a demob centre for servicemen, some of whom had been released ahead of schedule to help rebuild bomb-damaged London. Indeed, servicemen had been associated with the stadium ever since the Dunkirk evacuation. In 1943, the doors of the restaurant had been thrown open to any member of the armed forces who could get there to enjoy a Christmas party. And in the Burmese jungle, soldiers of the so-called Forgotten Army thought about dear old Wembley and prayed that one day they would see her again.

The final football season of the Second World War kicked off on 25 August 1945. Officially the war still had a few days to run because the Japanese would not surrender with a signed document until 2 September, but the dropping of two atomic bombs on their country had signalled the end. Ten days before football again rang up the curtain, the Allies celebrated VJ Day; as with VE Day in May, there were celebration matches between a handful of clubs, but now proper competitive football was back for 1946–47, the fixture list a replica of the one that had been rudely interrupted seven years earlier. There were hard times ahead, as promised by both Winston Churchill and his successor, Clement Attlee, but that December, one million servicemen would be demobbed and a million people would be released from munitions work. Some of them would be footballers, back in the only full-time employment they had ever wanted.

When the 1939–40 peacetime Rugby League competition was abandoned after the declaration of war, clubs faced the problem of what to do about supporters who had paid in advance for season tickets. Barrow resolved to give refunds, but would deduct for games already played. Oldham decided to keep all the money: 'We are up against it and must appeal to our members to make this sacrifice.' The Rugby Football League established a War Emergency League, with clubs playing separate Yorkshire and Lancashire sections to reduce the need for travel. The winners of each section played a two-legged final to determine the overall champions. The minimum entrance fee was set at sixpence (2.5p). As in soccer, clubs could use guest players There was also a temporary relaxation of the regulations prohibiting players of Rugby Union – a devoutly amateur sport – from contact with Rugby League that was seen as a professional devil incarnate. Any Union player so doing was hitherto 'contaminated' for life. In January 1943, however, there came a remarkable development when a Rugby League team met a Rugby Union team at Headingly, Leeds, in a game under Union rules. Both teams were drawn from soldiers of the army's Northern Command and the League side won. Eight thousand spectators paid £470 (worth £27,420 in 2023) to Northern Command's Welfare Fund. The *Bradford Observer* commented, 'Professionalism has been scattered to the winds.' The event was considered so successful that in April 1944, a second game was organised at Odsal Stadium in Bradford. Again, the League team emerged victorious before a crowd reported to number between 15,000 and 18,000 which the *Halifax Evening Courier* regarded as 'disappointing', although charity again benefited, this time by £1,500 (worth £87,500 today).

On 15 June 1938, a David Low cartoon in the London *Evening Standard* had depicted Prime Minister Neville Chamberlain as a quivering batsman defending a wicket that was the Rock of Gibraltar.

In conference at the other end were Hitler, Mussolini and Franco. They were about to bowl Chamberlain a hand grenade. Fourteen months later, on Wednesday, 30 August 1939, six County Cricket Championship matches got under way. Two days later, Germany invaded Poland and the cricket season stuttered to a halt. Reviewing the 1939 cricket season in *Wisden Cricketers' Almanack*, author R. C. Robertson-Glasgow, the Oxford Blue who had played for Somerset from 1920 to 1935, wrote that it was 'like peeping curiously through the wrong end of a telescope at a very small but very happy world'.

Once war had been declared, there was little hope of staging a meaningful County Championship, and the following 1940 season ended without Lancashire's suggestion, of a regionalised championship to include the Minor Counties, being taken up. Several county clubs closed down for the duration and spectators had to make do with inter-service matches and those games played by teams like the newly formed British Empire XI, although these were often of a high standard. The Empire XI featured mostly English county players along with the West Indian Test player Carlos 'Bertie' Clarke. The London Counties XI were also formidable opponents. Many service and Civil Defence organisation teams were formed, their matches keeping up morale as well as raising funds for wartime charities. On 7 September 1940, the government ruled that cricketers taking part in matches in London must take cover during the period of an air-raid warning. A match between Middlesex and a Lord's XI was held up for some time after the sirens wailed. When it finally resumed, the right-arm fast-medium bowler Laurie Gray ended the game in dramatic fashion, taking four Lord's XI wickets in only seven balls to win the match.

Although sport – even the alternative 'ersatz' versions such as the regional football competitions that had little in common with pre-war fare – was considered to be an important factor in maintaining morale, horseracing was considered by many to be nothing more than a wasteful luxury. In 1941, the MP Emanuel Shinwell asked, 'Is it desirable to allow these insane and unseemly spectacles to continue?'

The previous year, the Home Office had agreed that the 1940 Grand National could be run at Aintree as usual, despite a letter from Captain A. F. Hordern, the chief constable of Lancashire, who strongly opposed the idea. He pointed out that the attendance would probably number around 25,000 and that there were practically no air-raid shelters for them. If there were an attack, then Aintree's stands and enclosure would make perfect targets for enemy bombers. In the event, the crowd turned up but the Luftwaffe stayed away. The race was won by Bogskar, a 25/1 shot ridden by RAF sergeant Mervyn Jones. Then the army moved in and the race would not be run there again until 1946.

The use of several racecourses for military purposes meant that as the war went on, the racing programme was minimal. Epsom was another venue commandeered – it accommodated an anti-aircraft battery and a Home Guard training school, an aircraft on a training flight crashed straight into the course, and parts of the grandstand were affected by bombing – and meetings there were abandoned until further notice. So, where to stage the 1940 Epsom Classics? Newbury was considered but there was strong opposition from the local council. The meeting was transferred to the July course at Newmarket – the Rowley Mile course there was being used by RAF Bomber Command – and in June the 'New Derby Stakes' and the 'New Oaks Stakes' were run on the summer course. A crowd of more than 10,000, hundreds of them walking from Newmarket town centre, watched the Derby. Many came in special coaches, clogging local roads, while two special trains brought 1,400 punters from King's Cross (was their journey really necessary?). It would be 1946 before the two classics returned to Epsom. Some racecourses were used as prisoner-of-war camps or internment camps for 'enemy aliens'. York was one such, and when racing was resumed there in 1945, the first meeting included the St Leger because Doncaster, which had also been also used as a camp, was not ready in time.

Then there was the question that would not go away: was it even right to allow horse racing in wartime? In 1940, the annual Cheltenham Festival was reduced to two days' racing. The course was used as training quarters for soldiers waiting to be sent into action. Nonetheless, the Gold Cup was still run there except for 1942 and 1943. In January 1942, Sir Waldron Smithers, the Conservative MP for Chislehurst, asked the Home Secretary, Herbert Morrison, what was the approximate number of people who attended Cheltenham Races on the Saturdays of 13 and 27 December 1941 respectively, and whether he could inform the House, approximately, of the number of motor cars present on those days.

Morrison replied that there were an estimated 3,150 and 4,000 racegoers and 893 and 1,270 cars. Smithers wanted to know whether those numbers were consistent 'with the policy of total effort laid down by the Prime Minister'. He said:

> In regard to the number of cars, is he aware that the Minister of War Transport is making an appeal for more lorries and for the saving of petrol, both as regards waste in this country and shipping space? Will he take steps to stop these activities?

Morrison told him:

> I cannot answer for the Ministry of War Transport or for the petrol administration. The only question for me is whether these types of recreation should be prohibited or not. I do not think it is right that my personal opinion about that should influence my decision. We have taken the view that there must be, within reasonable limitation, recreation for the people. I do not think that we had better too readily or extensively adopt the philosophy or policy of progressive misery.

That dogged critic of horseracing in wartime, Emanuel Shinwell, followed up:

> Does my right honourable friend or the government pretend that the presence of over 1,000 cars at a race meeting is consistent with total effort? Is that Government policy?

'That is not a question for the Home Secretary,' Morrison replied.

Smithers would not let the matter rest. Two weeks later, he was asking Morrison for the number of cars present at the National Hunt meetings at Worcester and Wetherby on Saturday, 10 January 1941.
Morrison:

> The number of cars in the racecourse car park at Worcester on 10 January was, I am informed, 148. The Worcester meeting was held at a course near the town and some of the cars parked in public car parks in the town may have conveyed passengers to the racecourse. At the Wetherby meeting the number of cars was, I am informed, approximately 550.

Smithers still was not finished. He wondered whether, in view of the fact that at a recent race meeting at Cheltenham, under National Hunt

Rules, there were sixty-four runners, and that the grand total investment of the totalisator was £17,000, he would issue an order prohibiting all betting transactions as inconsistent with the prime minister's appeal for total war effort.

Morrison did not want to be a killjoy. He told Smithers:

> Whatever arguments there may be for amendment of the laws relating to betting, I do not think that the war powers conferred on the Government could properly be used to effect the changes desired by my honourable friend. As regards the number of horses running at the race meeting to which he refers, the reduced opportunities for racing have, as I explained on 27 November, resulted in an increase in the number of entries at individual meetings.

Horse racing was not the only sport that existed purely so that people could gamble that troubled some MPs. In January 1942, Cecil Wilson, the Labour MP for Sheffield Attercliffe, asked the Home Secretary for the number of greyhound racing meetings held each week throughout the country; an estimate of attendance or the average thereof; the total amount of money passing in bets through the totalisator; the amount of paper used for race-card programmes; the amount subsequently collected at the meeting places; and the total number of cars used by persons attending these meetings during the week.

Morrison was not minded to waste much time on the subject:

> Since June, 1940, dog racing has been restricted to one meeting a week on each track and I understand that the number of tracks is less than 150. The particulars required to answer the remainder of the Question are not available and, even where they could be obtained, would involve widespread inquiries which would not in present circumstances be justified.

The sport was certainly popular. On 4 March 1942, three meetings, at Harringay, Wimbledon and Wembley, attracted crowds of 7,500, 6,700 and 4,000 respectively. Seven months later, Viscountess Astor was asking whether the Home Secretary would obtain from the clerks to the county councils and county borough councils concerned full returns of the totalisator receipts at greyhound racing tracks for the years 1938, 1939, 1940 and 1941. Again, Morrison had more important things to do: 'I regret that I do not feel justified in asking for these returns in present conditions.'

Even in wartime – perhaps especially in wartime – people liked a flutter but the football pools seemed to have taken a hit. In July 1942, Robert Morgan, the Conservative member for Stourbridge, asked the Home Secretary whether, in view of the need for saving paper, utilising the workforce on the most useful lines, and promoting war savings, he would take action for the suppression of football pools in wartime.

Morrison told Morgan that the amount of business transacted by the football pool companies had greatly decreased since the outbreak of war. For example, the amount paid into the pools by the public in the form of postal orders was in the 1941–42 season 80 per cent less than in 1938–39. 'On the information before me I hardly think there are any sufficient grounds to justify singling out this particular form of amusement for repressive measures.'

Captain Leonard Plugge, Tory member for Chatham and a man who in 1931 had created the International Broadcasting Company that bought airtime from European radio stations as a rival to the BBC, asked, 'Would not the suppression of football pools result in a great loss of revenue to the Post Office and, therefore, to the Exchequer, and ought not everything be done to encourage a hobby which occupies people at home, saving transport and other wasteful expenditure?'

Morrison declined to offer an opinion: 'I am afraid my honourable and gallant friend is trying morally to draw me in the opposite direction; I think I had better not get there either.'

The boxing programme was severely curtailed during the war, but one fight stands out. On 20 June 1942, 23-year-old RAF sergeant Freddie Mills faced RAF pilot officer Len Harvey, who was within a week of his 35th birthday, for the British and British Empire light-heavyweight titles and, in many people's eyes, for the world championship as well.

Mills, a former Bournemouth milkman, had made his name fighting on local bills before becoming a full-time professional who battled his way around the halls and fairgrounds of the South Coast. But as his career was taking shape, so the world was sliding into war. Harvey, meanwhile, would be fighting the last of over 400 professional bouts.

The time was 7.00 pm, the skies were blue, the sun still evident on the kind of English midsummer's day about which *Dad's Army*'s

Captain Mainwaring might have said: 'It's what we are fighting for.' The ring was erected in the centre of the pitch at White Hart Lane, where generations of Tottenham footballers had entertained their fans. Seats were set on the grass, and then spread away to the more conventional accommodation of a football stadium. There was a crowd of more than 40,000 boxing fans, an attendance that would have pleased the Spurs' directors any Saturday peacetime afternoon.

The swarthy, snub-nosed Mills was first to enter the ring, to be greeted by a wall of sound from tens of thousands of sports-starved spectators. The champion received a similar welcome as he strode over to Mills and gave him a pat on the back and a gentle smile. Harvey had not had a serious fight for three years. But he was infinitely more experienced than his opponent.

The first round passed uneventfully enough as the boxers measured each other up, but within a minute of the second round, Mills had the crowd on their feet and Len Harvey on his knees after exploding a tremendous left hook on the champion's jaw.

Referee Eugene Henderson was within hundredths of a second of counting Harvey out when the champion made a final, seemingly superhuman, effort to climb to his feet. Mills went in again, arms working like piston rods. Harvey could not defend himself and when Mills landed a right-hander on his opponent's cheekbone, Harvey leaned back on the ropes for support, sitting on the middle hemp that he flattened against the bottom rope to make an unsteady seat.

Suddenly, the champion of Britain and its empire – and possibly of the world – disappeared from view. As Henderson took up the count again, an almighty drama was being played out down below. Some spectators were wondering whether to help Harvey to his feet; others pointed out that to do so would see him disqualified. It didn't really matter. By the time Harvey's dazed features eventually reappeared above the canvas, Henderson had reached 'ten'. Freddie Mills was the new champion. It took Len Harvey six months to announce that his boxing career was over. After the war, Mills would become the undisputed world champion after an epic battle with the American, Gus Lesnevitch.

After retiring from the ring, he remained in the public eye, not least with walk-on parts in films and TV programmes.

In July 1965, Freddie Mills was found shot dead in his car outside his London nightclub. The circumstances surrounding his death have given rise to many theories – suicide, a gangland murder, even that that

Mills was a vicious serial killer, responsible for the brutal deaths of at least eight young women whose naked bodies were found in or around the River Thames between 1959 and his own death. Always on the sports pages after that sensational wartime victory over Len Harvey, in death Freddie Mills had finally made front-page news in the saddest of circumstances.

In September 1940, Richmond Golf Club in Surrey conceded, 'In all competitions, during gunfire, or when bombs are falling, players may take cover without penalty for ceasing play.' However, another rule said, 'A player whose stroke is affected by simultaneous explosion of bomb or shell, or by machine-gun fire, may play the ball from the same place. Penalty: 1 stroke.' A typical example of golfers' sang-froid was shown by the following rules: 'The position of known delayed action bombs are marked by red flags at a reasonable – but not guaranteed – safe distance therefrom.' And: 'A ball moved by enemy action may be placed as near as possible where it lay, or if lost or destroyed, a ball may be dropped not nearer the hole, without penalty.'

Whether Richmond's rules revisions were serious, or whether they were meant simply to amuse, they were republished in several newspapers in the United States as a classic example of British pluck and resilience. Sport certainly helped Britain to keep smiling through.

Chapter 19

A Land of Begin Again...

> After one heavy raid a block of flats were damaged and sticking out of the rubble was the remains of a grand piano. No wood – just the insides. One of the local kids asked the demolition men, 'If you don't want that old harp, can we have it?' During the war, everyone was looking for ways to entertain themselves and others. It seemed strange when it was all over.
>
> June Buckle, London

As the Second World War entered its final months, the entertainment industry began to plan for a new beginning. After D-Day, the Forces Programme that was broadcast on long wave became the BBC's Light Programme, while the service continued broadcasting on shortwave to troops still fighting in the Far East, and after VJ Day to occupying forces in vanquished countries until civilian rule was restored. The Forces Programme closed altogether on 31 December 1946.

Listeners at home, meanwhile, had already seen a major change in their entertainment on the wireless. In July 1945, radio critic Harold Watkins said:

> Getting any information about the new regional alphabetical programmes from the BBC is rather like asking a censor not to be a censor. But I have discovered the reason why. The wavelength problem has been a major difficulty, and the BBC powers are truly anxious to use what new wavelengths can be spared from war and propaganda service to the best entertainment purpose.

There would soon be three, not two, BBC radio stations from which to choose. The *Gloucester Citizen* reported, 'The third station will cater for highbrows only – those who like opera, chamber music, symphonies, and long plays. The Light Programme will be for people who prefer variety, thrillers, bands, and comedians. The Home station will steer a middle-of-the-road course … the regions, seven of them, are also to come back.'

On Saturday, 28 July 1946, the Allied Expeditionary Force programme, which had been on air since 7 June 1944 – D plus One Day – had closed down with an outstanding tribute paid by General Eisenhower to all the British, Canadian, and American personnel who had operated that service. The next day, the Light Programme was launched to the sound of Big Ben and the words, 'Good morning, everyone. This is the BBC Light Programme … It's the first time we have said those words, "BBC Light Programme", which we hope are going to mean for you now and in the days to come all that is best in radio entertainment, from nine o'clock in the morning until midnight.' Then came the first news bulletin of the day, followed by a wide selection of programmes including *Transatlantic Quiz: Britain versus America*; the drama *Alf's Dream* by W. W. Jacobs; *Sandy McPherson at the Theatre Organ*; *As The Commentator Saw It: Cricket and Tennis*; *Variety Bandbox* starring comedian Issy Bonn, ventriloquist Peter Brough, and Edmundo Ros and his Rumba Band; a concert – *Tyneside Salutes the Merchant Navy*; and the religious programme *Sunday Half Hour*. The day ended with *In a Sentimental Mood*, and *Songs of Three Decades*, before the late-evening news and Big Ben once more.

The BBC's television service, which had been closed down on 1 September 1939, and remained in cold storage throughout the war, began broadcasting again at 3.00 pm on 7 June 1946, when it was estimated that there were 20,000 TV sets in Britain, all within the London area. The *News Chronicle* reported, 'The first transmission this afternoon will show the television mast, accompanied by a drum-roll and fanfare, and then cars will be seen arriving for the ceremony.'

The first words heard were those of Jasmine Bligh, one of three BBC TV presenters of pre-war days – Leslie Mitchell and Elizabeth Cowell were the others – who said, 'Good afternoon, everybody. How are you? Do you remember me, Jasmine Bligh?' The final programme shown before the service shut down on the eve of war was the Mickey Mouse cartoon, *Mickey's Gala Premier*, and it was shown again on the day of the BBC television's resumption, along with ballet featuring Margot Fonteyn from Sadler's Wells, and a talk, with drawings, by cartoonist David Low. At 8.30 pm, broadcasting resumed, showing Geraldo and his Orchestra, and a play entitled *The Silence of the Sea* by Vercors, the pseudonym of French writer Jean Marcel Bruller.

The following day, on tiny screens, viewers could watch black and white pictures of the nation's Victory Parade through London, and over the coming months a regular programming schedule was established with an hour's television between 3.00 pm and 4.00 pm (that could be extended to accommodate plays and outside broadcasts of special events) and two hours from 8.30 pm.

June 1946 also saw the return of the televising of Wimbledon; the All-England Tennis Championships had first been televised in 1937. In July, children's television returned, and in August, *Muffin the Mule* made his small-screen debut. In October, part of the Athenian Football League match between Barnet and Wealdstone was televised. The *Harrow Observer* reported that with the 'added attraction' of television cameras, the ground was packed to capacity. But television viewers missed the best bit. The newspaper said, 'The last twenty minutes proved the most exciting of all and produced two further goals, neither of which were televised, the service having to close down on account of bad light and a steady downpour of rain.'

On the West End stage in 1946, *Song of Norway*, an operetta based on the life of Edvard Grieg, opened at the Palace Theatre, and *Pacific 1860*, a musical by Noël Coward set in a fictional British colony during the reign of Queen Victoria, started its run at the Theatre Royal, Drury Lane. Unlike *Song of Norway*, which ran for 526 performances, *Pacific 1860* closed after only four months. After starting life in Los Angeles in 1944, *Song of Norway* was the first Broadway show to cross the Atlantic after the war.

An Inspector Calls also opened in the London in 1946. J. B. Priestley's three-act play set on a single night in 1912 is the story of an upper-middle-class family who find themselves questioned by a police inspector about the suicide of a young working-class woman. As guilty secrets are revealed, the play aims to deliver a strong moral message. Remarkably, it had premiered not in London but in Russia, first in Leningrad as *This You Will Not Forget* and then in Moscow as simply *He Came*. It was suggested that no London theatre would touch the subject; the more likely explanation is that none were available. A Russian translator approached Russian theatre producers and Priestley's story was snapped up by those who liked its message of communal responsibility.

When *An Inspector Calls* eventually found a home in London, it was to mixed reviews. The *Daily Mail*'s Leslie Hale revealed that 'only self-control prevented hollow groans rising through the last act from seat No E1 in the stalls: my seat. It was early on in this act that Mr Priestley disclosed that his moralising play had no theatrical ethics ... the stage demands a theatrical solution.' In *The Observer*, J. C. Trewin thought that the play 'could have been stripped of half its length'.

Not everyone was critical. James Agate in the *Sunday Times* praised the acting of Alec Guinness and Ralph Richardson, while Stephen Potter of the *New Statesman* thought the ending was 'the best coup de thétre of the year'. The *News Chronicle* theatre critic regarded 'Mr Priestley's examination of a North Midlands manufacturer's household in the year 1912 ingenious, improbable, and exceedingly well-acted by seven of the Old Vic's new company'. The *Daily Herald* called it 'an absorbing, finely-acted piece of stagecraft ... J.B. Priestley explains away coincidences, dissects consciences and rounds of his special sermon with fantasy'.

In 1946, theatre was popular but if radio was still the cheapest mass entertainment medium, only cinema came near to it. Picture houses were packed, people watching films through a haze of blue tobacco smoke during what was to become the 'golden era' of British film with Ealing Studios leading the way. In 1944, Ealing had been taken over by the Rank Organisation which now controlled a large proportion of the British film industry. Ealing had come to the fore during the war, with comedies starring George Formby, Tommy Trinder and Will Hay. In 1946, Formby made his final appearance on the big screen in *George in Civvy Street*. It was a box office flop and he returned to his music hall and variety theatre career.

Great Expectations, starring John Mills and Valerie Hobson, was a version of Charles Dickens's novel. The film, written by David Lean and produced by his Cineguild company, went on general release in December 1946 and was on its way to being named the fifth-best British films of all time. Alec Guinness played the part of Herbert Pocket, and the *Daily Herald* liked him: 'This is Alec's first film role, apart from a day's work, over ten years ago, in Evelyn Laye's *Evensong*. It must not be his last, for truly this Guinness is good for us all.'

It had been too late to arrange a normal football season for 1945–46 but on Saturday, 31 August 1946, for over a million people there was only one place to be: at a Football League ground. Unusually for the first day of the football season, the weather was cloudy and overcast, the forecast for rain. The previous week had seen gale-force winds and torrential downpours, rivers swollen, roads blocked by fallen trees. In Germany, the Nuremberg war crimes trials entered their last day and that afternoon Goering, Hess and Ribbentrop were among major Nazi leaders making their final impassioned pleas. In Britain, the days when football matches were interrupted by air raids, and teams made up their numbers by borrowing from their opponents, or even from the crowd, were over. Now there were no guest players, but there was promotion and relegation. Now there was a return to the old ways of football.

The fixtures were a replica of the 1939–40 season and Liverpool effectively won the title on 31 May, when they beat their closest rivals, Wolves, on a scorching day at Molineux, but they had to wait another two weeks to be sure; thanks to yet another dreadful winter, the 1946–47 season went on until 14 June.

The FA Cup, however, had resumed for the previous season, and on 9 March 1946, all roads leading to Burnden Park were packed. Bolton Wanderers were playing host to Stoke City in the second leg of their FA Cup quarter-final tie, and the visitors had the great Stanley Matthews in their ranks. Over 85,000 people wanted to see the outcome at first hand. But the capacity for the ground was just under 70,000. Thirty-three people died in the resultant crush – remarkably, the game had continued uninterrupted by the tragedy being played out on the terraces – and a Home Office enquiry, chaired by Ronw Moelwyn Hughes KC, found that while the Bolton club and the police had taken proper steps, procedures were inadequate. The real trouble lay in the fact that there had been no scientific assessment of the ground's capacity – this was simply regarded as the greatest number of people to have been safely accommodated there on a previous occasion. There was also no means of knowing when that figure was about to be reached, nor were there facilities for the immediate closing of the turnstiles. An attempt had been made to open exit doors, but the keys could not be found.

The first full season of first-class cricket to be played in England for seven years got under way in 1946 – Yorkshire would retain the County Championship they had won in 1939 – while a three-match Test series was hastily arranged against India, who were captained by a pre-war England player, the Nawab of Pataudi, and whose party contained Hindus, Muslims, a Parsi and a Christian. It would also be the last team to represent an undivided India. The players arrived in England in different groups, travelling by various means including an RAF Dakota, a BOAC Avro York, and a flying boat from Karachi to Poole.

After England won the first match, the last two were drawn, the third being ruined by persistent rain. But people were desperate for 'proper' sport, and in its review of the season, an era of Len Hutton, Denis Compton, Wally Hammond and Cyril Washbrook, *Wisden Cricketers' Almanack* commented, 'The weather in 1946 might have been dreadful, but it didn't stop the crowds flocking to games.' It was one of wettest of English summers.

In 1946, the Northern Rugby League began its longest season on record, again thanks to the appalling winter, and in Rugby Union – then strictly an amateur game – the remarkable Dr Kevin O'Flanagan played rugby for Ireland against France (in an unofficial international) and then soccer for the Ireland national football team against Scotland seven days later. He then won an official rugby international cap, against Australia.

In February 1946, the last of 16,000 troops left Aintree racecourse, which had been used a vehicle depot during the war. The remarkable Mirabel Topham, owner of Aintree, then achieved something that few thought possible: by the first weekend in April she had the racecourse ready for the first true Grand National since 1940. Racing fans, starved of their sport, poured towards Aintree – some estimates give the crowd that Friday (the last time that the race would be run on a Friday) at 300,000. The race was won by the 25/1 shot Lovely Cottage, ridden by Captain Bobby Petre and coming home four lengths ahead of the second-placed runner, Jack Finlay, a 100/1 chance.

When, in June 1946, the Derby was run at Epsom for the first time since 1939 – the course had accommodated an anti-aircraft battery – an estimated half a million people, including the king and queen, saw – in fact, most of them probably did not see very much at all – the grey colt Airborne, at 50/1 and ridden by Tommy Lowrey, catch Gulf Stream in the final furlong to win by a length. The race was filmed by Movietone, using a precarious-looking 120 ft-high (36.5 m) tower of scaffolding.

The 1946 University Boat Race returned to the Thames and was won by Oxford, by three lengths. No official races had been conducted between 1940 and 1945, which meant that none of the rowers had previously participated in a Boat Race.

Seaside resorts could fully reopen after the war – even in the summer of 1944, after the D-Day landings, swimming was allowed on some small beaches – but only after clearance work had been carried out, particularly on the South Coast, which had been heavily defended against a German invasion. Removing barbed wire and barricades was easy enough, but when it came to clearing mines sown during the early years of the war, there were plenty of challenges. As late as May 1955, five schoolboys were killed when a wartime mine exploded on the beach where they were walking in Swanage, Dorset.

When it came to holidays, for those who wanted something more than the pre-war seaside boarding house experience, there were holiday camps, although in and around them there were still plenty of reminders of the war itself, for several had been taken over by the military.

In 1946, Fred Pontin, who during the war had been involved in establishing hostels for construction workers, opened his first holiday camp on the site of a former US Army base at Brean Sands, near Weston-super-Mare. To help raise the £25,280 cost to restore it, Pontin formed a syndicate in which he owned 50 per cent. Osmington Camp, near Weymouth, soon followed, and within a year Pontin had six camps, each run by him for a year to get them into shape before selling them to the syndicate, in which he still owned 50 per cent. The Pontins company was formed in July 1946, with 400,000 shares, all of them placed in one day. Over the years, his empire grew to thirty sites. The post-war boom also saw new Butlin's camps at Minehead, Bognor Regis, Barry Island, and Mosney in the Republic of Ireland.

Radio, cinema, theatre, sport, holidays away from home at last – after six long, war-weary years, 1946 was a fresh start, a new beginning for Britain. There would be plenty of toils and efforts ahead. Winston Churchill had promised so, and his successor, Clement Attlee, had agreed. But there was also a chance to enjoy oneself without the threat of bombs or the worry of loved ones overseas.

At Christmas 1941, Vera Lynn had released a new recording. The song was 'There's a Land of Begin Again'. It promised new beginnings on the horizon, just over the hill, 'where we learn to love and live again…' Now it seemed that time had finally come.

Sources

During the research for this book, the following newspapers and periodicals were consulted:

Belfast Telegraph, Birmingham Evening Despatch, Birmingham Gazette, Birmingham Mail, Birmingham Sports Argus, Britannia and Eve, Bradford Observer, Chelmsford Chronicle, Coventry Standard, Daily Dispatch, Daily Express, Daily Herald, Daily Mail, Daily Mirror, Daily Record, Derby Evening Telegraph, Edinburgh Evening News, Halifax Evening Courier, Hampstead and St John's Wood News and Golders Green Gazette, Hartlepool Northern Daily Mail, Hull Daily Mail, Kinematograph Weekly, Lancashire Evening Post, Leicester Chronicle, Leicester Evening Mail, Lincolnshire Echo, Liverpool Echo, Liverpool Daily Post, London Daily News, London Evening Standard, Manchester Evening News, Melody Maker, Middlesex County Times, Nelson Leader, Newark Herald, Newcastle Chronicle, News Chronicle, Northamptonshire Evening Telegraph, Nottingham Evening Post, Picturegoer & Film Weekly, St Pancras Gazette, Sheffield Evening Telegraph, Shields Daily Gazette, Sheerness Guardian and East Kent Advertiser, Sheerness Times, Sunday Dispatch, Sunday Express, Sunday Pictorial, Sunderland Echo, Thanet Advertiser, The Hernando Sun, The Scotsman, The Tatler and Bystander, The Sketch, The Spectator, The Stage, Weekly Dispatch, West Ham and South Essex Mail, West Middlesex Gazette, Western Mail, Yorkshire Post and Leeds.

Index

Abbey, Beryl, 154
Abbot, Bud, 53
Adamson, Harold, 53
Agate, James, 187
Alexander, Norah, 40
Allen, Chesney, 36, 53
Allen, Gracie, 26
Allen, Les, 49
Allistone, Jean, 24
Ambrose, Bert, 41, 45, 45, 53, 54, 73
Anderson, Sir John, 171
Anderson, Lawler, 117, 118
Andrews, John Miller, 32
Andrews, Julie, 63
Andrews Sisters, 53, 73
Astell, Betty, 46–47
Astor, Viscountess, 180
Atkinson, Harold, 173
Attenborough, Richard, 104
Attlee, Clement, 176, 190

Bacall, Lauren, 105
Badger, Private John, 44
Baessell, Lieutenant-Colonel Norman F., 86
Bailleux, Christine, 129
Baker, Howard, 41
Banks, Monty, 35, 36, 52
Barker, Gordon, 89
Barnett, Fred, 132
Barrie, Wendy, 89
Baum, L. Frank, 93
BBC Symphony Orchestra, 15, 58, 66
Bearne, C., 166
Beaton, Anne, 2, 5
Beaven, Dudley, 20, 49
Benjamin, Bennie, 56
Benny, Jack, 23, 28
Bergman, Ingrid, 95, 105
Bergner, Elisabeth, 114
Bernard Crook Quintet, 4
Beste, Vernon, 79–80
Black, George, 56
Black, Stanley, 56
Bligh, Jasmine, 186
Bonn, Issy, 185
Bonnalie, Colonel F. J., 72
Boston Symphony Orchestra, 83
Boult, Sir Adrian, 16, 66
Boyer, Charles, 95
Bowly, Al, 55
Bracken, Brendan, 12, 23, 118
Brackpool, Herbert, 101
Brackpool, Michael, 101
Bronte, Emily, 91
Brotherton, Fusilier Donald, 43
Brough, Peter, 185
Brown, Joe E., 89
Browne, Sam, 49
Bruller, Jean Marcel, 186

Buchanan, Jack, 148
Buckham, Bernard, 20, 25, 26, 45, 129
Buckle, June, 184
Budgeon, Frank, 75
Burns, George, 26
Burton, Nat, 50
Butler, Frank, 175
Butler, Ralph, 54
Butlin, Billy, 190
Byam, Guy, 11
Byrne, Ted, 98

Cameron, Basil, 61, 62
Campbell, Jimmy, 55
Campbell, Stuart, 144
Capra, Frank, 95
Carr, Michael, 54
Carter, Raich, 4, 5
Casson, Lewis, 125
Chamberlain, Neville, 1, 3, 5, 7, 15, 141, 176, 177
Chaplin, Charles, 28, 97
Charles, Hughie, 49, 54
Chenhalls, Alfred, 103
Chevalier, Maurice, 18
Churchill, Winston, 44, 48, 55, 103, 105, 176, 190
Claes, Johnny, 78
Clague, Sergeant William Norman, 116
Clarke, Carlos 'Bertie', 177
Clarke, Sir Kenneth, 63
Clitheroe, Jimmy, 149
Coates, Eric, 21
Cochrane, C. B., 40–41
Collinson, Walter, 71
Collodi, Carlo, 95
Coleman, Serjeant Edward Arthur, 117
Colman, Ronald, 88
Compton, Denis, 189
Congreve, William, 125
Connelly, Reg, 55
Cooper, St John, 54
Costello, Lou, 53
Cotton, Billy, 41, 50, 53, 55
Cottrell, Jack, 31
Coulter, Vera, 157
Coward, Noël, 55, 103, 106, 120, 126, 127, 186
Cowell, Elizabeth, 185
Crazy Gang, The, 35, 36, 53
Crosby, Bing, 46, 55, 56, 66, 73, 136, 146
Curtiz, Michael, 105
Cutler, N. W., 30

Daladier, Édouard, 5
Daniels, Bebe, 10, 19–20
Davies, Glyn, 50
Daw, Leslie, 157
de Havilland, Olivia, 94
du Maurier, Daphne, 91, 95
Dean, Basil, 31, 36
Dennis, Denny, 73
Desmond, Florence, 35, 36
Dickie, Edgar Primrose, 147
Dietrich, Marlene, 66, 95
Dimbleby, Richard, 11
Disney, Walt, 94
Donat, Robert, 91–92
Dorman-Smith, Sir Reginald, 153
D'Orsay, Marlene, 131
Dorsey, Tommy, 55
Douglas, Keith, 61
Dougall, Robert, 12

Drake, Ted, 169–170
Durban, Deanna, 93

Eddy, Nelson, 89
Edwards, Miss C. M., 151
Eisenhower, General Dwight D., 84, 185
Elgar, Sir Edward, 58, 62

Fain, Sammy, 55
Farmer, Harry, 21
Fields, Gracie, 35–36, 41, 46, 48, 51–52, 54, 55, 92–93, 141, 149
Flanagan, Bud, 36, 53, 54
Fleming, Victor, 93
Fletcher, Cyril, 20, 46
Flynn, Errol, 88
Fontaine, Joan, 95
Fonteyn, Margot, 185
Ford, Private Charles Oliver, 117
Ford, John, 95
Forde, Walter, 43
Formby, Beryl, 31, 34, 38
Formby, George, 30–39, 103, 187
Franco, Francisco, 177
Frankau, Ronald, 25
Fraser, Morton, 20

Gable, Clark, 93
Gail, Zoe, 56
Gallai-Hatchard, Flight Lieutenant Donald, 116
Gannon, Kim, 136
Gardner, Charles, 10–11
Garland, Judy, 50, 89, 93
Garson, Greer, 91, 92, 93
Gates, Bill, 22
Gay, Noel, 54
Geraldo, 55, 185
Goebbels, Joseph, 56, 103
Goering, Hermann, 188
Goodliffe, Canon J. B., 30
Goodman, Benny, 83
Gordon, Dick, 133
Gorham, Maurice, 85
Goring, Marius, 117
Gottlieb, Marian, 94
Grant, Cary, 88
Gray, Barry (see Pountain, Eric)
Gray, Laurie, 177
Greene, Graham, 104
Gregg, Hubert, 56
Grenfell, Joyce, 27
Grisewood, Freddie, 156
Guinness, Alec, 187

Hale, Binnie, 54–55
Hale, Leslie, 187
Hall, Henry, 22
Hallé Orchestra, 63
Hallmark Dance Band, 146
Hamilton, Patrick, 95
Hammond, Wally, 189
Handley, Jack, 27
Handley, Tommy, 24–29
Harben, Joan, 26, 27
Hardy, Oliver, 89
Harrison, Rex, 96
Harrison, Suzanne, 136
Harrisson, Tom, 69
Harvey, Len, 181–183
Haskins, Minnie, 141
Hathcock, Cleother, 78
Haw-Haw, Lord (see Joyce, William)
Hay, Will, 103, 148, 187
Hayworth, Rita, 134
Heath, Moira, 56

Heath, Ted, 56
Helliwell, Arthur, 38
Henderson, Eugene, 182
Henderson, Laura, 129, 133–134
Henderson, Sir Neville, 3, 5
Heneker, David, 54
Henn, William, 100
Henson, Leslie, 31
Hepburn, Katharine, 88
Herbert, A. P., 54
Hess, Dame Myra, 62–63
Hess, Rudolf, 188
Hibberd, Stuart, 8
Hintze, First Oberleutnant Herbert, 103
Hitchcock, Alfred, 91, 95
Hitler, Adolf, 1, 2, 5, 15, 16, 20, 24, 31, 58, 89, 90, 97, 103, 119, 125, 148, 157, 177
Hobman, Molly, 115
Hobson, Valerie, 187
Holiday, Billie, 55
Holloway, Stanley, 35
Holmes, J. B., 116
Hordern, Captain A. F., 177
Horne, Kenneth, 18–19
Horton, Sir Max, 119, 120
Horton, W., 165
Howard, Leslie, 94, 102, 114
Howard, Trevor, 106
Howson, Pat, 39
Hughes, Ronw Moelwyn, KC, 188
Hughes, Spike, 23
Hutchinson, Leslie ('Hutch'), 55
Hutton, Len, 189
Hylton, Jack, 4

Iremonger, Very Reverend F. A., 21

Jack, Robert, 99
Jackson, Pat, 120
Jay, Joan, 49
Jennings, Humphrey, 69, 112, 114, 117
Johnson, Celia, 104, 106
Johnson, Ken 'Snakehips', 73–74
Johnson, Len, 167
Jones, Mervyn, 178
Joubert, Air Chief Marshal Sir Philip, 115
Joyce, William, 10

Kahal, Irving, 65
Kavanagh, Ted, 24, 27
Kaye, Danny, 28
Kelly, HMS, 104
Kendall, Denis, 83
Kennedy, Jimmy, 54
Kent, Walter, 50–51
Kimmins, Lieutenant Commander Anthony, 109
King George VI, 112
Kingdom, Arthur, 146
Kirby Flying Ballet, 149

Lambert, Constant, 111
Lamour, Dorothy, 89, 98
Lansbury, Angela, 95
Laughton, Charles, 91
Laurel, Stan, 89
Lawson, Evertt, 108
Leach, Jimmy, 21
Leach, William, 158
Lean, David, 103, 106, 120, 187
Leigh, Vivien, 94
Leip, Hans, 117
Lejeune, C. A., 106
Lennox-Boyd, Alan Tindal, 140

Lennox-Boyd, Lady Patricia, 140
Lennox-Boyd, Simon, 140
Leslie Bridgewater Quintet, 6
Lesnevitch, Gus, 182
Levis, Carroll, 50
Levy, Thomas, 159
Lewis, Harry, 44
Lewis-Jones, Virginia, 44
Liddell, Alvar, 7
Liverpool Philharmonic Orchestra, 63
Llewellin, Colonel John, 148
Lloyd, Geoffrey, 158–159
Lloyd, Olive, 140
Lockwood, Margaret, 88, 96
Lombard, Carole, 90
London Symphony Orchestra, 58
Low, David, 176
Lowrey, Tommy, 189
Lynn, Vera, 40–45, 47, 49–51, 56, 57, 66, 190
Lyon, Ben, 10, 19, 20

McCormack, Corporal S. T., 42
McCracken, Esther, 128
McCrea, Judy, 132
McGee, Driver Malcolm, 117
McHugh, Jimmy, 53
McLurg, Bill, 18
McPherson, Sandy, 2, 15, 185
Madden, Cecil, 42, 85
Madge, Charles, 69
Mannheim, Lucie, 117
Marchant, Hilde, 133
Marcus, Sol, 56
Markle, Sergeant Fletcher, 120
Martin, Bram, 4
Martin, Sergeant D. H., 35
Martin-Harvey, Sir John, 124
Marshall, Howard, 11
Marshall, Nugent, 130
Maschwitz, Eric, 56
Matthew, W. P., 2
Matthews, H., 166
Matthews, Jessie, 89, 114
Matthews, Stanley, 188
Mayo, Eileen, 147
Merry Macs, 55
Miller, Glenn, 46, 51, 53, 56, 66, 83–87
Miller, Max, 35
Mills, Freddie, 181–183
Mills, John, 104, 187
Mitchell, Leslie, 185
Mitchell, R. J., 102
Monroe, Vaughn, 57
Montgomery, General Bernard, 36, 119
Moore, Doreen, 129
Morgan, Guy, 90
Morgan, Flight Officer John R. S. 'Nipper', 86–87
Morgan, Robert, 181
Moriarty, Cecil, 171
Morrison, Diana, 27
Morrison, Herbert, 68, 178–181
Morton, Hugh, 27
Moss, Jack, 21
Mountbatten, Louis, 104
Murdoch, Richard 'Stinker', 19
Murphy, Danny, 79
Murphy, Jesse, 79
Mussolini, Benito, 52, 177
Myers, Denis, 106

Neagle, Anna, 114
Newman, Robert, 58, 60
Niven, David, 91, 102–103

Noble, Ray, 55
Noel, Art, 53
Nolan, Lloyd, 89
Novello, Ivor, 126, 128

Oatley, Edwin Albert, 72
Oberon, Merle, 91
O'Connor, Tommie, 45
O'Flanagan, Kevin, 189
O'Hara, Maureen, 91
Oliver, Vic, 20, 129
Olivier, Laurence, 91, 95, 102, 105, 112, 126

Pargiter, Isobel, 114
Park, Phil, 52
Parker, Ross, 49, 54
Parr-Davies, Harry, 51, 52
Parsons, Eric, 101
Parsons, John, 99
Pataudi, Nawab of, 188
Payne, Jack, 45
Pearcey, Kathleen, 142
Pelosi, Don, 53
Pepper, Harry S., 17
Percival, Horace, 26
Peters, T. P., 100
Petersen, Joe, 49
Philadelphia Orchestra, 83
Phillips, Frank, 8
Pickford, Percy 'Pick', 111
Pickles, Wilfred, 12
Pinero, Arthur Wing, 125
Plugge, Captain Leonard, 181
Pollard, A. H., 170
Pontin, Fred, 190
Potter, Stephen, 187
Poulsen, Martinus, 74
Pountain, Eric, 73
Powell, Michael, 102
Pressburger, Emeric, 102
Priestley, J. B., 2, 51, 186–187
Prince, Hughie, 53
Princess Elizabeth, 112
Princess Margaret, 112, 149

Queen Elizabeth, 112
Queen Elizabeth II, 49
Queen Elizabeth, RMS, 85

Ram, Buck, 136
Randolph, Elsie, 148
Rattigan, Terrence, 127
Raye, Don, 53
Read, Ivy, 146
Redgrave, Michael, 89, 114, 126
Reed, Carol, 96
Reekie, Yvonne, 154
Reid, Private David, 72
Reid, Lieutenant Commander David, 46
Revnell, Ethel, 149
Reynolds, Quentin, 42
Richardson, Ralph, 126, 187
Ridley, Arnold, 127
Rignold, Captain Harry, 117
Robertson-Glasgow, R. C., 177
Robinson, A. L., 70
Rommel, Erwin, 116, 119
Rooney, Mickey, 89
Ros, Edmundo, 185
Rudsdale, Eric, 146

Salisbury, Arthur, 4
Sanders, George, 89
Sarony, Leslie, 35
Secombe, Harry, 44
Seiler, Eddie, 56

Selznick, David O., 94
Shadwell, Charles, 17
Shakespeare, William, 90, 105, 112, 125, 132, 141
Shaw, Fred, 87
Shaw, George Bernard, 89, 136
Shelton, Anne, 40, 45–47, 63, 55–56
Sherwin, Manning, 56
Shinwell, Emanuel, 177, 179
Sim, Alistair, 89
Sinatra, Frank, 55
Slater, Brigadier John Durnford, 109
Slater, Sergeant William, 72
Smith, Kate, 51
Smith, Poppy, 97
Smithers, Sir Waldron, 178–180
Snagge, John, 7, 12–13
Snow, James Daniel, 72
Song Spinners, 53
Stafford, Jo, 55
Stead, Lance Corporal P., 43
Stevenson, Kent, 12
Stewart, James, 90, 95
Stiles-Allen, Lilian, 63–64
Strode, Robert, 19
Sullivan, Henry, 54
Summers, Dorothy, 26
Sunnucks, Anthony, 121–122
Swarthout, Gladys, 89
Sylvester, Victor, 49

Tarnowski, Grzegorz, 72
Taylor, Driver John Robert, 117
Teasdale, Ken, 172
Temple, Shirley, 88, 93
Thomas, Gunner Fred, 44
Thompson, C. Patrick, 144
Thompson, Gordon, 54
Thorndike, Sybil, 125
Tillett, Bob, 9
Topham, Mirabel, 189
Train, Jack, 26, 27
Trinder, Tommy, 35, 36, 84, 103, 112–113, 187

Van Damm, Vivian, 129, 130, 135
Vaughan-Thomas, Wynford, 11
von Ribbentrop, Joachim, 188

Wakefield, Duggie, 149
Walbrook, Anton, 95, 102
Walker, Norman, 21
Walker, Ronald, 115
Walker, Syd, 89
Walton, William, 105, 111
Wand, Dr William, 29
Ward, Susie, 132
Warner, Jack, 16–18
Warnock, Judy, 77
Washbrook, Cyril, 189
Waters, Doris, 17
Waters, Elsie, 17
Watkins, Harold, 184
Watt, John, 8
Wayne, John, 89
Weaver, Albert, 74
Weldon, Maisie, 132
West, Gracie, 149
Wilbur, Jay, 49
Williams, Captain J. J. Lloyd, 90
Williams, Ursula Moray, 147
Wilmot, Chester, 11
Wilson, Cecil, 180
Wilson, Keppel and Betty, 149
Winskill, Flight Lieutenant Archibald, 129
Winters, Joan, 17–18

Withers, Jane, 89
Wolfit, Donald, 125
Wood, Sir Henry, 58, 59–62, 65, 66, 67
Woodward, Lynda, 49
Woodward, Mona, 49
Woodward, Thomas, 49
Woolton, Lord, 144, 148, 154, 155, 156
Worsley, Francis, 26–27
Wyler, William, 91

Young, Arthur, 49
Yule, Fred, 27

Zec, Donald, 49

Films

Always in Trouble, 89
Ambush, 89
Bees in Paradise, 46
Bell Bottom George, 103
Blotto, 89
Brief Encounter, 106–107
Builders, 113
Casablanca, 105
Christmas Under Fire, 142
Climbing High, 89
Coastal Command, 115–116
Destry Rides Again, 95
Discoveries, 50
Eating Out with Tommy Trinder, 112–113
Evensong, 187
First of the Few, The, 102
Flirting with Fate, 89
Foreman Went to France, The, 103
Gaslight, 95
George In Civvy Street, 187
Get Cracking, 103
Gone With The Wind, 93, 94
Goodbye Mr Chips, 91–92
Goose Steps Out, The, 103
Grapes of Wrath, 95
Great Dictator, The, 97
Great Expectations, 187
Heart of Britain, 110
Henry V, 105
Henry VI, Part 2, 141
Hopalong Cassidy, 98
Huckleberry Finn, 89
I Killed the Count, 89
I Was a Fireman, 114
In Which We Serve, 103–104
Inspector Hornleigh, 89
Invaders, The, 102
It's That Man Again, 28
Jamaica Inn, 91
King Arthur was a Gentleman, 46
Lambeth Walk, The, 93
Lawless Valley, 89
Let Freedom Ring, 89
Let George Do It!, 31
Listen Darling, 89
Listen to Britain, 114
Lofoten, 109
Made for Each Other, 90
Me and My Girl, 93
Merchant Seamen, 110
Mickey's Gala Premier, 2
Miss London Ltd, 46
Mr Smith Goes to Washington, 95
Mrs Miniver, 105
Night Mail, 110
Night Train to Munich, 96
One Exciting Night, 43–44

Orchestra Wives, 84
Peck's Bad Boy With the Circus, 89
Pinocchio, 94–95
Rebecca, 95
Rhythm Serenade, 43
Rookies, 53
Saint Strikes Back, The, 89
Shipyard Sally, 52, 92–93
Sing As We Go, 52
Snow White and the Seven Dwarfs, 95
South Riding, 89
Spare a Copper, 103
St Louis Blues, 89
Stagecoach, 88–89, 91
Still Life, 106
Sun Valley Serenade, 84
Target For Tonight, 111–112
Thanks for Everything, 89
The 49th Parallel, 102
Arsenal Stadium Mystery, 92
Times Flies, 28
To Have and To Have Not, 105
Tonight and Every Night, 134
Tunisian Victory, 116–117
Typhoon, 98
We'll Meet Again, 43
Went the Day Well?, 104–105
Western Approaches, 119–121, 123
Wizard of Oz, The, 50, 93
Words for Battle, 112
Wuthering Heights, 91

Songs and Instrumentals

'A Nice Cup of Tea', 54
'A Nightingale Sang in Berkeley Square', 56
'American Patrol', 84
'Auf Wiederseh'n Sweetheart', 44
'Bee Song, The', 53
'Biggest Aspidistra in the World, The', 46
'Bless 'Em All', 33
'Boogie Woogie Bugle Boy', 53
'Calling All Workers', 21
'Chattanooga Choo Choo', 84
'Chinese Laundry Blues', 31
'Cockaigne Overture', 58
'Comin' In On a Wing and a Prayer', 53
'Dam Busters March', 21
'Deep in the Heart of Texas', 21
'Ding Dong Merrily on High', 142
'Don't Let's Be Beastly to the Germans', 55
'Fools Rush In', 45
'Get In Your Shelter', 53
'God Bless America', 51
'Good Night Sweetheart', 55
'Happy Go Lucky Me', 39
'Harbour Lights', 54
'Hey Little Hen', 55
'I Can't Love You Any More', 45
'I Did What I Could With My Gas Mask', 31
'I'll Be Home For Christmas', 136
'I'll Be Seeing You', 55
'I'm Going to Get Lit Up (When The Lights Go Up In London)', 56
'I'm Sending You the Siegfried Line', 54
'In the Mood', 84
'It's a Long Way to Tipperary', 52
'It's Home', 41

'Kiss Me Goodnight Sergeant Major', 53
'Lay Down Your Arms', 46
'Let the Curtain Come Down', 45
'Lili Marlene', 45, 117–118
'Little Stick of Blackpool Rock', 34
'Mairzy Doats and Dozy Doats', 55
'Maybe It's Because I'm A Londoner', 56
'Moonlight Serenade', 84
'Mr Wu's a Window Cleaner Now', 32
'Mr Wu's an Air Raid Warden Now', 32
'Pennsylvania 6-5000', 84
'Red Sails in the Sunset', 54
'Run Rabbit Run', 54
'Sing As We Go', 52
'Somewhere Over the Rainbow', 50, 93
'South of the Border', 48
'String of Pearls', 84
'Teddy Bear's Picnic, The', 54
'That Lovely Weekend', 56
'There'll Always Be an England', 49–50
'Thing-ummy-bob, The', 54
'Tuxedo Junction', 84
'We'll Gather Lilacs', 128
'We'll Meet Again', 41
'We're Gonna Hang Out the Washing on the Siegfried Line', 54
'When the Lights Go On Again (All Over the World)', 57
'White Cliffs of Dover, The', 40, 50–51
'Wish Me Luck As You Wave Me Goodbye', 52
'Wishing', 40
'Yours', 40

Books

Cocktails, 144
Let The People Sing, 2
Nature's ABC, 147
The Good Little Christmas Tree, 147
The Paper Boat, 147
The Wonderful Wizard of Oz, 93

Stage plays, operas, pantomimes and musicals

Aladdin, 39, 149
An Inspector Calls, 186–187
Babes in the Wood, 140, 149
Blithe Spirit, 127, 128
Count of Monte Cristo, The, 4
Flare Path, 127
Ghost Train, The, 127
Glad Tidings, 140
Heart of the City, 134
Home & Beauty, 54
Humpty Dumpty, 149
Jack and the Beanstalk, 149
Keep Going, 46
King John, 125
Little Dog Laughed, The, 54
Love for Love, 125
Magistrate, The, 125
Marriage of Figaro, The, 60
Old Mother Red-Riding Boots, 149

Pacific 1860, 186
Perchance to Dream, 128
Present Laughter, 127
Quiet Weekend, 128
Revudeville, 129–130, 131, 132, 135
Robinson Crusoe, 141, 149
Song of Norway, 186
Star Variety, 41
Strike a New Note, 56
Sunny, 148
This Happy Breed, 127
While The Sun Shines, 127–128
Zip Goes a Million, 39

Radio Programmes

Ack Ack, Beer Beer, 16–17, 18–19
AEF Christmas Show, 86
Alf's Dream, 185
All Sorts of Music, 20
As The Commentator Saw It: Cricket and Tennis, 185
Band Waggon, 19
Beyond Our Ken, 19
Bob Hope Show, The, 22–23
Calling Malta, 46
Children's Hour, 15
Desert Island Discs, 130
Garrison Theatre, 16–18
Hi Gang!, 19–20
In a Sentimental Mood, 185
In Town Tonight, 148
Introducing Anne, 45
It's That Man Again (ITMA), 15, 24–29
Jack Benny Programme, The, 22–23
Journey Home, The, 148
Merry-go-Round, 19
Monday Night at Eight, 45
Moods Modernistic, 45
Much-Binding-in-the-Marsh, 19
Music While You Work, 20–22
Private Smith Entertains, 17
Round the Horne, 19
Sandy McPherson at the Theatre Organ, 185
Shadow of the Swastika, The, 17
Sincerely Yours, 40–41, 42
Songs of Three Decades, 185
Starlight, 42
Sunday Half Hour, 185
Transatlantic Quiz, Britain versus America, 185
Tyneside Salutes the Merchant Navy, 185
Variety Bandbox, 46, 185
War Report, 12
Workers' Playtime, 22
Works Wonders, 22

Television programmes

Friday Show, The, 39
Muffin the Mule, 186
Silence of the Sea, 186